THE COMPLETE BOOK OF DREAMS

T0159266

OTHER BOOKS IN THIS SERIES
BY LEONARD R. N. ASHLEY

The Complete Book of Superstition, Prophecy and Luck

The Complete Book of Magic and Witchcraft

The Complete Book of Devils and Demons

The Complete Book of the Devil's Disciples

The Complete Book of Spells, Curses, and Magical Recipes

The Complete Book of Vampires

The Complete Book of Ghosts and Poltergeists

The Complete Book of Werewolves

I have had a most rare vision.
I have had a dream past the wit of man to say what dream it was.
Man is but an ass if he go about t'expound this dream.
—Bottom the Weaver in Shakespeare's
A Midsummer Night's Dream, IV, i.

THE COMPLETE BOOK OF

DREAMS

AND WHAT THEY MEAN

Leonard R. N. Ashley

PROFESSOR *EMERITUS*, BROOKLYN COLLEGE
OF THE CITY UNIVERSITY OF NEW YORK

BARRICADE BOOKS / NEW JERSEY

Published by Barricade Books Inc.
Fort Lee, NJ 07024
www.barricadebooks.com

Copyright © 2002 by Leonard R N. Ashley
All Rights Reserved.

No part of this book may be reproduced, stored in a retrieval system, or transmitted in any form, by any means, including mechanical, electronic, photocopying, recording, or otherwise, without the prior written permission of the publisher, except by a reviewer who wishes to quote brief passages in connection with a review written for inclusion in a magazine, newspaper, or broadcast.

Library of Congress Cataloging-in-Publication Data
Ashley, Leonard R N.
The complete book of dreams / Leonard RN. Ashley
p.cm.
1. Dreams. 2. Dream interpretation. I. Title.

ISBN: 1-56980-211-4 (alk. paper) 2002
ISBN: 978-1-56980-523-7 (paper) 2016

BFI091 .A735 2002
154.6'3--dc21

2001043037

10 9 8 7 6

Printed in the United States of America

Table of Contents

PREFACE

CHAPTER ONE
A SAMPLING OF DREAMS AND DREAMING   13

CHAPTER TWO
DREAMS AND SCIENCE   61

CHAPTER THREE
RELIGION, MAGIC AND DREAMS   95

CHAPTER FOUR
DREAMS IN ART, LITERATURE, AND FOLKLORE   129

CHAPTER FIVE
DREAMS AND THE CINEMA   187

CHAPTER SIX
A LITTLE TREASURY OF SHORT STORIES   229

CHAPTER SEVEN
THE INTERPRETATION OF DREAMS   287

INDEX   341

Nightmare (1782)
by Henry Fuseli

In Memoriam

GUY WILLIAM LAMBERT, CB
1889–1983
President of The Society for Psychical Research, 1955–1958

Preface

This reprint of one of my books from Barricade Books offers me an opportunity to say something extra about dreams from the scientific point of view because dreams are to science only occult ("hidden") insofar as we still lack so much basic information about sleep, to which the average person devotes six years of life, and the dreams that come to all of us.

"I don't dream," you say? You do. For some reason you do not recall what you have dreamt. Why, do you think? Perhaps if you could be awakened during REM sleep you would recall your dreams. RM (Rapid Eye Movement) is said to have been discovered by Keitman and his associates in 1953, but surely people noticed the twitching eyelids of sleepers long before that, even if they did not know what it meant. Something strange, maybe weird, was surely going on. From the earliest recorded times, sleep has always been quite a mystery and dreams have been given prophetical reputations as well, of course, being dreams or imaginings in the sense of a goal or expectation. After all, dreams seem quite similar to visions that religion says are vouchsafed by supernatural powers to people supposedly wide awake, if sometimes in an odd state because of fasting or pain and so on.

Superstition says that dreams deal in symbols and tells us on no authority that so-called dream books can reveal to you what your dreams are trying to tell you, provided you do lucid dreaming and can remember dreams. In this book I mention dream books because so many people superstitiously turn to them but naturally I think them to be ridiculously unreliable. Perhaps if you read enough of them they can actually influence the content of your dreams because there is some connection between waking experience and sleeping mind activity.

What the mind is up to when we dream we do not fully understand. Of course there are theories. The ancients thought we might be getting messages from superior powers. Freud thought we might be dealing with ideas and emotions that in waking life were socially unacceptable, personally shameful, repressed. With an emphasis on sex, he built on slight earlier German speculation about mind, and undertook psychoanalysis, trying to get to so-called latent significance in dreams that somehow connect the ego to the subconscious and deal in symbols that he was sure demanded and would respond to interpretation.

Freud's theories are now almost totally dismissed by the leading scientists of mind and cognition. Jung was a bit better at "practical dream analysis"; he also was interested in how the spirit and its human container might be understood, but he put more emphasis on the obvious symbols than on guesswork interpretation.

Scientific research has concentrated now not on superstition about how dreams can foretell the future or deliver messages from higher powers but on the physiology and psychology of sleep and dreams. Science has actively pursued knowledge into how and why we go to sleep, how we dream, how and why we wake up, how much sleep a person needs, how insomnia can be fought (night lights work, and the colors matter), why we have nightmares (diet may be a factor), how environment can affect sleep (dripping water shapes dreams, noises may wake us or certain noises guarantee sounder sleep), many disorders from narcolepsy to sleep apnea can be treated, sleeping medications can be both helpful and dangerous, etc.

The medical world is just commencing to realize that men and women and the young and the old are different and may need different treatment in the world of sleep medicine. Rakesh Bhattacharjee (University of Chicago) is working on children's sleep problems (and pediatricians want school to start later for the very young), Helene Emseller and others are studying the sleep problems of adolescents, and people generally think that the elderly need, or at least, get less sleep than the adult and middle-aged, but that they may need more.

Roger Ekirk at Virginia Tech is studying insomnia and others elsewhere are investigating the impact of sleep of the lack of it in sports medicine. There is a huge amount about dreams still to be explored. In the United States there are scientific journals such as *Dreaming* and *Journal of Sleep Research*, organizations such as the National Sleep Foundation and DREAMS Foundation and the Sleep Research Society, medical programs and pharmaceutical trials dedicated to sleep and dreaming, publications from newspapers such as the *The New York Times* and the *Huffington Post*, a variety of popular magazines such as *Psychology Today*, Internet sites, blogs, and more – all examining sleep and dreaming.

At Harvard there is a Division of Sleep Medicine, at Stanford, a Center for Sleep Sciences. Everywhere, sleep is accepted as the "third pillar" of health (along with diet and exercise) and key to what we have come to call "wellness" and longevity. Repeatedly, we hear that driven, multitasking Americans do not get enough sleep. There is disagreement over so-called "power naps" (no time for REM to start) and whether the traditional eight hours a night is enough. In fact, the eight hours rule is as wrong as the traditional eight glasses of water a day. But what is right? Science is working on that. Meanwhile, as a wise man once said, "It is not what we don't know that hurts us as what we think we know 'that ain't so,'" superstition, that in a Barricade book I called a "religion for the ignorant."

Thus far, science is still unsure whether it is safe to say that sleep has "no adaptive function." But we sleep, well or badly, and we benefit some and suffer some from that. Some dreams that recur are extremely hard on us, as some war veterans attest. Some inspire us to do great things. The way that the dizzying pace of modern life keeps us from enough or enjoying enough sound sleep worries us. That can keep us awake at nights.

We worry about that if not about the fact that dreams, it seems, can be implanted in our waking hours (see Kelly Bulkeley's Big Dreams and theology in her Dreaming in the Worlds' Religions) if not invaded, our ideas stolen, while we sleep (the movie "Inception"). Dreams are related to evolutionary psychology, neurobiology, sex difference (*Journal of Psychology* 138:6) prophecy, problem solving (Alfred Adler and others), fantasy, phantasmagoric images, wish fulfillment, the regulation of mood, the incorporating of information, political goals ("I have a dream"), innovative ideas ("It came to me in a dream"), and much more. We all dream and have a couple of hours on average of dreaming every night of eight hours sleep, as many as six or seven separate dreams, seconds long or as much as half an hour long. Dreams are a considerable part of life.

This book was not and is not now the place for neurobiology or the minutiae of the operation of mind, but we can at least cite Fritz Perl (who suggested that dreams present rejected or suppressed matter from waking life) and some few other experts who comment on everything from cognition to cortisol.

William Dement is often mentioned as the father of this branch of science. J. Alan Hobson traced REM signals to the brainstem and described how limbic systems work with emotion, sensation, and memory. The amygdala (that science discovers has something to do with some sex-life variations) and hippocampus, Hobson showed in the 1970s to be involved in seeking meaning from a mass of input. Mark Solms located dreaming in the forebrain and it was he who discovered that parietal lobe damage ends dreaming. He saw that ordinary dreaming draws on long-term memory and functions to incorporate new information.

Yes, sleep produces some excitement in the genitals, but Freud did not know that only ten percent of male dreams are sexual (less than that in women) and that dreams of sex are chiefly in hormone-happy adolescents.

By the way, do you dream in Technicolor or in black-and-white or both? And are your daydreams or even your night flights quite like movies? Who is influencing whom? At least you are not only Dickens' hero of your own life but leading man (or female star) of your own personal Indie feature. For daytime you may need earphones for background music. Do you like action movies, fright night movies, romance, comedy, or what? Where do you get your scenery and costumes and FX experts and supporting cast? Do you think the Great Big Producer in the sky is supervising your movie, constantly watching the rushes?

Cinephiles will know all the "it was just a dream" movies (*The Wizard of Oz*, 1939 and *The Woman in the Window*, 1944 among them) these days are regarded as cop outs and so are the films with dream sequences (but in *Rosemary's Baby* 1968 when she wakes from a nightmare there are claw marks on her back) are almost as common as the dream ballets used to be in Broadway musicals.

Of course one has to distinguish sleep from daydreaming (*The Secret Life of Walter Mitty*), remade in 2013 but not nearly as good as the Danny Kay version or James Thurber's fine short story) and hallucinations (which figure in a number of movies). Invading your minds/dreams is the subject of the likes of *Dreamcatcher* (2003) and *Paprika* (2006) and more, lucid dreaming hits Tom Cruise in *Vanilla Sky* and Jim Carey in *Eternal Sunshine of the Spotless Mind*. We learn how to escape a nightmare in the foo-fah on Elm Street series, we get a lot of nightmarish matter in fright night pics and I get deeply into the zombie craze and dare to relate it to political reality, the fear of the revolt of the underclass that is dead to the likes of the 1%.

There are few horror movies dealing with actual nightmares and most cannot get into the twisted minds of extremely violent people, dead or alive. The nightmare mind of serial killer James Gumm in Thomas Harris' the *Silence of the Lambs* is brilliantly captured in the awful cellar of his house as shown in the award-winning film. The viewer feels trapped in a horrible dream. What will happen next? We are given predictive dreams in *Minority Report* (2002). You might have a peek at the short *Abre los Ojos* (Open the Eyes). Movies are eye-openers and mind trips, visual voyages, fictional flix but also often as significant as our dreams. The cinema is often called The Dream Palace. We have our own dream palaces right in our heads.

Meanwhile, sleep centers study health problems, Adam Schneder & G. A. Domhof have conducted a quantitative study of dreams, and neuroscientists ponder whether dreams are produced by randomly firing neutrons and perhaps some consolidating mechanism that rather relates in our wetware to our computer's hard drive and RAM. Jie Zhang has a promising continued-activation theory (*Journal of Theoretics*, 2005) and there are other hypotheses. Much, however, remains unmapped and unexplored let alone unexploited. Meanwhile, we can actively pursue answers to such questions as why there are people who are "not morning persons" and what to do about it besides handing them coffee and staying awake as we have learned is advisable. We can learn how to "get a good night's sleep" and rise refreshed. We can learn from our dreams (sleeping) to help realize our dreams (aspirations).

You can learn from this book. This book in reprint continues to do what the dozen books, from *The Complete Book of Superstition, Prophecy, and Luck*, to the present have done, which is to tell as objectively as any individual can the extraordinary history of unfounded belief. I have sought to record honestly the imagination and misunderstanding that so many have greedily grasped for when fact and rationality eluded them. Now that we Google, the new contributions to the matters I wrote fifteen years ago require no added bibliography here even to the pages in the original on the march of science. In fact, scholars such as myself, who amassed and communicated massive erudition, are out of date in the cyber age.

In the *Dream Dictionary* part of the book (somewhat mocking the old gypsy guides) under Book it says "wisdom, authority" but today professors are seldom credited with much of either. Times change.

As to superstition, there is nothing to add but a repeated warning: do not allow yourself to be deceived because you are uncomfortable not knowing. Maybe some ignorance is handy. The poet says that "in dreams begin responsibilities."

We must agree with Shakespeare's Puck about "what fools these mortals be" but also sympathize a little with our human weaknesses and vain but valiant hopes for comprehending everything in our universe, unequipped for that omniscience as we are. We still have our human limits and die-by date. After all, however, as Hamlet says, we are "godlike in reason" if merely mortal human beings and not divine. Recall and rely upon the "good news" that we are all, the bible says, descended from Noah. Maybe you have forgotten that Noah's father was not human. Noah's father was an angel! So somewhat super powers, to some extent, may still be within our grasp, especially if we rely on science and not on baseless superstition.

—Leonard R. N. Ashley, PhD, LHD
December 2016

Read This First

Lend your ears to hear the sayings.
Lend your heart to comprehend them.
It will profit you to take them to your heart.

—Amenemope

All evidence to the contrary, I continue to hope that readers will begin at the preface, to get some idea of what a book is about. You can learn a little more right here of this book's purpose than a glance at the table of contents or the back cover blurb will afford. Yes, this is a book about interpreting your dreams—but it is much more.

My subject is dreams and dreamers. My purpose is to integrate well-researched information with my personal opinions, about the materials I have found, to open up a dialogue with both the scholar and the casual reader about some important things that occur in that third of our lives we spend in sleep, unconscious of the rest of the world and alone with our most intimate selves.

In the course of this I will touch on science and art, myth and religion and superstition ("the religion of the ignorant"), and a number of other fascinating topics, from an unusual perspective.

I excuse the existence of this book the way every book should be excused: there is no other book like it and there ought to be such a book available. So here it is.

This book follows a whole series of books I have written on the occult. Those I published with Barricade Books (New Jersey) include: *The Complete Book of Superstition, Prophecy and Luck*; *The Complete Book of Magic and Witchcraft*; *The Complete Book of Devils and Demons*; *The Complete Book of the Devil's Disciples*; *The Complete Book of Vampires*; *The Complete Book of Spells, Curses, and Magical Recipes*; *The Complete Book of Ghosts and Poltergeists*; and *The Complete Book of Werewolves*.

These add up to a kind of general encyclopedia of the occult. This book continues the series on a high note, with a subject of more than curious interest. I propose to explain what dreams have meant historically and contemporarily to our waking lives.

Once again I have presented my arcane materials in a ready-friendly way. I have broken things up into tiny essays suitable to our age of grazing on ideas and short attention spans, when, more than ever, enlightenment must be accompanied by entertainment. That is not a bad thing. One of the greatest of the ancients told us to "teach delightfully." I hope you will find this book educational and enthralling, profitable and pleasurable to read.

It is possible to read this book straight through, but I expect that most readers will begin by opening it at the last chapter—interpretation—or more or less at random and, finding something that catches their attention, read in fits and starts until, ideally, they have not only read it all but read it with such pauses as will enable them to relate my facts and comments to their own experiences and opinions.I should like this book to be a conversation with the reader rather than a lecture. You can even read parts of it when you cannot sleep. More than half of all Americans suffer from insomnia and twenty-nine percent wake up too early and cannot go back to sleep. Here is an ideal bedside book.

Dip in. After some investigative sampling, some readers may even adopt the good old-fashioned advice given by Lewis Carroll that we should begin at the beginning, go on until the end, and then stop. Also, as the Duchess says in *Alice's Adventures in Wonderland*, "Everything's got a moral if only you can find it," so you may look for one, too.

As with my other books that attempt discussions amusing enough for the ordinary reader but authoritative enough for the scholar, I have taken care (without footnotes) to document sources in the text. I offer brief bibliographies of useful books in which some readers may wish to continue their reading. For that purpose I have made certain to cite only sources you are likely to lay your hands on. The book actually contains an extensive research guide, but don't let lists of books trouble you. If you aren't interested, ignore them. If and when you want to do more reading, the names of authors and the titles of useful books will help you at the library or online. I have, as usual, included illustrations to accompany and enliven the text. By now this format has taken readers' suggestions to heart and become, I hope, something like ideal for the purpose.

As always, I welcome response from readers. I cannot promise to answer all correspondence. I have learned that from the earlier books published in America and abroad. I assure you, however, that I read all communications. All useful suggestions have a chance of being incorporated in a gathering, some day, of all the books in the series into a uniform set or one big compendium.

The Complete Book of Dreams and What They Mean deconstructs something that happens to each and every one of us consistently, and that is dreaming. Although the previous volumes examine every aspect of the occult, the truth is we may never encounter black magicians, devils and demons, vampires and werewolves, table rappers and noisy ghosts. But we all dream.

With dreams and dreaming I continue a series that has ranged over most the major aspects of the occult. In discussing dreams I address the occult at least in the sense of the word that stresses the hidden. There is not as much superstition connected with dreams and dreamers as there is in some other eerie matters but even with dreams and dreamers there are mysteries and the very things with which the series began, which is to say "superstition, prophecy, and luck." THe series will end with the forthcoming *Complete Book of Sex Magic.*

There are still many things about dreaming that even science does not fully understand, and whenever there is a lack of fact there is always the danger of superstition. The unconscious has at times been connected with the irrational, as you are well aware. It is just part of the miracle of daily existence.

With H. L. Mencken, "I have found existence on this meanest of planets extremely amusing," thus far, and I trust that this present book of mine will amuse you. As we say in Brooklyn, Enjoy!

The Feast of St. Boniface, 2001

1
A Sampling of Dreams and Dreaming

There are more things in heaven and earth, Horatio,
Than are dreamt of in your philosophy.
—William Shakespeare, *Hamlet*

WHAT DO YOUR DREAMS MEAN?

That's what this book will help you to discover. Let me say right off the bat that this book goes beyond the This equals That gypsy dream-book approach and puts the whole thing in a more sensible and broader context, as you will find if you start here rather than the last chapter on the dream-book manner of interpretation. So read on now to prepare yourself, first with a *pot pourri* of dream-related matters and then with chapters on dreams in science, religion, literature, folklore, and the cinema. After all that, you will be much better prepared to make the most of the final chapter.

EN TOUTOI NIKA

In the history of Christianity there is probably no single dream more important than one of the Emperor Constantine. He was the one who took the revolutionary new version of the ancient religion of the Jews and made it the cornerstone of the greatest empire of its time, as well as one of the most significant factors in world history.

In 312 AD Constantine advanced against one of half a dozen competitors for the imperium of Rome, named Maxentius. Maxentius had the backing of the powerful Praetorian Guard. Constantine's forces met them at The Tiber. Against the sun Constantine saw a flaming cross and the Greek motto, more familiar to us in Latin as *In Hoc Signo Vinces*, "In This Sign You will be Victorious." Then Constantine had a dream. It strengthened his belief and indeed changed the history of the Roman Empire and the world. In his dream Constantine was commanded to have his soldiers put two Greek letters on their shields, *chi* and *ro*, standing for *Christ*.

He so ordered his troops, advanced against the army of Maxentius, and won the battle and the empire. Thereafter the empire was known as "Christian," a word introduced by St. Peter while preaching in Turkey.

WHY DO WE DREAM?

The scientific jury is still out on a number of questions. For example:

- Do we sleep to rest or to do necessary work of the unconscious?
- Do we retreat in darkness from nocturnal threats remembered from primitive times?
- Do we dream to solve problems not otherwise known or understood?
- Do we somehow get in touch with spiritual forces when we are asleep?
- Are the symbols of dreams personal or part of humanity's collective memory?
- Precisely what is consciousness and what are the mechanisms by which various states of consciousness are achieved?

I think dreaming can be summed up by the terms used for teaching: remedial, compensatory, practical, career training, intellectually stimulating, character building, entertaining, inspiring, and wish fulfilling.

MAYBE WE DREAM FOR DOLLARS

The modern world has touched every aspect of dreaming. Not only is there a 900 number to help you decipher your dreams but also a "dream community [that] has begun to sell itself to the public." Entrepreneurs tell us we can dream our way to success on Wall Street or on Main Street, dream which way the market is going to go, dream up a new product, or take a course on how to solve management problems overnight.

Soon they will be offering DDs (Doctor of Dreams) to MBAs, or MD (Merchandising Dreams) degrees. Pamela Weintraub writes of "Dreaming for Dollars" in *Omni* 15 (September 1993). Hers is a fairly early entry in the dreams in business trend.

In many senses, business success has been founded on a dream.

LOAVES AND WISHES

A classical statue of Sleep, in the Vatican.

Dreams are so fascinating because they hold the secrets of our desire at the deepest levels of our being, but are only revealed in the third of our lives spent in oblivion. In dreams we participate in experience in a way that may be different from the experience of waking life. You might say that in daily life we film the world and that in dreams we edit and add the music.

I recall a famous story, "Borges and Myself," commenting on duality in literature, in characters like William Wilson and Dr. Jekyll and Mr. Hyde. Luis Borges writes: "According to one of the Indian schools of philosophy, the ego is merely an onlooker who has identified himself with the man he is continually looking at."

What is the precise relationship between the dreamer and the man or woman who experiences the dream? Exactly whose wishes are fulfilled, and for whom? To what extent are the needs of the person in reality met by dreams? Do we have two separate lives; one waking and the other asleep?

> "I do not know whether I was then a man dreaming I was a butterfly, or whether I am now a butterfly dreaming I am a man."
> —Confucius (369-286 BC)

ANCIENT AUTHORS

The scholarship on dreams and dreaming has filled shelves over the centuries, from literary classics to psychology journals and books. Some samples:

Aelius Aristides. Charles A. Behr, *Aelius Aristides and the Sacred Tales* (1968).

Aristotle. Mark A. Holowchak, "Aristotle on Dreams..." *Ancient Philosophy* 16 (Fall 1996), 405–423.

Asclepius: *Asclepius: A Collection and Interpretation of the Testimonies* (ed. Emma J. & Ludwig Edelstein, 1976).

Herodotus. Stephanie West, "And It Came to Pass that Pharoah Dreamed: Notes On Herodotus 2.139, 141," *Classical Quarterly* 37:2 (1987), 262–271.

Iambilicus. *"Polyhymnia Athanassiadi, Dreams, Theurgy and Freelance Divination..." Journal of Roman Studies* 83 (1993), 115–130.

Lucretius. P. H. Schrijvers, *"Die Traumtheorie des Lucrez* [Dream Theory of Lucretius]," *Mnemosyne* 33 Fasc. 1-2 (1980), 128–151, and Howard Jacobson, "Lucretius 1. 102–105 [on a short passage in Lucretius]," *Classical Quarterly* 32:1 (1982), 237.

Petronius: H. Musurello, "Dream Symbolism in Petronius," *Classical Philology* 53 (1958), 108–110, and Patrick Kragelund, "Epicurus, Priapus, and Dreams in Petronius," *Classical Quarterly* 39:2 (1989), 436–450.

Plato: David Gallop. "Dreaming and Waking in Plato" in *Essays on Ancient Greek Philosophy* (ed. J.P. Anton, 1971), 187–201.

Propertius: James L. Burtica. "Propertius 3.3. 7-12 and Ennius," *Classical Quarterly* 33:2 (1983), 464–468.

Roman Historians: Christopher Pelling. "Tragical Dreamer," *Greece & Rome* 44 (October 1997), 197–213.

A standard book in the field is E. R. Dodds, *The Greeks and the Irrational* (1951).

AMERINDIAN DREAMS

The earliest people in the Americas brought from Asia shamanism, vision seeking, dream interpretation, dream prophecy, and much more. Here is a sample of the twentieth-century scholars on this vast topic:

Lydia Nakashima Degarrod, *Dream Interpretation among the Mapuche Indians of Chile* (1989).

Laura R. Graham, *Performing Dreams...* [Xavante of Brazil] (1980).

Gerald Hausman (illustrated by Sid Hausman), *Turtle Dream: Collected Stories from the Hopi, Navajo, Pueblo, and Havasupai People* (1989).

Paul Radin, "Ojibwa and Ottawa Puberty Dreams" in *Essays in Anthropology Presented to A. L. Kroeber* (1936).

Jonathan R. Spinney, *The Awakening of Red Feather: Dream, Prophecy, and Earth Changes* (1996).

John James Stewart, *Dream Catchers: A Journey into Native American Spirituality* (1999).

Barbara Tedlock, ed., *Dreaming: Anthropological and Psychological Interpretations* (1992).

Merilyn Tunneshende (ed. John Nelson), *Medicine Dream: A Naqual Woman's Energetic Healing* (1996).

Vine Deloria, Jr. & Lee Irwin, *The Dream Seekers: Native American Visionary Traditions of the Great Plains* (1996).

Virgil J. Vogel, *American Indian Medicine* (1970).

James R. Walker, *Lakota Belief and Ritual* (1980).

AMERINDIAN FOLKLORE OF DREAMS

A folktale, a Native American dance, and two dream songs from the First Nations of Canada can stand as examples of the rich Amerindian dream lore. In dreams the Native Americans found out about their own natures and the future and reinforced their connections with the spirit world and with nature, of which they considered themselves a part, not apart.

P. F. Baum, "The Three Dreamers; or, The Dream Bread Story," *Journal of American Folk Lore* 30 (1917), 378–410 (see also *JAFL* 34, 1921, 327–328).

"Dream Song of the Creator of the White Dog Sacrifice," sung by Chief Joseph Logan of the Onondaga at the Six Nations Reserve (Canada). Library of Congress Records AAFS26B2 (1943), Album 6.

"Dream Song of Our Two Uncles, The Big Heads," sung by Joshua Buck of the Seneca. Same album.

"The Dream Dance of the Chippewa and Memominee Indians of

Northern Wisconsin, *Bulletin of the Public Museum of The City of Milwaukee* 1: 4 (1911), 251–306.

AMERINDIAN FOLKLORE

Here are some older references. More modern ones can more easily be located in online and other bibliographies. In the Time-Life *The American Indians: The Spirit World* (1992) we read: "In the world of the Indians, the dream is real."

Eighteenth-century books include *The History of the American Indians* (1775, by James Adair *c.*1709–*c.* 1783) and in the nineteenth century there were many studies, notably *Letters and Notes on the Manners, Customs and Conditions of the North American Indians* (2 vols. 1841 by George Catlin 1796–1872) and *Historical and Statistical Information Respecting the History, Condition and Prospects of the Indian Tribes of the United States* (6 vols. 1851–1857, Henry Rowe Schoolcraft 1793–1864). In the twentieth century a huge store of writing on the subject was assembled. A few items relative to Amerindian dreams:

D. D. Mitchell, "Remarkable Dream and Prediction," *Southern Literary Magazine* 1 (August 1835), 658–660

"The Dream in Mohave Life," *Journal of American Folk Lore* 60 (1947), 252-258.

"Navaho Dreams," *American Anthropologist* 34 (1932), 390–405

Ernest S. Burch, Jr. *The Eskimos* (1988).

Sam D. Gill, *Native American Religions: An Introduction* (1982).

St. Jean de Crevecoeur, "Indian Dreams, "*Port-Folio* 3 (4 June 1843), 103.

Jackson Seward Lincoln, *The Dream in Primitive Cultures* (1935).

Paul Rudin, "Ojibway and Ottawa Puberty Dreams" in *Essays in Anthropology Presented to A[lfred]. L{ewis]. Kroeber* (1936).

Ruth M. Underhill, *Red Man's Religion: Beliefs and Practices of the Indians North of Mexico* (1965).

THE WORD *DREAM*

The word *dreme* in Old English, *dream* since Middle English, traces back to earlier Continental words referring not only to dreams, but music, joy, or a shout of joy.

Dream has a number of meanings, from aspiration and inspiration to the images of sleep. We really have to stop thinking of sleep as simply the body at rest. While we sleep we exercise our minds, reviewing and revealing our most personal secrets.

To be a dreamer when awake is to be the sort of Shavian idealist who goes beyond asking "why?" to demanding "why not?" To be a dreamer while asleep is to access the most profound knowledge of human being, in which the greatest achievements of have their impetus.

IS IT ALL A DREAM?

"How can you determine," asked Plato in the *Theætetus* 158, "whether at this moment we are sleeping, and all our thoughts are a dream, or whether we are awake, and conversing with each other in the waking state?" That resembles what Confucious said.

Descartes addressed the problem of how we can tell whether we are in a dream world or what we consider to be the real world. In his *Sixth Meditation* of sleep and wakefulness he wrote, "I find a very notable difference between the two, inasmuch as our memory can never connect our dreams with one another, or with the whole course of our lives, in the way that it unites events which happen to us when we are awake."

But that just proves you have dreamed in the past. It does not guarantee that you are not currently in a dream. You could be dreaming that you are reading this book.

A TERRIBLE DREAM

The Russian writer Andrei Biely (1880–1934) has a powerful short story imbued with the same elements found in his Symbolist poetry and prose.

In "From St. Petersburg" there is the line: "A terrible dream…. He could not remember it." Like Nikolai Appollonovich of the story, do you have some nightmares from which you awake in fear unable to remember any of the details that frightened you? Why have you repressed the dream? What do you think the purpose of such dreams may be?

On the other hand, do you have recurrent nightmares that are in all their terrors completely memorable? Do you think if you could decode them they would stop? Science says that anything so repeated must be important and psychoanalysis wants to get to the root of the problem. Because your dreams are so private, only you can uncover them, examine them, and recover (if necessary) from them.

Remember: dreams are part of your life. Dreams are part of your identity.

WORKING NIGHTS

Girolamo Cardano (1501–1576, known to the French as Jerôme Cardan) was a typically Renaissance man. He was astrologer, casting many famous horoscopes, including that of Jesus Christ; mathematician, a major force in algebra; a philosopher and reputed magician; a physician, first to describe the symptoms of typhoid fever. He authored *De subtilitate rerum* (The Subtlety of Things, 1551) and *De varietate rerum* (The Variety of Things, 1557).

His big book came to him in a dream, all laid out for him. His dreams both nagged and encouraged him until he completed the work. Once the book was in print they completely stopped. Today we authors have generally to make do with agents and editors. Some writers get complete stories from nightmares—Kafka and Robert Louis Stevenson of *Dr. Jekyll and Mr. Hyde* most notably—but few have their unconscious driving them on. Even nightmares that terrify us help by stressing the need to cope with some repressed problem.

LUCID DREAMS

You are not powerless when it comes dreams although it takes some practice to manipulate them. In lucid dreams you are in charge: you know you are dreaming and can take control. Here are a few examples of the scholarship on this fascinating aspect of dreams. It suggests the wealth of material in published books, unpublished dissertations, and articles.

This is one of the most interesting of dreams, to me. You not only have to dream but you can take charge of your dreaming and your life! You can do dream work in concert with other people—even just listening to your reports of your dreams can empower them to deal with their own.

Go to sleep having thought about, willed, and taken charge of your dreams. Wake up and write them down. Think them over later. Try to look at them as messages. You have e-mail (empowerment-mail)!

Make up your mind to put your dreams to work for you today. Or tonight. Be aware, however, that you may get not truth but what the prophet Jeremiah called "the wish of the heart," not real revelation.

Ahsen, Akhter. *Prolucid Dreaming* (1992).

Cartwright, Rosalind Dymond & Lynne Lamberg, "Directing Your Dreams," *Psychology Today* 25 (November/December 1992), 32–37.

Queen Catherine's Dream, by William Blake

Flagg, Allen. "Dream Education and General Semantics" in *Developing Sanity in Human Affairs* (ed. Susan Presby Kodish *et al.*, 1998).

Gackenbach, Jayne & Jane Bosveld. "Take Control of Your Dreams..." *Psychology Today* 23 (October 1989), 27-32.

Green, C. E. *Lucid Dreams* (1968).

Harary, Keith. *Lucid Dreams in 30 Days* (1999).

Hearne, Keith M. T. "Lucid Dreams: An Electrophysiological and Physiological Study" (unpublished dissertation, University of Liverpool, 1978).

Kaplan-Williams, S. *Elements of Dreamwork* (1997).

LaBerge, Stephen & Jayne Gackenbach. "Lucid Dreaming" in *Handbook of States of Consciousness* (ed. B. B. Wolman & Montague Ullman, 1986).

Ogilvie, Robert D. *et al.* "Lucid Dreaming and Alpha [Brain Wave] Activity: A Preliminary Report," *Perceptual and Motor Skills* 55 (December 1982), 795–808.

Prescott, James A. & C. Gary Pettigrew. "Lucid Dreaming and Control in Waking Life," *Perceptual and Motor Skills* 81 (October 1995), 658.

Weiss, Lillie. *Practical Dreaming* (1999).

PSYCHIC POWERS

I do not telephone those annoying TV psychics. If they really are psychic, they will know how to get to me. Also, if they have to scramble for a living, most people say, psychics cannot have much power.

Magicians insist that they cannot conjure for themselves, only for others, which is why they are not comfortably retired to Boca Raton. (They do not seem the type for The Riviera). But I have never heard psychics seriously argue that their psychic powers work only for the benefit of others. Personally, I think we all have some powers that will evolve in time. But a psychic is a whole different animal. I'm not the only skeptic, as evidenced by a hilarious "CLOSED" sign I saw on the storefront psychic shop, to which someone had added "DUE TO UNFORESEEN CIRCUMSTANCES."

The US government believes in psychics more than this taxpayer does. Military intelligence has dabbled in psychics. The police have also consulted psychics who claim to see, in dreams or otherwise, the location of murder victims, lost articles, missing persons, and so on.

When the Lindberg baby was kidnapped—a famous case in 1932—1,300 persons responded to a police request for dream information about the whereabouts of the baby.

It was eventually found buried under a tree, naked and mutilated. Only 5% of the dreamers "saw" the baby dead, four persons "saw" the baby buried under a tree. No one "saw" that the baby had been hastily buried naked and mutilated. In the Lindberg case, not a single psychic soul recorded "seeing" the most striking details of all.

Infrequently, but disturbingly, some alleged psychics or dreams provide the police with facts. My local 70th Precinct gets offers of this sort from time to time. New York City's phone line offers cash rewards for good leads in police work and gets occasional offers on speculation. They could be lucky guesses or something else.

There are dream-books that deal in luck. One offers to help you win at casinos; another suggests it can assist in picking winning lottery numbers.

We can do nothing with comments like "I knew that but I was afraid to come forward" or "I knew I was going to win this time," uttered after the truth comes out. People often assert after the fact that they had a "feeling." I have often convinced myself that I had a premonition, a "feeling", haven't you?

As I confessed elsewhere, a few of my premonitions or predictions have been amazing—but most of these "feelings"were way off the mark. My scores are so low I cannot attribute a few successes to anything but dumb luck.

However, a lot of people disagree. Hans Holtzer, prolific writer about ghost busting, has a book called *Psychic* that includes test sheets so you can see if you have extra-sensory perception. I sense you think you do.

THE PROBLEM OF PSYCHIC RESEARCH

As I said in the first book of my occult series, *The Complete Book of Superstition, Prophecy, and Luck,* we put ourselves in a bad position when we consider the occult because we believe too little and too much. To some extent we are unwilling to open our eyes and scientifically investigate incidents that may or may not be connected to the paranormal, and, at the same time we attribute far too much validity to the uninvestigated, superstitious, and purely coincidental.

There must be laws of nature beyond the laws we know. Science keeps working on the problem. Religion in the east involves a world of marvels. Religion in the west from the Doctors of the Church onwards have assured us that even magic and miracles cannot counter the laws of God, though they may speed things up.

We could investigate but that same Church forbids the faithful to do so. If we have, or can develop, psychic powers, and if these really can be used for the benefit of mankind (in the service of God), let's approach the matter with reason and ethics.

Consider what is happening in the field of biology, for instance. Cloning, gene manipulation, and other discoveries challenge us to consider what it is to be human. Are we simply virtual computers processing information and contained in randomly-evolved biological machines?

I suggest you rely not on fate but faith:

> Where ask is have,
> Where seek is find,
> Where knock is open wide.

KUAN YIN

Though dressed in female garb, this is a god, not a goddess, The Compassionate One, known by other names in other oriental beliefs, such as Tara in Tibet. In his/her helpful, even savior, capacity, Kuan Yin was sought out to cure diseases, answer queries, grant blessings, etc., through dreams.

You went to sleep in the temple of this dignitary, usually for a certain period, the way people follow novenas to The Blessed Virgin. There was also a set time, say seven nights or some multiple of seven or even 100. By the last night in a dream you might be vouchsafed a cure for your illness, given life path directions, relieved of some worry, improved. If there was a question that troubled you, you could state it before going to sleep in the sacred precincts and might receive the answer in your dreams. Many stories are told of the efficacy of this sleeping cure and there are those who still have absolute faith in it. They publish their thanks for favors granted in somewhat the same way the devoted put thank-you ads to St. Jude in the newspapers.

This tradition is very old. Printing (from wood blocks) was actually invented to produce religious images. You will find statues of Kuan Yin for sale in every Chinatown in America.

ETHIOPIA

Jim Rogers in *Worth* (December/January 2001, p. 55): "According to legend, 12th-century Ethiopian King Lalibela has a dream in which God ordered him to build a holy city to rival Jerusalem. The story goes that angels aided the king in building the city. Witnessing the incredible craftsmanship firsthand, I was tempted to believe the story."

DREAM AS PORTENT

The pieces in this book will usually be brief. However, here is a rather complex tale of William Rufus. He was the second of the Norman kings of England. My story is taken from the legend of his time, almost a thousand years ago. You will find its length justified by its inherent worth.

We commence with the chronicler Roger of Wendover, a monk of St. Albans—and prior of Belvoir until demoted for "extravagance"—who died in 1236. He left a chronicle called *Flores historiarum* (Flowers of History), which chronicled the history of the world from the Creation to his time. Such a sizable project was typical of medieval times.

Roger, like other early historians, strove to record the events but integrated legends and superstitions compiling the "lie agreed upon" that is historical record. Here is Roger of Wendover's year 1100 chronicle of strange signs and occurrences surrounding the death of William Rufus (The Red-Haired), successor to his father, William the Bastard (or The Conqueror).

King William Rufus held his court in Gloucester at Christmas, at Winchester in Easter and at Whitsuntide in London.

On the morrow of St. Peter *ad vincula* ["in chains," 2 August 1100] he went to shoot in the New Forest, where Walter Tyrrel, aiming at a stag, unintentionally struck the king and thus by a miserable death ended his cruel life. Pierced to the heart, he fell without uttering a word. Many signs prefigured his departure, for the day before his death he dreamed of being bled by a physician, and the stream of his blood reaching to Heaven, obscuring the sky.

After the dream he'd sprung from sleep, invoking the name of St.

Mary and calling for a light. He kept his chamberlains with him for the rest of the night. In the morning, a foreign monk at court for business related a dream to Robert FitzHamon [d. 1107 at Falaise], a powerful nobleman intimate with the king. In the dream, the king went into a church and cast his usual haughty look on the congregation round about, after which he took the crucifix between his teeth and nearly bit off its arms and legs. The crucifix was at first passive but afterwards kicked the king with its right foot so that he fell down on the pavement, and emitted such a huge flame from his mouth that the smoke of it rose in a cloud even up to the stars.

Robert told this dream to the king, who said with a laugh, "He is a monk and, like all monks, dreamed this to get something by it; give him a hundred shillings so that he may not say he has dreamed in vain."

When St. Anselm [1033–1109], archbishop of Canterbury, was exiled because of his tyranny, he traveled from Rome to Marcenniac to

visit Hugh, the abbot of Cluny. There a dialogue arose concerning King William, and the abbot swore that on the previous night he had seen the king summoned before the Throne of God in a dream. He was accused of his crimes and sentenced by the Judge to eternal damnation but did not explain how he was informed of it. (To speak of prophetical dreams of the monarch's death was in the Middle Ages punished as treason or as the witchcraft which sometimes tried to produce such a death. Even in twentieth-century Malaysia prophetic dreams threatened the stability of the state.) Neither the archbishop [Anselm] nor any of the others present asked him, out of respect to his great holiness or to prevent trouble for him.

The following day the archbishop went to Lyons, and when the monks who had accompanied him chanted matins, a young man, in simple dress and of a mild countenance, stood beside one of the clerks of the archbishop, who had his eyes closed. "Adam," he said, "are you asleep?" The clerk responded "No," and the young man continued, "Do you want to hear some news?"

"Most willingly," said Adam.

"Then," said the young man, "be informed that most certainly the quarrel between the archbishop and King William has now been put at an end." The clerk, roused by these words, looked up, and opened his eyes, but he saw no one.

The next night, one of the clerks of the same archbishop was standing at his post and chanting matins when someone held out to him a paper, on which the monk read the words "King William is dead." He immediately looked around but saw no one except his companions. A short time after, two of his [the archbishop's] monks came to him, telling him of the king's death, and earnestly advised him to return to his see.

It was also said that on the day of William Rufus' death (news of which could never have traveled so quickly to Rome), the pope himself learned of the death of William Rufus and said a requiem Mass for his soul. This also sounds unlikely, considering the king's opposition to the church.

Several people have argued that the death of the king had been planned, which would have explained why people knew of it some distance from England. The king, Dr. Margaret Murray argued, was of the Old Religion, which on occasion called for the king to die as a sacrifice to his people. It is possible Tyrrel's arrow was no accident.

Dr. Murray's views on the Old Religion and the history of witchcraft have been challenged for a long time. If indeed William Rufus was a sacrifice it would have explained how the day of his death, made more dramatic by the report of prophetic dreams, was known so soon by so many. Some have suggested Charles I or even Joan or Arc and Gilles de Rais were substitute sacrifices for a king.

In my view, Charles I was not a king sacrificed for his people any more than Louis XVI was. They were simply victims of their own politics. Joan of Arc went to the stake because of political enemies, despite her claims of visions. She said the Archangel Michael had appeared to her, when she was awake, which led to accusations of witchcraft and helped to seal her fate.

Whether William Rufus died by accident or by design, pious Christians were eager to believe the stories of prophetic dreams about his sudden demise.

William Rufus, William II of England, was born in Normandy in 1056. He succeeded his father William the Conqueror as king of England on 26 September 1087. The church disliked him for many reasons but not because of the Old Religion, rather because when a bishopric fell vacant William Rufus, desiring its revenues for the crown, was slow to fill it.

Nevertheless, he was buried in the Christian cathedral at Winchester. He was succeeded by his younger brother Henry I, called Henry Beauclerc because he could write. Henry tried to get along better with ecclesiastical authorities but in some ways was no improvement over William Rufus. With half a dozen mistresses, he produced more illegitimate children than any other British monarch. The score stands at least a score, and that is 20.

Henry I was married to Matilda for political reasons. Matilda was the granddaughter of King Edmund Ironside, who had a brief reign from April to November in 1016. Her father was the king of Scotland and her mother was Margaret, of the royal English lineage. Moreover Matilda was descended from Alfred the Great.

When Matilda died in 1118, Henry Beauclerc married Adela of Louvain. By that time he started masking Norman connections, which may explain why William Rufus was hated when alive and why his death was a subject of fascination and superstition.

Finally, on the subject of William Rufus and his brother Henry Beauclerc, there is a legend that William the Conqueror once consulted wise men as to the fates of his sons.

The wise men foretold that his eldest son, named Robert Curthose for his clothing, would not succeed him and that the second son, Richard, would die young. A stag killed Richard while he hunted in the New Forest, in 1081.

The wise men asked William Rufus what kind of bird he would want to be. William Rufus replied, "I would want to be an eagle, because it is a strong and powerful bird, feared by other birds, and therefore king of them all." When asked the same question, Henry Beauclerc responded that he would like to be a starling because "it gains its living without injuring anyone and never seeks to grieve or to rob its neighbor."

So the wise men told the Conqueror that William Rufus would be a strong but violent king and die a harsh death while Henry Beauclerc, because William would die without an heir, would have a peaceful reign and a peaceful death.

History is of full of dreams that happened to coincide with future events, or were thought up afterwards in an attempt to explain or enhance them. Hindsight is very useful. Sometimes, as Oscar Wilde said, "our only duty to history is to rewrite it."

Do you believe in prophetic dreams that some deeper personal or divine consciousness speaking to us? If our lives are written for us, is it possible that from time to time we are able to sneak a look at the later pages of the script? Do we all know at some very secret level what is going to happen to us? I should hate to think so. That would be extremely depressing.

SOME PHILOSOPHERS

In the *Timæus* (46a), Plato says dreams are "visions within us,…which are remembered by us when we are awake and in the external world" but ever since then philosophers as well as scientists have worried about how well we recall what we dream and even how we can be sure we are not dreaming and actually conscious in "the external world" (however you define that).

In the *Thætetus* (158), Plato asks: "How can you determine whether at this moment we are sleeping, and all our thoughts are a dream; or whether we are awake, and talking to each other." Many philosophers have attempted to answer that question but even René Descartes' solution to the problem does not appeal to everyone.

In the Middle Ages people worried that demons might attack us in our dreams; science and superstition, philosophy and theology all had various positions about dreams and the extent to which we were responsible for them or could learn from them.

Thomas Hobbes was suspicious of dreams, claiming that they lacked coherence because they were mere phantasms and not really experience, "in the silence of sense there is no new motion from the objects, and therefore no new phantasm." Later thinkers were to value and

Imaginary portraits of Plato and Aristotle, by Raphael.

encourage the rehashing of real experience that dreams are supposed to accomplish. But Hobbes said dreams had no defense against absurdity, that they were prone to illogic, and worst of all that they were not really experience but musing or imagining, though at the time they seem to be experience. Dreams do often convince us that we are having real experiences. To what extent are we doing so?

If dreams are simply fanciful, no wonder Emmanuel Kant denounced them as too metaphysical. In *Dreams of a Spirit-Seer* (1766) he suggested that dreams were as fragile and fantastic as Swedenborg's ideas (of which he greatly disapproved). Kant wanted a metaphysics (if any at all) that was devoted to the hard facts of human sense experience and aware of the limits of human knowledge so derived.

Freud looked on dreams are reports from the unconscious, aware, of course, that these reports might be manipulated or misleading. He had to deal not with dreams themselves but with the stories of their dreams his patients told him. Later in the twentieth century A.J. Ayer (among others) stressed that reports of dreams are not dreams but interpretations of dreams. Ayer said we can really know nothing about dream content but "only wake with delusive memories of experiences we have never had." Others claim that dreaming is indeed experience and can even be controlled and accurately recalled. Or that our delusions are interesting in any case.

Bertrand Russell in *Our Knowledge of the External World* (1949) and Norman Malcolm in *Dreaming* (1959) presented their views forcefully but Ayer argued with Malcolm in the *Journal of Philosophy* (1960) and others have gone on to take one side or the other in a continuing debate. Philosophy still does not have an absolute grip on what reality is.

Meanwhile, scientists have made progress in detecting when we dream (rapid eye movement), investigated what happens when we are deprived of dreams (sleep deprivation), and gone on attempting to decode the meaning of dreaming and of dreams (psychoanalysis) with the use of word associations and other means.

Start with something fairly easy from a philosopher: M. MacDonald's "Sleeping and Waking" in *Mind* 62 (April 1953), 202-215, which, for what it attempts, probably has not been improved upon in the last half century or so. Philosophers like to deal in eternal verities— and to spend eternities coming to conclusions. Some go so far as to say that conclusions are impossible. They claim that believing you have found or can find truth is just daydreaming.

As for daydreaming, some people boasting of pragmatism condemn it roundly, but I am on the side of Leonardo da Vinci when it comes to daydreams. "If you pay close attention to them," Leonardo said, "you will hit on some truly marvelous ideas." He did.

A woodcut from Dr. Johannes Weirus' *De Præstigiis dæmonum* (1586) presents various images of medieval and Renaissance witchcraft, especially the witch riding a goat to the sabbat. She really ought to have been seated backwards (as in Albrecht Dürer's engraving of 1511); witches did many things backwards (rejecting orthodoxy), at the Black Mass the crucifix is inverted, the coven dances counter-clockwise in a circle, and so on. The goat (as with the horns and hooves attributed to the Devil) represents bestial instincts. Some witches were said to ride on broomsticksand indeed a dildo annointed with "flying ointment"'s hallucinogens may have given witches dreams of flying. Much of what was soberly reported in accounts of witchcraft may have been experienced only in dreams or other altered states of conciousness.

NIGHT OF THE LIVING DREAD

Argargün, Mehmed Yücel, *et al.* "Repetitive and Frightening Dreams and Suicidal Behavior in Patients with Major Depression," *Comprehensive Psychiatry* 39:4 (July/August 1998), 198–202.

Bower, Bruce. "The Fragile, Creative Side of Nightmares," *Science News* 131 (17 January 1987), 37.

————————-. "Nightmare Numbers Surprisingly High," *Science News* 137 (3 March 1990), 132.

Claridge, Gordon *et al.* "Nightmares, Dreams, and Schizotypy," *British Journal of Clinical Psychology* 36: 3 (September 1997), 377–386.

Hartmann, Ernest. *Dreams and Nightmares: The New Theory on the Origin and Meaning of Dreams* (1998).

————————-. "Nightmare after Trauma as Paradigm for All Dreams: A New Approach to the Nature and Functions of Dreaming," *Psychiatry: Interpersonal and Biological Processes* 61: 3 (Fall 1998), 223–238.

————————-. "What Dreams, Nightmares Tell You about Yourself. Interview with Ernest Hartmann," *US News & World Report* 96 (16 January 1984), 49–50.

Levin, Ross & Rebecca Stiritz Daly, "Nightmares and Psychotic Decompensation: A Case Study, "*Psychiatry: Interpersonal and Biological Processes* 61: 3 (Fall 1998), 217–222.

Neidhardt, Joseph. "The Do-It-Yourself Nightmare Cure," *Prevention* 45 (March 1993), 62–64.

Nightmares by Henry Fuseli

Sabini, Meredith. "Imagery in Dreams of Illness," *Quadrant* 14: 2 (Fall 1981), 85–104.

Sage, Londa. "Night of the Living Dread," *Health* 19 (August 1987), 20.

Schredl, Michael & Ruth Pallmer. *"Alpträume bei Kindern"* (Nightmares in Children), *Praxis der Kinderpsychologie und Kinderpsychiatrie* 46:1 (January 1997), 36–56.

Stockholder, Kay. "The Wedding Guest's Nightmare: An Oneiric Reading of Coleridge's 'The Rime of the Ancient Mariner,'" *Dreaming* 7: 1 (March 1977), 29–46.

von Krteisler, Kristin. "The Dream that Haunts You..." *Redbook* 178 (April 1992), 108–110.

Wilson, S. J. *et al.* "Adult Night Terrors and Paroxetine [a drug]," *Lancet* [North American Edition] 350 (19 July 1997), 185.

DID YOU KNOW...?

- All across America (and in many other countries) Sleep Disorder Centers are booming? Americans spend staggering amounts on drugs to put them asleep and to get them awake or keep them awake.

- Young children do not put themselves into their dreams, and American dreams (according to Dr. Milton Kramer of Cincinnati, in *Newsweek* for 14 August 1989) had begun to show less sexual differentiation years before the new millennium?

- That men and women dream about different things? According to psychologist Christopher Evans (*Landscapes of the Night*) and neuroscientist Jonathan Winson (*Brain and Psyche*) the principal reason for sleep is to order the information collected by the brain during the consciousness of the day.

- That dreams, according to researchers at The State University of New York and Bell Laboratories (reported in *Science News* 126, 15 September 1984, 173), do not vanish from memory any faster than other kinds of information? Recall may be prompted by some kind of waking experience.

- The Senoi of Malaysia consider dreams a community resource and in the U.S. we have communities such as at the San

Francisco Dream House, where dreamers discuss, paint and sculpt their dream images as a means of self-understanding?

- That dreaming about eggs or eagles can be very significant—and you can be different ages in different dreams?

- That fetuses not only hear and see in the womb but dream?

By the way, what *do* you look like in your dreams?

EMOTIONS

These are the principle source material in dreams. For the best study of emotions, so crucial to the understanding of dreams, I suggest a surprising source. It is not any modern psychologist or philosopher but Adam Smith's *The Theory of the Moral Sentiments* (1759). Smith (1723–1790) is known in the field of economics for *The Wealth of Nations* (1776), but *Moral Sentiments* may be his best book, in its philosophical approach to emotions.

Even after more than 200 years psychology tries to reinvent the wheel every generation. Its proponents are often abysmally ignorant of anything written before they went to college. After Aristotle, then Freud and Jung, discoveries have been minimal.

There is a lot of sleep disorder research, but not enough to understand emotional states, or the lack of them, in dreams. The understanding of human psychology surely has a bright future, but so much is to be learned. The brightest practitioners of the present appear to ignore psychology's past.

This book will give you some idea of that past. The bibliographies are a main feature of this book, as I have been researching for years. I have cited fairly recent books that you can find.

DAYDREAMING

The old joke goes that everyone builds castles in the air; neurotics and psychotics live in them; and psychiatrists collect the rent.

There is nothing wrong with daydreams, what Henrik Ibsen calls "life lies" or Eugene O'Neill calls "pipe dreams." They keep us going. Castles in the air are okay—no one can foreclose on the mortgages. Use them as vacation homes only!

Sometimes we are actually asleep we are aware that we are dreaming. Novalis calls this "near waking." In these situations as in daydreams we can learn a lot from our unconscious. Freud, of course, says it's all about sex. In *The Interpretation of Dreams*, he writes of daydreams:

> They occur with perhaps equal frequency in both sexes, though it seems that while in girls and women they are invariably of an erotic nature, in men they may be either erotic or ambitious. Nevertheless, the importance of the erotic factor in men, too, should not be given a secondary rating; a closer investigation of a man's day-dreams generally shows that all his heroic exploits are carried out and all his successes achieved only in order to please a woman and to be preferred...to other men. These fantasies are satisfactions of wishes proceeding from deprivation and longing.

F. Diane Barth has a whole book on the subject: *Daydreaming* (1997). What's the difference between daydreaming, dozing, ruminating, fantasizing, being in a reverie, and just chilling?

A REALLY NASTY IDEA

Ethelred the Unready (meaning he would not be advised not that he was unprepared) first reigned in England from 978 to 1013. He was deposed, and then restored to reign from 1014 to 1016. Ethelred's eldest son by his first wife had died, so Edmund Ironside succeeded him in 1016, but lasted only a few months. Then came Ethelred's second wife's new husband, Canute (1016–1035), king of Denmark, Norway and then England.

When Ethelred the Unready died, his oldest son Alfred Atheling was killed by those who wanted him out of the way, in favor of a man named Harold Harefoot. Stay with me now because here comes the gruesome event of 1036.

It is said that the Earl Godwin had a dream in which he saw a violent way of getting rid of Alfred Atheling. Godwin's men cut open Alfred's belly, tore out his guts and nailed them to a post. Then they chased Alfred around, sticking him with daggers, until he died. This did not take long, as the dream had foretold. Harold Harefoot got the throne, and after him came Hardicanute.

DREAMING AND THINKING

Descartes and Leibnitz argued that "the soul is always thinking," but Locke denied this. Then a Victorian student of the paranormal, F.W.H.

Meyers, suggested that dreams are what he called "uprushes" of a sub-level. On that Freud, Jung, and other scientists based the concept of the unconscious and even a collective unconscious.

If you ever dream or think, and I know that you do, you might want to look into courses from IMAGO at 24 Maryon Mews, London NW3 2PU, ten monthly sessions. Here's the pitch:

> Social Dreaming is a method whereby people come together and share their dreams. It is based on the assumption that all dreamers are thinkers. The focus is on the dream not the dreamer.

There is nothing wrong with telling people your dreams and getting their reactions, but I doubt this is a business for amateurs. Dreams can be so tricky.

Freud dreamed that his brother released their mother from a cupboard. If you know German you might be able to connect the German noun *Kasten* (cupboard, closet, box) with the German adjective that translates "boxed up." That is, confined or in a predicament, but not in a real box or closet. Mom was not in a closet but in a quandary. An Englishman might dream of a piece of luggage in a closet as a "closet case."

Is that stranger in your dream perhaps a shadow version of yourself? Or could he or she be visiting (as some peoples believe is possible) from someone else's dream world? Never jump to conclusions, though. Freud warned: "It remains an essential rule always to leave out of all account the ostensible continuity of a dream as being of suspect origin." It's in code, any coherence you may be adding in remembering or reporting.

INTERPRETING

Your friends have all the answers, but to more complex symbols? Are you able to tell them about the dream reliably? This stuff is a game for pros, in my opinion. I agree with Adam Phillips, however, that dream interpretation is not a science but an art form.

You might take a friend's advice on how to stop hiccoughs. But would you take a friend's advice on how to cure psoriasis? Or would you follow your vague feeling that it must be caused by beets and stop eating them?

DREAMING AT A DISTANCE

From a Mrs. Montgomery of Beaulieu (Co. Louth, Ireland) dated February 1884:

> Nearly 30 years ago I lost a sister. The place where she died being at some distance, my husband went to the funeral without me. I went to bed early, and had a frightful dream of the funeral ceremony. I saw my brother faint away at the service, and fall into the grave. I awoke with the horror of the dream, just as my husband entered the room on his return from the funeral, which had taken place at least eight hours before...I related [the dream]. He said, "Who in the world told you that? I never intended telling you." I said, "I only dreamt it. Just as you were coming in I awoke."

Was it a veridical dream from the brother in his altered state of faint, or was she reading the husband's thoughts as he entered the room? What do you believe?

LAWRENCE OF ARABIA IN *SEVEN PILLARS OF WISDOM*

"All men dream, but not equally. Those who dream by night in the dusty recesses of their recesses of their minds wake in the day to find that it was vanity; but the dreamers of the day are dangerous men, for they may act their dream with open eyes, to make it possible."

A RATIONALE OF PROPHETIC DREAMS

Felix E. Planer, in the revised edition of his *Superstition* (1988), referred to J. W. Dunne's *An Experiment with Time* (1927) in connection with prophetic dreams (p. 77):

> Dunne believed...that over a period of time the majority of his dreams contained elements of events that were later to materialize. After consultations with his friends on the subject he eventually took this to be a general phenomenon, and proposed a worldview centering upon a novel conception of time. According to this theory the events on this earth are presumed to be part of a preconceived scheme, embracing past, present and future. This plan was thought to unfold continuously, in the way a cinematographic film unrolls. The picture actually being

projected, according to this somewhat simplified analogue, represents our experience of the present. Past, present and future are thus assumed to exist simultaneously, whereby the present is being spotlighted in a mysterious way, marking it off from past and future.

Gifted or privileged persons, according to this concept, are able to glimpse, or even become immersed in, episodes of the past in the course of their dreams, represented here by the roles of film already unrolled.

The way time is speeded up or slowed down in dreams demands investigation. If time is a human construct, possibly we will be able to construct something to beat it.

EXTERIOR INFLUENCE ON DREAMS

The story is told about two travelers who pause for a rest. One falls asleep and the other sees a bee creep into a hole in a nearby wall, reaches out his staff, and traps the bee. When he removes the staff, the bee flies into the ear of the sleeping man. His companion then awakens him and hears that the sleeper dreamed his friend had trapped him in a dark cave. Had the "bee entered into the soul of the dreamer," as the story claims?

The soul (Hebrew *ruach*, Greek *pneuma*) is a "spirit" independent of the body—except maybe in Swedish, where the word for "soul" is the same as that for "mind." Do transient souls visit humans in sleep and influence dreams? Important questions; sleep on them.

WHEN TO DREAM

Whether you believe dreams can foretell the future or just interpret the past you definitely are going to have a lot of them. They will all be in the present tense. They are not expressed as stories but as experiences.

In an hour or hour and a half nap, you probably won't dream. Dreams visit about three-quarters of your night's sleep, but only 5%, if any, takes place during the last quarter.

So you could sleep 25% less and still not miss much dreaming. At the start you are too deeply asleep to dream.

Some people have managed to get by on a few hours of sleep each day. Napoleon and other men of action have been credited with the ability to sleep in snatches, and Buckminster Fuller once spent a whole year sleeping for half an hour every three hours. Such people must have had trouble finding time to dream and process the day's information. Maybe they did that when they were awake.

WRITE IT DOWN

"The horror of that moment I shall never forget," says a character of Lewis Carroll. Another responds that he will forget it "unless you make a memorandum of it." I remind you of that.

You have a number of dreams every night and if you should happen to wake up from one, you have a fighting chance of being able to get it down in paper if you act swiftly. Freud feared you might elaborate on the dream or try to make sense of it and thereby distort it, so take a few notes but do not try to straighten it all out as you record what you recall.

Eventually you'll need to put your dream in the context of what Hugh of St. Victor (1096–1141) called *cogitatio* (thinking), *meditatio* (meditation), and *contemplatio* (contemplation), by which a soul gains a supernatural intimation of God. This medieval thinker gave some good advice in connection with dreams and dreaming when he advised people to "learn everything, and afterwards you will see that nothing is useless."

Medieval religion and ancient myth are not so far from what I like to call the reformed religion of Freudian psychoanalysis. Freud may not

have been orthodox or a lawgiver, but Freud was a priest, in his way, of the new faith—the religion of science.

Psychoanalysis offers a new kind of sacrament of confession and absolution. It even has its holy books, and Freud wrote some of them. He once said near the end of his brilliant career, that if he had the opportunity to do it all over he would specialize in parapsychology.

There is always something magical at the highest reaches of science. Dreams in particular deal in transformations and the magical connection between levels. "As above, so below" is a standard magical credo, which fits neatly into Freud's concepts of the way dream symbols connect with reality. He felt that dreams create a sort of third reality.

Freud also demonstrated that the interpretation of dreams identifies and cures neuroses. By understanding dreams, we can understand ourselves in our daily actions and in the deepest wellsprings of our personalities, but also something larger in the origins of human consciousness.

We must try to learn everything we can about our dreams. However, when a dream doesn't rise into the conscious mind, how are you ever going to recall it?

At the other end of the spectrum is James Thurber. Objecting to faddish psychology, which Freud could not help launching and surely would have deplored as his doctrines became distorted, Thurber once collaborated on a book entitled *Leave Your Mind Alone*.

THE CATEGORIES OF DREAMS

In Britain, "sorting things out" is tantamount to solving the problem. Naturally, just getting the pieces of the puzzle sorted is not the same thing as putting it together. But sorting into categories is a useful first step.

Ambrosius Macrobius was the author of the *Saturnalia*, a work resembling a compilation by Aulus Gellius in Athens called *Attic Nights* and *The Dream of Scipio* (c. 390). Macrobius categorized dreams in the following way:

visum: (apparition): the dreamer thinks himself awake and sees specters.
insomnium: the dreamer has disturbed dreams or nightmares caused by mental or physical stress.
somnium: (dream): the dreamer experiences information which "conceals with strange shapes, and veils with ambiguity" the true meaning of the information offered, and requires an interpretation for its understanding.
visio: (vision): the dreamer is vouchsafed a dream that comes true.
oraculum: (oracle): a (dead) parent offers advice or some other revered figure makes a prophecy.

During the Middle Ages, Macrobius was hailed by theologians such as John of Salisbury and Alexander of Hales as influential in philosophy and theology but also in literature on dream visions and premonitory apparitions. Macrobius also affected Chaucer. Chaucer extended St. Augustine's division of *visio* into:

visio corporale: vision of sensory and realistic images
visio spirituale: the sensory images shaped by spiritual powers
visio intellectuale: a direct appeal to the intellect, revealing something
  of the divine *mysterium* (mystery) without the mediation of images,
  direct apprehension of the Divine Will such as that experienced by
  the prophets

Informative dreams were considered a revelation of holy truths. There could be, however, false dreams deriving from evil, designed to lead mankind astray. Satan (The Adversary) was just as real to pious believers as God Almighty. Thus, in addition to piety, there existed a fear of The Devil, who roamed "through the world seeking the ruin of souls."

For more on dreams and the Fathers of the Church, see Patricia Cox Miller's "'A Dubious Twilight:' Reflections on Dreams in Patristic Literature," *Church History* 55 (June 1986), 153–164.

DAYDREAMS

We all have them, especially dreams of sex, escape, power, and glory. T.S. Eliot used to say the reason he did not frequent the movies was that they interfered with his daydreams.

ROBERT HERRICK ON THE INDIVIDUALITY OF DREAMS

Here we are all by day; by night we are hurled
By dreams, each one into a several world.

WILLIAM FOXLEY'S LONG SLEEP

One American detective writer calls death the "long sleep," but living persons have slept remarkable amounts of time. Take, for example, William Foxley, an employee of the Mint in London, who, says John Stow in his *Survey of London* (1598), slept for 14 days and 15 nights in 1546. He became a curiosity, though, rather than a catastrophe, and did not lose his job.

A Roman copy of a third-century BC Greek statue of a Sleeping Faun.

BAD DREAM COME TRUE

Franz Kafka's opening sentence in *Metamorphosis* (1915): *Als Gregor Samsa eines Morgens aus unruhigen Traüme erwachte, fand er sich in seinem Bett zu einem ungehueuren Ungeziefer verwandelt* [As Gregor Samsa woke one morning from uneasy dreams he found himself in his bed transformed into a giant insect].

Have you ever awakened from a dream and found yourself vastly changed? You need not look like a cockroach; perhaps you are just certainly and suddenly older, or melancholy or happy. Maybe you're freed of some burden you carried all your life.

Dreams can be watersheds of emotion, as sudden as a stab to the heart. We do not grow older gradually. We grow older now and then, in jumps, as it were, which might be symbolized by such a dramatic appearance as Kafka describes, but more often in ways that are internal and imperceptible.

A VISION

In 1603 the famous playwright and poet Ben Jonson stayed in the country at the home of a friend while the plague raged in London. There he had "a vision" of the death of his "best piece of poetry," his young son, who stayed back in the city. Presumably the "vision" came in a dream. Here is the story as William Drummond of Hawthornden reported it:

> At that time the pest was in London, he [Jonson] being in the country at Sir Robert Cotton's house with old [William] Camden, he saw in a vision his eldest son, then a child and at London, appear unto him with the mark of a bloody cross on his forehead, as if it had been cutted with a sword....

It was the custom to mark a cross on the doors of those who had died of the plague so carts collecting bodies could identify the houses. Metaphors and symbols in dreams are often derived from popular customs and beliefs. The story continues:

> at which, amazed, he prayed unto God, and in the morning he came to Mr. Camden's chamber to tell him, who persuaded him it was but an apprehension of his fancy at which he should not be dejected. In the mean time comes three letters from his wife of the death of the boy in the plague. He appeared to him (he said)

of a manly shape, and of that growth that he thinks he shall be at the resurrection.

If, as The Creed says, we shall rise again "with the same bodies as in this life," there's no reason why Jonson would think that Benjamin Junior, age seven, would appear at the resurrection as a grown man. But that is the least striking part of the report, surely.

SHORT STORIES OF G.A. HENTY

As the author of a recent book on Henty, I cannot miss the opportunity to choose him as a representative of dreams in the short story of the nineteenth century. Dennis Butts, writing on "The Short Stories of G.A. Henty" in *Henty Society Bulletin 93* (2000), 16, notes that "Henty is particularly fond of the device of the dream or vision that ultimately comes true to suggest experiences that cannot be explained rationally."

Leonard R. N. Ashley, *George Alfred Henty and the Victorian Mind* (1999).
Peter Newbolt, *G. A. Henty 1832–1902: A Bibliographical Study* (1996).
Harold Orel, *The Victorian Short Story...* (1986).

A PREMONITORY DREAM

In the week before he was shot at Ford's Theater in Washington, President Abraham Lincoln had a dream that he discussed with several people. Lincoln said he dreamed he was walking through the White House and saw a catafalque covered in a black pall.
"Who is dead?" asked Lincoln.
"The president," replied a soldier on duty.

A DREAM, BY WILLIAM ALLINGHAM (1824–1889)

I heard the dogs howl in the moonlight night;
I went to the window to see the sight;
    All the Dead that ever I knew
Going one by one and two by two.

On they pass'd, and on they pass'd;
Townsfellows all, from first to last;
    Born in the moonlight of the lane,
Quench'd in the heavy shadow again.

Schoolmates, marching as when we play'd
At soldiers once—but now more staid;
   Those were the strangest sight to me
Who were drown'd, I knew, in the awful sea.

Straight and handsome folk; bent and weak, too;
Some that I lov'd, and gasp'd to speak to;
   Some but a day in their churchyard bed;
Some that I had not known were dead.

A long, long crowd—where each seem'd lonely,
Yet of them all there was one, one only,
   Rais'd a head or look'd my way.
She linger'd a moment—she might not stay.

How long since I saw that fair pale face!
Ah! Mother dear! Might I only place
   My head on thy breast, a moment to rest,
While thy hand on my tearful cheek were press'd!

On, on, a moving bridge they made
Across the moon-stream, from shade to shade,
   Young and old, women and men;
Many long-forgot, but remember'd then.

And first there came a bitter laughter;
A sound of tears the moment after;
   And then a music so lofty and gay
That every morning, day by day,
   I strive to recall it if I may.

SWEDENBORG

When he was over 50, Emmanuel Swedenborg, as the result of dreams, switched his work from science to mysticism. Signe Toksvig's biography calls him *Emmanuel Swedenborg: Scientist and Mystic* (1948). Swedenborg was utterly convinced that the Last Judgment had taken place in 1757 and that he was the prophet of the New Church. He claimed to have visions of distant planets and conversations with angels and the dead. He also had dreams telling him where to find hidden documents and knowledge about far off events.

At a party in Gothenberg in July 1759, he told people that

Stockholm was experiencing a great fire but it had been put out, sparing his house. He said the fire had stopped only three doors away. This was confirmed later when news arrived from the capital, some 300 miles from Gothenberg.

Emmanuel Swedenborg (or Svedberg, 1688–1772) is an astounding character in world history. He still exerts an influence, has a religious following, and is excitingly presented in William Wunch's *An Outline of Swedenborg's Teaching* (1975).

HAVE YOU HEARD THIS ONE?

A man dreamed that he had died and, when he did not wake up, he had.

OUT IN SPACE

"While I was out in orbit," said Soviet astronaut Vladimir Lyakhov, "my dreams were usually about earth." To what extent are our dreams limited or not limited to our personal experience? It is difficult to remember dreams because, while we dream, our memory-making devices are, as it were, turned off to provide more power for the imagination. (Seratonin is also produced in smaller quantity, making dreams less like hallucinations. Noradrenalin production is almost completely shut down, making dreams less likely to be affected by exterior influences.) How much of dreaming is memory, how much is chemistry, and how much is something else? Precisely what *is* that something else?

AN AUTHOR'S NIGHTMARE

The philosopher Bertrand Russell (Earl Russell, 1872-1970) once dreamed that he was in a big library of the future. It was 2010. A library employee was going along with a large container into which he dropped books selected from the shelves for what is politely called de-acquisition. Russell watched in horror as the library employee took down from the shelf the three volumes of Russell's *Principia Mathematica*, turned a few pages and blithely chucked the volumes into the garbage.

TECHNICOLOR

Science tells me that most dreamers dream in old-fashioned black and white. I distinctly recall color in my own dreams. Maybe they are basically black and white, or gray, but burst into color to make important points, like *The Picture of Dorian Gray*. What about your dreams? Do you dream in full color with *Sensurround*?

My dog, an Old English sheepdog, dreams. You can see his feet move, for (as Tennyson says) "he hunts in dreams." But I also know he does not dream in color. Dogs only see in black and white.

A nasty scientist in Lyons named Michel Jouvet killed laboratory cats by keeping them from dreaming for about three weeks. Cats nap so often that they must require a lot of dreamtime. Or maybe they're lazy.

Dorothy (Judy Garland) with the Scarecrow (Ray Bolger) on the Yellow Brick Road (1939), mercifully without the wooden Tin Man and the Mugging Lion.

MURDER AT THE RED BARN

Based on a true story of a poor girl's murder, this melodrama of 1828 was immensely popular. The mystery was solved by a dream.

ON THE SILENT SCREEN

Sometimes dreams present us with a sort of silent film. Charles Baudelaire in *Les fleurs du mal* (Flowers of Evil) writes of a "Parisian Dream" in a splendid palace—he later wakes up to "the horror of my garret"—that is entirely without sound. The poem begins:

De cette terrible passage,	Of that terrible landscape,
Tel que jamais mortel n'en vit,	Such as mortal never saw,

Ce matin encore l'image,	This morning the image,
Vague et lointaine, me ravit.	Vague and far off, excites me.

Then he describes the vision and comments:

Et sur ces mouvements merveilles	And over these moving marvels
Planait (terrible nouvéaute!	Hovered (terrifying novelty!)
Tout pour l'oeil, rien pour	Everything for the eye, nothing for
les oreilles!)	the ears!
Un silence d'eternité	A silence of eternity!

In the original French there is such a wonderful music, lost in English translation!

UPAS

This tree is said to produce a poisonous vapor that can kill those who sleep beneath it. Actually it does produce a strong poison used on arrowheads. See: William A. Emboden's *Bizarre Plants: Magical, Monstrous, Mythical* (1974).

GETTING WHAT YOU WANT

Every one of us dreams from time to time about getting what we want. Here is a story from Edmund Fuller's *25,000 Anecdotes for All Occasions* (1943). It is about two people who claimed to have dreams that actually got them what they wanted:

> Sir William Johnson [Bart, 1715–1774, superintendent of Indian affairs in North America] had ordered some suits of rich clothing from England. When they were unpacked, the Mohawk chief Hendrick admired them greatly. Shortly afterward he told Sir William that he had had a dream in which Sir William had given him one of the suits. Sir William took the hint and presented Hendrick with one of the handsomest outfits. Not long after that when Sir William and Hendrick were together, Sir William said that he too had had a dream. Hendrick asked him what it was. Sir William explained that he had dreamed that Hendrick had presented him with a certain tract of land on the Mohawk River, comprising about 5,000 acres of the most fertile terrain. Immediately Hendrick present-

ed the land to Sir William, remarking as he did so that he would dream no more with him. "You dream too hard for me, Sir William," he observed.

A THOUGHT

If people could fly people would walk in their dreams.

—*Egg*, the television arts show

AMONG THE POETS

Atlas, James. *Delmore Schwartz: The Life of an American Poet.* New York: Harcourt Brace Jovanovich (1985).

Kauvar, Elaine M. "Blake's Interpretation of Dreams...," *American Imago* 41 (1984), 19–45.

Mann, John S. "Dream in Emily Dickinson's Poetry," *Dickinson Studies* 34 (1978), 19–26.

Martin, Robert K. "Whitman's 'Song of Myself:' Homosexual Dream and Vision," *Partisan Review* 42 (1975), 80–96.

Mezel, Kathy. "Émile Nelligan," *Canadian Literature* 87 (1980), 81 – 99.

Zoltow, Maurice. "'I Brake for Delmore Schwartz:' Portrait of the Artist as a Young Liar," *Michigan Quarterly Review* 25 (1986), 1–22.

FROM *PIERRE, OR THE CONFIDENCE MAN*

"One trembles to think of that mysterious thing in the soul, which seems to acknowledge no human jurisdiction, but in spite of the individual's own innocent self, will still dream horrid dreams, and mutter unmentionable thoughts."

—Herman Melville

MASTER OF THE NIGHT

My late friend Dennis Williams treasured a small book by Takashi Ohta and Margaret Sperry called *The Golden Wind* (1929). I have never met anyone else who has heard of it. In it a Japanese youth named Takawo Muto encounters three unusual women. One of them says to him, "...trade will be master of my days; at night I am master of myself!"

It is this sense that in dreams we enjoy a freedom denied us in waking life that encourages some to so value the world of sleep and live chiefly in their dreams.

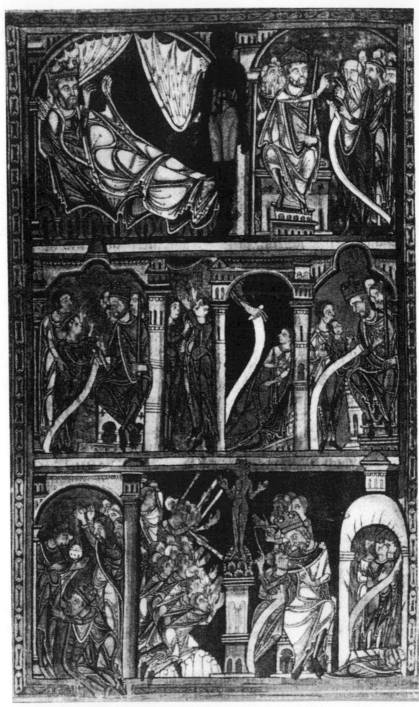

Daniel interprets Nebuchadnasser's Dream.

FANTASTIC ENTERTAINMENT

The way that a dream presents a series of exciting, fantastic scenes in rapid succession acts as a muse for many narratives and spectacles. For instance, the show that preceded the 2000 Olympic Games used dreams as its framework.

Thirteen-year-old Nikki Webster starred in the show at the Olympic stadium in Sydney. She spread a beach towel on the ground, put some zinc on her nose, and lay down to dream.

Her dream included aborigines like herself: Djakapurra Munyarryun (the song spinner) and the communities of Manningrida, Numbulwar, Ramingining, and Yirrkala in the traditional bush march.

There were also the Wandjinas (creators of the Universe) regenerating the earth with a lightning bolt simulated by 140 fire-breathers, 20 stilt walkers with flames, and 20 jugglers of fiery clubs. The desert women of Ngannyatjarra walked five days to take part in the festivities.

There was a Dream of Nature; a Tin Symphony, the violence of an early white settlement complete with 1,162 stomping dancers and the bandit Ned Kelly; and a final Eternity Dream.

EARLY TO BED AND EARLY TO RISE

From George Ade, author of *Fables in Slang*:

> Early to bed and early to rise is a bad rule for anyone who wishes to become acquainted with our most prominent and influential people."

A MAGICAL RECIPE

From one of the interludes of the sixteenth-century Bishop Bale we learn of an ancient recipe connected with St. Uncumber (*ohne Kummer, Without Anxiety*):

> If ye cannot slepe, but slumber,
> Geve Otes unto Saynt Uncumber,
> And Beans in a certain number
> Unto Saynt Blase and Saint Blythe.

As in most magical recipes, the "certain number" is vague. I would guess nine, for that number of beans goes all the way back to Roman magic of which I have written in *The Complete Book of Spells, Curses, and Magical Recipes*. Try nine.

The suggestion that oats be offered to St. Uncumber is disturbing because it suggests the subject cannot get a good night sleep due to an unwanted husband. St. Uncumber was a very popular old saint called upon by wives who were tired of their spouses. She herself had trouble with a man and defended her chastity to the death.

At one point she was asked to marry a man she did not want and grew a beard to put him off. That worked. Originally called St. Wigefort, you sacrificed to her (get this!) wild oats.

One old English writer suggested this actually worked, and emphasized that you got the desired effect if you offered the oats at "Poules" (St. Paul's) in London.

This saint went by a confusing number of names: St. Wilgefort, St. Wilgefortus, St. Comera, St. Cumerana, St. Dignefortis, St. Eutropia, St. Hulfe, St. Komina, St. Kummernis, St. Liberata, St. Livrada, St. Ontcommene, St. Ontcommer, and St. Uncumber. She was supposed to have been the daughter of a king of Portugal who wanted her to marry a pagan prince.

Her father killed her for avoiding marriage by growing that beard. The Old Testament says parents are enjoined to kill children who will not obey them. Her death gave her the status of virgin martyr. She was a *Virgo Fortis* (Strong Virgin) or a *Heilige Fratz* (Holy Face) and resembled, with her beard, the pure Christ crucified, and is often mistaken for a man. Her existence under so many names suggests to me that there must have been a lot of unhappy married women in the old days.

LUNATIC IDEAS

Does the moon have an effect on our dreams? Some people say so. Folklore is confidant that evil may come to one who dreams outdoors by moonlight. Superstition says that because our body is mostly water and the moon affects tides, it must also produce physiological effects on us that shape our dreams. Science is not so sure, but *The Farmer's Almanac* still directs us to consider phases of the moon when planting. Should we look for good dreams and bad dreams depending on moon phases too?

COULD SLEEP BE DANGEROUS?

A security guard told the management that they needed to beef up protection of the plant, as he had dreamed of burglars the previous night. They fired him. Nobody needs a watchman dreaming anything on the night shift.

A COUNTRY DOCTOR

In this brief but powerful story is the symbolism typical of nightmares: rose red, allusion (a wound like Christ's, in the side), narrative style, frustration, and fear of inadequacy.

This is Franz Kafka's tale of "A Country Doctor," drawn directly from his dreams. The district doctor is "called out needlessly" in a storm late at night to treat a patient. He is a young man, who begs the doctor, "Let me die." The relatives want him to help the lad. Meanwhile, the horses of the gig look in the windows of the sickroom, while the doctor accepts a drink from the patient's father.

At first the doctor thinks the patient ought to be dragged out of bed and reprimanded for unnecessarily worrying his poor parents but sees a huge wound, crawling with rosy maggots. He tells the boy "it is not so bad" and escapes. The story ends with the distraught doctor saying that once a false alarm is answered there is no chance of putting things right.

Many people suffer dreams in which they are faced with difficult decisions, impossible problems, frustration and shame at not being able to cope. The details differ, but the dreams are the same.

ANOTHER BLOODY REFERENCE TO PARACELSUS

The readers of my occult series want to see the name Theophrastus Bombastus von Hohenheim in every volume. He called himself Paracelsus and compared himself with the famous Greek physician Celsus. So here he is, with the news that Paracelsus claimed menstruation causes nightmares. I should think that occasionally men have nightmares when they discover that a woman of their acquaintance has ceased to menstruate.

C.G. JUNG DESCRIBES THE DREAM

"The whole creation is essentially subjective, and the dream is the theater where the dreamer is at once scene, actor, prompter, stage manager."

HOLLYWOOD WITH BROADWAY DREAMS

Lady in the Dark (1944) saw Ginger Rogers swanning around in the role made famous on stage by Gertrude Lawrence. It was a Moss Hart musical about a career girl undergoing psychoanalysis, which has since been the subject of serious psychoanalytic publication.

All movies are a kind of daydream; the psychiatrists have been writing about it in the professional journals for years. Indeed, so intensely

Paracelsus. From the frontispiece of Meric Causabon's *A True & Faithful Relation of What Passed for many Years Between Dr. John Dee...and Some Spirits* (1659)

do we sometimes enter into films that they become our real world. William James said dreams occur "whilst we are sleeping, because our attention then lapses from the sensible world."

What Hollywood can do that Broadway cannot is invade other character's dreams with elaborate fantasy worlds like Oz. Film can even create waking nightmare situations, as in *Seconds* (1966), a John Frankenheimer horror film that must have given unpleasant dreams to a good many who saw it.

The most amusing Hollywood product related to sleep, for my money, is Woody Allen's *Sleeper* (1973). Allen has always said he is not sure whether there is an afterlife but he is taking along a change of underwear, just in case. In this hit film he undergoes an operation, is frozen, awakens in 2173. The future takes place in a police state that forces hapless citizens to watch reruns of Howard Cosell on television.

THOREAU ON OUR REAL SELVES IN DREAMS

"In dreams we see ourselves revealed and acting out our real characters even more clearly than when awake." People have said that your true character is what you do when you don't think anyone is watching. Your true character may be darker than you think and act out in the privacy of dreams. As we say carelessly, we never would have *dreamed* of such a thing.

This is especially true in regard to sex. Michel de Chazal pointed out that sex is the mediator between birth and death. Just don't tell anyone your "worst nightmare" if you value your reputation over peace of mind.

The therapists have debated how much of our dreams is our own and how much is collective unconscious, archetypal material. It is comforting to believe that some of the bad stuff is not personal.

WATCH YOUR LANGUAGE

"Language is culture" is often quoted. Here I want simply to remind you that what we say can reveal assumptions and ideas about our society. Haven't you heard these following expressions without really examining what they contain?

Dream on!
Quit your dreaming!
I would never have dreamed it!
Not in my wildest dreams!
It was like a dream come true!
I must be dreaming!

"THERE ARE DREAMERS AND DREAMERS"

Jenny Diski, "Thank You, Disney," *London Review of Books*, 24 August 2000:

There are dreamers and dreamers. Great dreamers, on the whole, are saints or sinners (the Marquis de Sade, Simon Stylites), variations on innocence, whom we revere or abhor, while your everyday, small-scale worldly dreamer (the bloke down the road who wants to build a conservatory, the woman saving up for a breast enhancement) is a more mundane figure for whom we are likely to feel contempt. The degree to which we admire or despise dreamers depends mainly on the size of the dream and the distance of the dreamer from our own lives. We are very pleased that Martin Luther King had a dream, and that Nelson Mandela held to his dream through 28 years in jail, mostly because we are grateful that we don't have to do it ourselves. Impractical dreaming that amounts to something in the world we positively venerate, at least in retrospect. But then very often what we call admiration is, on closer examination, a special form of contempt.

Ms. Diski must mean impractical dreaming, because both King and Mandela actually did transform their societies. Bismarck dreamed of the success of the Prussian state and gained confidence from it.

A vision of what might be accomplished in real life often comes to the idealist, as it did for Bismarck, in a dream.

THE OLD HAG

Ancient folklore said that an old hag (or *mare*) could come in the night (whence *nightmare*) to sit on your chest and make it difficult for you to breathe. In the US, one encyclopedia says, "about 15 percent of the population suffers from this.

> The syndrome is characterized by a person awaking to find himself paralyzed and in the presence of a nonhuman entity, sometimes humanoid in shape and with prominent eyes, which often sits on his chest and causes feelings of suffocation. The experience is sometimes accompanied by musty smells and shuffling sounds. Occultists still attribute such attacks to evil spirits.

THE DREAMERS

From Anaïs Nin in *The Novel of the Future:* "In the old collective culture there was always room for the dreamer, the one who dreamed for the villagers, the one who interpreted dreams, omens, and myths, told tales, and preserved the history, ballads, and myths of the clan."

HALF A DOZEN IMPORTANT REFERENCES ON DREAMS

Aristotle. *De somniis* (On Dreams), translated by J. I. Beare in *Works of Aristotle* III (1931).
Chappell, V. C. "The Concept of Dreaming," *Philosophical Quarterly* 13 (July 1963), 193–213.
Dement, W. & N. Kleitman. "The Relation of Eye Movements during Sleep to Dream Activity: An Objective Method for the Study of Dreaming," *Journal of Experimental Psychology* 53 (1957), 339–346.
Freud, Sigmund. *The Interpretation of Dreams*, translated by James Strachey (1963).
Malcolm, Norman. *Dreaming* (1959).
Manser, A. R. & L. E. Thomas. "Dreams," *Proceedings of the Aristotelian Society* Supplement. Vol. 30 (1956), 197–228.

IN AFRICA

Among the Yoruba, a juice or powder is placed in or near the eyes to induce prophetic dreams, but the dream must be interpreted by a witch doctor. If a dream indicates a certain action, it is usually best to perform it. Watch out, though, the Yoruba say, some dreams may work by contraries.

DREAM DIARY

I suggest you keep a dream diary. Look at it every night before you hit the hay. Gail Delaney, a physician who writes about dreams, says "[T]he very act of placing a piece of paper beside your bed before you go to sleep with the intention of recording your dreams in the morning will increase your recall."

I think a bound book instead of pieces of paper is the right idea; you will want to thumb through and reconsider your interpretations. You ought to write interpretations down too, with the date, maybe leaving space for later comments as well.

These are your secrets. Nobody ought to read your dream book but you. If you are sleeping with anybody you don't trust not to peek, sleep at his or her place (or replace them!). If you are away from home, you can make notes in the bathroom.

NIGHTMARES

Various people (like Fred Alan Wolf in *The Dreaming Universe*) list the Top 10 Nightmare Topics, but my list runs to half a dozen frequent bad dreams, in no particular order:

- Death (yours or another's).
- Being chased or cornered.
- A situation or vehicle out of control.
- Danger of bodily harm, harm to reputation, property, etc.
- Frustration at not being able to do something important.
- Loss of something, from an object to a sex object.

TAKE CONTROL OF YOUR DREAMS

You cannot really arrange to dream this or that, although some people claim to. Sometimes in a dream you can become aware you are dreaming and urge the action in the direction you would like.

Gary K. Yamamoto, who is chiefly interested in dream interpretation (*Creative Dream Analysis: A Guide to Self-Development*, 1988), suggests one might be able to gain control in a dream by biting their tongue. "Attempting to bite my tongue, a task which I find impossible, triggers awareness within my dream…a different kind of consciousness….There is such a heightened state of awareness, such a feeling of euphoria, that words fail to describe it." Well, *his* words.

You could try it. Anything that puts you in the driver's seat in a dream could prove useful.

GETTING BETTER EVERY NIGHT

There are shelves and shelves of self-improvement books related to dreams:

> Louis Breger, *Freud: Darkness in the Midst of Vision*
> Ann Faraday, *Dream Power*
> Patricia Garfield, *Creative Dreaming*
> Gillian Holloway, *Dreaming Insights*
> Joan Mazza, *Dreaming Your Real Self*
> Alan B. Siegel, *Dreams that Can Change Your Life*
> Jeremy Taylor, *Dream Work Techniques for Discovering the Creative Power in Dreams*

…to name a few.

These paperback publications offer mostly common sense and the power of positive thinking but they do ask you to think about dreams, and thinking is always good for you. I do not approve of Indira Shankar's Spanish *Dream and Win the Lottery*, but I see nothing wrong with Siegel's *Dreamcatching* or Dr. Delaney's guide to interpretation as a hobby, *All about Dreams*.

There is even a book for pregnant women, Raína M. Paris' *The Mother-to-Be's Dream Book* (2000), in case mommy dreams of baking, cats, chocolate, flowers that need watering, mislaying the baby, swimming with dolphins, etc. For instance, dreaming of a fire in a fireplace is cozy but dreaming of a fire raging where it ought not is a sign of hormones on the rampage.

Online or in libraries you can find almost endless lists of books on dreaming. But none like this one!

FRIEDERICKE HAUFFE

Some people's dreams lead them into weird waking lives. There was one neurotic young girl who came from an obscure village near Heilbronn in mid-nineteenth-century Germany. She was greatly disturbed, asleep and awake, and said she saw and chatted with spirits, performed astral projection, and could see with her stomach. According to Dr. Justinius A. C. Kerner (her skeptical, then devoted physician), she could read documents placed face down on her stomach. He wrote a whole book about her.

A British author of some popular novels, Catherine Crowe (1800?–1876), translated the doctor's book as *The Seeress of Prevorst* (1845), though Friedericke was long dead by then. Poor Freidericke, haunted by ghosts, plagued by poltergeists, terrified by powers she did not understand, died at age 28 in 1829.

Ms. Crowe's book far outshone her novels. It was a sensation. She followed up with *The Night Side of Nature* (1848) and *Spiritualism and the Age We Live In* (1859). She contributed significantly to the great nineteenth-century interest in spiritualism on both sides of the Atlantic. Out of the SFPR came the huge collection of dreams and visions published in 1886, which I edited in the reprint of *Phantasms of the Living*.

On the other hand, fake mediums and heated debates over hysteria, possession, and other frauds may have steered real scientists away from serious dream research.

Crowe herself beseeched the science world to conduct investigations:

And by *investigation* I do not mean the hasty, captious, angry notice of an unwelcoming fact…but the slow, modest painstaking examination that is content to wait upon nature, and humbly follow out her disclosures, however opposed to preconceived theories or mortifying to human pride.

Science was slow to respond. Rational investigation was obscured by late Victorian prejudices, then a dedication, more superstitious than scientific, to spiritualism occasioned by the victims of the Great War. As the twenty-first century dawned all aspects of parapsychology and even of dream research remained tainted. Too many kooks spoil the broth.

The Creator of the universe is shown on the lotus which issues from the navel of the Hindu god Vishnu, sleeping lower left. All creation is Vishnu's dream.

2
Science and Dreams

Mehr Licht! (More Light!)
—alleged dying words of Johann
Wolfgang von Goethe

SCIENCE AND DREAM DISCOVERIES

Before you get to the business of interpreting your own puzzling dreams, here is some information about how science has benefited from the dreams of others. It may make you look harder at yours to discern some valuable truth.

Joseph Bryan III's delightful second book of bits and pieces, *Hodgepodge Two* (1989), notes:

> A number of great discoveries were hit upon during the night, [Pierre] Fluchaire points out [in *Bien dormir pour mieux vivre*, Sleeping Well for Better Living, where he recommends four hours a night]. Dreaming, Einstein discovered relativity; Fleming found penicillin; Rutherford understood the constitution of the atom; Gauss formulated the laws of induction; Mendel revealed the laws of heredity....

I've heard that Einstein got the idea of relativity watching one streetcar pass another on a Swiss street. Fleming came back from a vacation to find mould killing off bacteria on a Petrie dish, but perhaps dreaming helped bring the ideas to fruition.

In dreams we can work things out. See the chapter on art, literature, and folklore for people composing in their dreams or using dreams in waking composition. All good art springs from the subconscious. The conscious mind just tries to manage what comes up.

Arguably, the most remarkable scientific discovery in the field of dreaming had nothing to do with the subconscious. It was the discovery that rapid eye movement (REM) accompanied dreams. E. Aserinsky & N. Kleitman's work was a milestone that increased psycho-physiological research for the next 15 years. REM research once seemed poised to assimilate psychiatry, psychoanalysis, psychological counseling, evolutionary psychology, neurophysiology, psychopathology and the nature of consciousness, as well as play up brain chemistry and function, and suggest treatment for conditions from autism to psychosis.

I believe the great discoveries of the future will take place in the field of psycho-physiological research. REM leads to a different explanation of the dream state than the one Freud advanced. It may be much closer to the truth. Freud, I think, was mistaken, but he did believe that science progresses by making and recognizing mistakes. Investigators should not fall in love with theories.

If dream investigations can make psychology more of a science, and psychiatry less of an art, they will confer tremendous benefits. Here are some highly technical samples to suggest the range of recent scientific literature on REM:

D'Cruz, O'Neill F & Bradley V. Vaughn. "Nocturnal Seizures Mimic REM Behavior Disorder," *American Journal of Electro-neurodiagnostic Technology* 37: 4 (December 1997), 258–264.

Hobson, J. Allan, *et al.* "The Neuropsychology of REM Sleep Dreaming," *Neuroreport* 9:3 (February 1998), R1–R14.

Melnechuk, Theodore. "The Dream Machine. REM Sleep Acts as Reverse Learning to Erase Memories: Theory of F. Crick and G. Mitchison," *Psychology Today* 17 (November 1983), 22–24.

Mestel, Rosie. "Noises from the Cellar: Dreaming Brain," *New Scientist* 154 (Supplement 26 April 1997), 14–17.

Miller, Laurence. "REM Sleep, Pilot Light of the Mind?," *Psychology Today* 21 (September 1987), 8.

Saredi, Roberto, *et al.* "Current Concerns and REM Dreams," *Dreaming* 7:3 (September 1997), 195–208.

Zborowski, Michael J. & Patrick McNamara. "Attachment

Hypothesis of REM Sleep...," *Psychoanalytic Psychology* 15: 1 (Winter 1998), 115–140.

TWENTIETH-CENTURY PSYCHOLOGICAL SCIENCE CONCERNING SLEEP AND DREAMS

Anch, A. M. *et al. Sleep: A Scientific Perspective* (1988).

Bergson, Henri. *The World of Dreams* (1958).

Boss, Medard. *I Dreamt Last Night* (1977).

Brook, Peter & Alex Woloch. *Whose Freud?* (2000).

Brubaker, Lowell L. "Note on the Relevance of Dreams for Evolutionary Psychology," *Psychological Reports* 82: 3 Part I (June 1998), 1006.

Campbell, Joseph. *The Portable Jung* (1971).

Christo, George & Christine Franey. "Addicts' Drug-Related Dreams...," *Substance Use and Misuse* 31: 1 (January 1996), 1–15.

Crews, Frederick C., ed. *Doubters Confront a Legend* [18 experts attack Freud] (1998).

Davis, Whitney. *Drawing the Dream of the Wolves: Homosexuality, Interpretation, and Freud's 'Wolf Man'* (1995).

Eisenbud, J. *Parapsychology and the Unconscious* (1983).

Empson, Jacob. *Sleeping and Dreaming* (1989).

Frankland, Graham. *Freud's Literary Culture* (2000).

Freud, Sigmund. *On Dreams* (trans. James Strachey, 1952).

——————. *The Interpretation of Dreams* (Standard Edition, 1958).

Grey, Loren. *Alfred Adler, the Forgotten Prophet* (1998).

Guralnik, Orna, *et al.* "Dreams of Personality Disordered Subjects," *Journal Of Nervous and Mental Disease* 187: 1 (January 1999), 40–46.

Hall, James A. *Jungian Dream Interpretation* (1985).

Hall, Manly P. *Studies in Dream Symbolism* (1993).

Hunt, Harry T. *Multiplicity of Dreams* (1989).

Jones, Richard M. *The New Psychology of Dreaming* (1970).

Jung, G. C. *The Archetypes and the Collective Unconscious* (trans. R. F. C. Hull, 1959).

——————. *Memories, Dreams, Reflections* (1989).

Kesey, Morton. *Dreams: The Dark Speech of the Spirit* (1968).

Kitcher, Patricia. *Freud's Dream: A Complete Interdisciplinary Science of Mind* (1992).

Kramer, Kenneth Paul. *Death Dreams* (1993).

LoConto, David G. "Death and Dreams...," *Omega* 37:3 (1998), 171–185.

Mahowald, Mark W., *et al.* "Sleeping Dreams, Walking Hallucinations, and the Central Nervous System," *Dreaming* 8:2 (June 1998), 89–102.

Maidenbaum, Areyh. "Dreams and Other Aspects of Jungian Psychology" in *Current Theory of Psychoanalysis* (Robert Lang, ed., 1998).

Mavromatic, A. *Hypnogogia: The Unique State of Consciousness between Waking And Sleeping* (1987).

Meltzer, Donald. *Dream-Life: A Re-Examination of the Psycho-Analytical Theory and Technique* (2000).

Piaget, Jean. *Play, Dreams and Imitation in Childhood* (1962).

Shulman, David, ed. *Dream Cultures* (1999).

Simon, Robert. *Bad Men Do What Good Men Dream: A Forensic Psychiatrist Illuminates the Darker Side of Human Behavior* (1999).

Squier, Leslie H. & G. William Domhoff. "The Presentation of Dreaming and Dreams in Introductory Psychology Textbooks...," *Dreaming* 8:3 (September 1998), 149–168.

States, Bert O. *Seeing in the Dark* (1997).

Tabori, Paul. *Crime and the Occult* (1974).

Tedlock, Barbara, ed. *Dreaming: Anthropological and Psychological Interpretations* (1992).

Carl Jung

Thaler, Stephen L. "The Death Dream and Near-Death Darwinism," *Journal of Near-Death Studies* 15: 1 (Fall 1996), 25–40.

Thurschwell, Pamela. *Sigmund Freud* (2001).

Ullman, Montague, ed. *The Variety of Dream Experience* (1999).

———————— & Stanley Kripner. *Dream Studies and Telepathy* (1970).

van de Castle, Robert L. *Our Dreaming Mind* (1994).

van Eeden, F. "A Study of Dreams," *Proceedings of The Society for Psychical Research* (1913).

von Franz, Marie-Luise, *et al. Dreams* (1998).

Young-Bruehl, Elizabeth. *Freud on Women* (1990).

I listed the standard Freud but I strongly suggest you read his *The Interpretation of Dreams* in Joyce Crick's translation; she translates the original text (1899), better (in my view) than the more cluttered, later versions. Here Freud is fresh, vital, excitingly finding his way, guided by his own dreams and those of his patients.

A SERIES IN DREAM STUDIES

The State University of New York Press publishes one of the most extensive of the series of scientific studies on dreams. Here are some titles in the series:

Bulkeley, Kelly. *Among All These Dreamers: Essays on Dreaming and Modern Society* (1996).

—————. *Visions of the Night: Dreams, Religion, and Psychology* (1999).

Delaney, Gayle, ed. *New Directions in Dream Interpretation* (1993).

Dombeck, Mary T. B. *Dreams and Professional Personhood: The Contexts of Dream Telling and Dream Interpretation among American Psychotherapists* (1991).

Koulack, David. *To Catch a Dream: Explorations of Dreaming* (1991).

Moffit, Alan, *et al. The Functions of Dreaming* (1993).

Strauch, Inge, *et al. In Search of Dreams: Results of Experimental Dream Research* (1996).

Scientists today are not content to assess the meaning and impact of dreams. They're experimenting to discover how dreams are produced. Many questions go unanswered in the fields of psychiatry and psychotherapy, but science is certain, as were people from centuries ago, that dreaming is significant human behavior and far more complex than the "gypsy dream-book" approach to interpretation would suggest.

PROFESSIONAL JOURNAL

The Association for the Study of Dreams publishes the quarterly periodical *Dreaming* (PO Box 1600, Vienna, VA 22183). It is not too technical for the average person.

SLEEP AND HEALTH

Sir Philip Sidney called sleep "the poor man's wealth." How much sleep do we actually need to be healthy? Monastic orders dictated how the monks' time was to be spent in sleeping, praying, working, eating, and resting. Now that "healthcare professionals" are more likely to be consulted for the cure of the body than ecclesiastics for the care of the soul, all sorts of traditional and alternative medical practitioners are volunteering guidelines for when and how long to sleep.

Alfred the Great divided the day into three eight-hour periods, for work, exercise and eating; for study and prayer; and for sleep. Different people need different amounts of sleep under different conditions, while sleeping too much can cause (or betray) depression. John Wesley (who could sleep as he rode a horse) was healthy right up to his death at 88. It is said that some active people, such as Frederick the Great and Napoleon, got by on three or four hour naps in every 24.

PHARMACY AND FANTASY

An indispensible book is J. Allan Hobson's *The Dream Drugstore: Chemically Altered States of Consciousness*. It is *the* guide to the neurobiology of the mind on all sorts of trips.

THE PRIMITIVE BRAIN

The reticular stem is where the action is, but it is so deep within the base of the brain that poking with electrodes or other intrusions is contraindicated. Thus we do not know a lot about it.

We know that's where the unconscious resides and where most of the creative stuff in dreams gets started. Other areas of the brain must be operating during sleep to produce sensations of taste, touch, smell, sight and hearing—all those peculiarly vivid aspects of the world of dreams.

THE TEMPLE OF ASCLEPIUS

Asclepius was a god (the god of healing); a physician who had been deified. At least that is Homer's story. Other sources say Asclepius was not a human but the child of Apollo (also associated with healing) and Coronis. I have visited his shrine at Epidaurus, and the sacred snakes are long gone. I did not sleep there.

Traditionally, a sick patient was to sleep in the temple precincts overnight and receive a diagnosis in a dream. In Rome the god was called Æsculapius; historians such as Livy and the poet Ovid speak of a sacred snake that embodied the god on the Isla Tiberina. The main shrine of Asclepius was located on the island of Cos, where the great Hippocrates took over the treatment of patients. When men stepped in to make Apollo a substitute for earlier, feminine religion at Delphi's shrine the snake reappeared. The snake, Freud would say, is a symbol of you-know-what: Male.

Have you incubated? That is what sleeping in sacred precincts and inviting the god to inform you is called. Have you ever found a treatment that came to you in a dream? Do dreams *simplify reality* and get to the heart of things? Is there a wisdom of the unconscious that reads the physical world?

A GEM OF AN IDEA

Scientific (or superstitious) claims are made for crystals, precious stones and semi-precious stones, and have been as long as records have been kept. The problem is that nobody attempts to explain how the "energy" from them works.

Just in case you want to know, rubies must be worn on the left side of the body but can be placed in the center of the forehead for a sort of third-eye prosthesis. They traditionally produce pleasant dreams. Crysolite is said to ward off nightmares. Here's something to think about: To what extent does belief in gems' powers resemble psychiatry and to what extent does superstition function to *police society?*

DREAMS AND OUR MENTAL PROBLEMS

"All the things one has forgotten," wrote Elias Canetti in *The Human Province* (1973), "scream for help in dreams."

DREAM STATES

Some dreams provide the illusion of having what we cannot get awake. Some inspire or inform, or, as Macbeth says, create "unreal mockery." Sometimes, as Mary Shelley says in *Frankenstein*, "a dream has power to poison sleep."

For a fairly simple idea of dream states, look in *The Emerging Mind*, edited and cowritten by Karen Nesbitt Shanor, Ph.D.

Jung in *Psychology and Alchemy* (1953) lets the dreamer off the hook: "The conscious mind allows itself to be trained like a parrot, but the unconscious mind does not—which is why St. Augustine thanked God for not making him responsible for his dreams." It took modern mavens of psychoanalysis to try that.

Science is most interested in the physiological states of the dreamer, and the chemistry and physics of thought. Science has to depend upon the dreamer's report, which means its experimental data is flawed.

Basically, we are stuck with consciousness to examine consciousness and the dream state being investigated by the waking state—not the ideal situation.

EARLY THEORIES OF DREAMS

For a very long time Aristotle (384–322 BC) was influential in the area of sleep and dreams. Two parts of what we call the *Parva naturale* (in Latin *De somno et vigilans*/Concerning Sleep and Wakefulness, and *De somniis*/Concerning Dreams) were still being discussed during the Renaissance.

At that time the alchemists were giving way to the chemists, and the astrologers to the astronomers. Modern science was being created; however, there was still a great dependence on ancient superstitions and practices as well as a revived interest in the occult.

Vesalius was advancing the study of anatomy, Ambrose Paré was founding modern surgery, herbalists were bringing plant medicines to the forefront, but when it came to the study of psychology and such, the most advanced thinkers were as old-fashioned as the doctors dispensing the prescriptions of Discorides. They were still dominated by Aristotle in science, as they were by Plato in philosophy.

Aristotle's belief was that sleep is common to all animals and essential to their health. He thought it related to the sanguineous and nutritional processes. He felt that when food is ingested it "evaporates," enters the blood, heats on its way to the heart and then goes to the brain, where it is cooled. Drowsiness then occurs as the nutrition goes back to the heart, causing the sensory organs to shut down, reducing perception and movement. Yet even when perception quiets down and the senses are dormant, the sleeper can react to interior and exterior stimuli, though the perceptions may be confused and irregular.

Dreams are produced, then, (according to Aristotle) by the sense organs dealing with changes in the blood. When the actual method of blood circulation was discovered during the Renaissance, the church declared it heresy and repressed it. It had to be discovered again, by William Harvey, in a more secular century.

Aristotle knew that blood was crucial, even if he may not have shared the ancient Jewish belief that "the blood is the life," containing the soul. For Aristotle, the blood may not have been the soul but it did control the intelligence.

The blood is one of four humours that, according to the theory of the Greek physician Galen, have to be maintained in proper balance. At least Galen knew that oxygen was important to both the blood and to combustion, but he did not know how it circulated.

Johann Weir (1515–1588), a leading German doctor of his day, addressed the questions of body and soul. Weir quotes the following passage from *De somno et vigilia* in his book on medicine and witchcraft, *De Præstigiis Dæmonum*, in my opinion one of the ten best books in the history of the world:

> When a great deal of blood descends to the originating point of sensation, the forms conceived in the imagination also descend. For the imagination is a sort of treasure house for the forms received through the senses. Therefore demons are able to move the humours and spirits of sensations both interior and exterior and thus bring certain forms and appearances to the sense organs as though the objects themselves were truly presenting themselves from without, whether in sleep or in wakefulness.

Thus our dreams come to us like experiences in the now. That is why they are so convincing. Consider dreams not so much as thoughts but as experiences. They are one of the products of what Djuana Barnes termed "that priceless galaxy of misinformation called the mind."

Dr. Weir fully believed in the occult. He was convinced that The Devil entered dreams on occasion. Weir reported that witches and wizards, whom nearly everyone in those days feared, could call upon The Devil to bring them oracles in dreams. They had to perform Satanic rites and concentrate on what questions they wanted answered before they went to sleep.

Johann Weir at age 60

Of course Dr. Weir also believed that people received useful information in ordinary dreams. Using the Galenic theory of humours, Dr. Weir explained how the four body fluids (corresponding to fire, water, earth and air) produced different kinds of dreams.

DE PRAESTIGIIS
DÆMONVM.

Von Teuffelge
spenst Zauberern vnd

Gifftbereytern/ Schwartzkünstlern/ He-
ren vnd Vnholden/ darzu jrer Straff/ auch von den Bezauberten/
vnd wie jhnen zuhelffen sey/ Ordentlich vnd eigentlich mit sonderm fleiß in
VI. Bücher getheilet: Darinnen gründlich vnd eigentlich darge-
than/ was von solchen jeder zeit disputiert/ vnd
gehalten worden.

Erstlich durch D. Johannem Weier in Latein beschrieben/ nachmals
von Johanne Fuglino verteutscht/ jetzund aber nach dem letzten Lateinischen außgange-
nen Original auffs neww vbersehen/ vnnd mit vielen heilsamen nützlichen stücken : Auch sonderlich
hochdienlich newen Zusätzen/ so im Lateinischen nicht gelesen/ als im folgenden Blat
zufinden/ so der Bodinus mit gutem grunde nicht widerlegen kan/
durchauß gemehret vnd gebessert.

Sampt zu endt angehencktem newem vnd volkommenen Register.

Mit Röm. Keyf. Maiest. Freyheit/ auff zehen Jahr nicht nachzudrucken/ begnadet.

Getruckt zu Franckfurt am Mayn/ durch Nicolaum Basseum.
M. D. LXXXVI.

Johan Weier or Weirus, German translation of *De Præstigis Dæmonum* (1586).

The following is an example of the science of the sixteenth century in this regard (translated by John Shea, 1991):

> Furthermore, in his work *On Dreams*, Aristotle says that the images which appear in dreams are carried to the head and the sense-organs just as cloud images are raised on high and the faces of various animals are represented in the vapor that comes from the water or the earth, which is then carried to mid-air by the heat of the sun. So, too, dream images take on various forms in consequence of the exhalations that arise. Choleric or jaundiced vapor, hot and dry, seems to cause flame; but a phlegmatic exhalation is recognized by its sweetness when it flows to the organ of taste, and it produces dreams relating to water. From black [bile] and melancholic vapor something horrible appears—a demon-image, as it were; accordingly, the Devil loves to insinuate himself into this vapor, as being a material most suited for his mocking allusions. That which ascends from burnt [yellow] bile or jaundice (which is *accidental* melancholia) is perceived as biting, painful, piercing, and imbued with a gall-like bitterness. And that which is dispersed in vapor from pure blood appears as beautiful and delightful, such as the sight of roses or [other] flowers, dances, music, and all sorts of pleasurable but insubstantial phenomena. In this way the illusion is created, and in proportion to the quality of the images (which are more strongly conveyed in sleep because of the exhalation of humours) the things thus seen are believed to be true....

QUINTUS SEPTIMUS FLORENS TERTULLIAN

This theologian from Carthage, who lived *c.* AD 155–*c.* 222, is a good example of the way theology, mythology, and science in the old days. In his treatise on the soul (written in Latin rather than the usual Greek of the time) he devoted a number of chapters to matters both theological and practical concerning dreams. He believed dreams could be caused by everything from weather conditions to the movements of the planets but essentially that they came from either God or from Satan.

One of the more encouraging arguments in his works, which are

naturally deeply imbued with the traditional Christian view of sex as sinful, is the assurance that we cannot be held responsible for wet dreams. Emphasis on dreams is less pronounced in later Doctors of the Church such as St. Thomas Aquinas, by whose time most sorts of dream interpretation were regarded as pagan.

AN UNUSUAL ELIZABETHAN THEORY OF DREAMS

From *The Terrors of the Night* by Thomas Nashe (1567–1601), written in the same year (1594) as his early picaresque novel, *The Unfortunate Traveller; or, The Life of Jacke Wilton*, comes this unusual theory of the causes and uses of dreams:

> A dream is nothing else but a bubbling scum or froth of the fancy, which the day hath left undigested; or an after feast made of the fragments of idle imaginations....Divers have written diversely of their [dreams'] causes, but the best reason among them all that I could ever pick out was this: that as an arrow which is shot out of a bow is sent forth many times with such force that it flyeth beyond the mark whereat it was aimed, so our thoughts intensively fixed all the daytime upon a mark which we are to hit are now and then overdrawn with such force that they fly beyond the mark of the day into the confines of the night. There is no man put to any torment but quaketh and trembleth a great while after the executioner [i.e. torturer] hath withdrawn his hand from him. In the daytime we torment our imaginations with sundry cares and devices; all the nighttime they quake and tremble after the terror of their late suffering and still continue thinking of the perplexities they have endured. To nothing more aptly can I compare the working of our brains after we have unyoked them and gone to bed than to the glimmering and dazzling of a man's eyes when he comes newly out of the bright sun into dark shadow.

Nashe is onto the concept of sleep as a time for processing the events and thoughts of the day. From this, science has logically come to the conclusion that sleep deprivation unhinges the mind.

OCCULT SCIENCES BY THE NINETEENTH CENTURY

Early history had seen books by Cornelius Agrippa von Nettelsheim, Paracelsus, Johannes Weir and others and in 1846 a translation, in two volumes appeared as *The Occult Sciences* of a major work by Eusébe Salverte (1771–1839). There is a whole library of such books, including histories of magic by Éliphas Lévi, Paul Christian and others and curiosities such as the book by Francis Barrett containing colored portraits of demons summoned by black magic. Occult works written under pseudonyms continued into the twentieth-century with David Conway, Orphiel and others.

The confusion of science and pseudoscience made interpretations more superstitious than scientific for a long time. Maybe psychoanalysis based on dreams is not quite science. See Thomas Hardy Leahy's *Psychology's Occult Double: Psychology and the Problem of Pseudoscience* (1983) and bibliographies online *re* more recent and more relevant materials.

Here are half a dozen modern books of some scientific interest:

Ben-Yehuda, Nachman. *Deviance and Moral Boundaries: Witchcraft, the Occult, Science Fiction…* (1985).
Devereux, George. *Psychoanalysis and the Occult* (1953).
Freud, Sigmund. *Delusion and Dream: An Interpretation in the Light of Psychoanalysis of Gradiva, a Novel* (1917).
Jung, C. G. *Psychology and the Occult*, trans. R. F. C. Hull (1977).
Klein, Aaron E. *Science and the Supernatural* (1979).
Rawcliffe, Donovan Hilton. *The Psychology of the Occult* (1952, reprinted 1969 as *Occult and Supernatural Phenomena*).

THE CONSCIOUS MIND

What human consciousness is and how it developed has challenged the best scientific minds. That we are more than our egos and that there is an unconscious as well as a conscious mind is not up for debate. See Oliver J. Flanagan's *Dreaming Souls: Sleep, Dreams, and the Evolution of the Conscious Mind* (2000). The unconscious mind seems to be running 24/7, as we now say, awake or asleep. We are not only subject to what we think but also to what Jung calls "collective thinking;" this is our patrimony from our culture. In other words, we know things we don't usually know that we know.

SWEET DREAMS

Sometimes what looks like science is mere superstition. Take the custom of removing flowers and plants from the room while a person sleeps. Just be careful that you do not bring flowers traditionally associated with death to someone who's sick in bed. Like all stimuli, the presence of flowers and plants may have some input into your dreams, but it is not unhealthy to have them around. The superstitions vary from one culture to another: for instance the Greeks would identify with death white chrysanthemums and the Mexicans yellow or orange flowers.

SELF HELP

Inevitably, there are books on how to do it yourself in your spare time for fun and profit. Two recent entries:

> Capacchione, Lucia. *Visioning: Ten Steps to Designing the Life of Your Dreams* (2000).
> Richmond, Cynthia. *Dream Power: How to Use Your Night Dreams to Change Your Life* (2000).

Other writers have contributed to the superstition industry in books such as these:

> Aveni, A. E. *Behind the Crystal Ball* (1996).
> Franklyn, Julian. *A Survey of the Occult* (1935).
> Freedland, Nat. *The Occult Explosion* (1972).
> Goodwin, John. *Occult America* (1972).

In my opinion, the confusion of real self-help with superstitious practices has damaged the reputation of dream work.

DEAD TO THE WORLD

This phrase is commonly used to describe someone in deep sleep, but when you are sleeping you may still react to the real world. When you are in the room with a dying person, though the person may be in a coma or "completely out of it." be careful what you say. They may be able to hear you. They could even recover and rewrite their will.

You may have realized that you can be sleeping and still not be entirely cut off from the world. It is not impossible to hear a telephone ring in your dream and wake up to discover that the telephone is actually ringing. A car backfiring in the street may cause you to work in a gunshot.

In 1861 the French scientist Alfred Maury noted a dreamer's account that he was in the French Revolution and taken to the guillotine to be beheaded. As the blade fell, he awoke in terror. The bedstead had fallen and struck him across the neck. Everyone wondered how a complete story about the Time of the Terror could have passed through the sleeper's mind in the instant it took the bedstead to strike him.

Science still has to demarcate the borders between the conscious and the unconscious, the wide-awake and the dozing, and the comatose person.

As the poet says, "Do I wake, or dream?"

DR. CHARCOT

Jean-Martin Charcot (1825–1893) was an early scientific investigator of the "animal magnetism" of Mesmerism, which had caught the attention of the public by the nineteenth century. Charcot studied the neurology and psychology of hypnotism (and its effect upon women chiefly) and concluded that there were three levels:

1. the cataleptic, in which the subject is rigid and oblivious to everything.
2. the lethargic, in which the subject is in a deep sleep.
3. the somnambulistic, in which the subject appears to be asleep but can be communicated with and respond to questions or suggestions.

Charcot's contributions to the new science of psychoanalysis were considerable but Freud didn't respect his views. Freud said Charcot "can find no rest till he has correctly described and classified some phenomenon with which he is concerned, but he can sleep quite soundly without having arrived at the physiological explanation of that phenomenon."

Charcot's interest was in the field of physiological effects of the "animal magnetism" exploited by Anton Mesmer.

He considered the extent to which the subconscious can be made to respond while hypnotized, a matter still in debate. The relationship between the person sleeping normally and the person in the lethargic state of hypnosis remains to be fully understood.

DREAMS, MYTHOLOGY, AND THE COLLECTIVE UNCONSCIOUS

Jung noticed that mythological heroes and symbols were to be found across a wide spectrum of time and civilizations. From this he deduced the theory of a collective unconscious, or "archetypes." His popular follower Joseph Campbell, author of *The Hero with a Thousand Faces* and *The Masks of Gods*, and famous subject of Bill Moyers' interviews, also probed the collective unconscious.

I think archetypes are related to the Swiss art historian Burckhardt's primordial symbols. In any case, they occur in literature such as mythology, fairytales, folktales and fantasies as well as in dreams—all of which spring from the unconscious.

But Jung, unlike Freud, did not see the unconscious as a mere repository of repressions. To him the archetypes were subconscious and so could not have been pushed down into the unconscious. They are older than any culture and its discontents, influenced by each and linking them all.

Campbell attempted to surpass Jung's opinion of mythological archetypes as fundamentally without interpretation. Through psychology and psychohistory, he attempted to explain the myths that shaped every mind despite age and language differences. This work was in the tradition of the nineteenth-century scientist Bachofen, who looked to mythology for spirituality and an understanding of ancient peoples.

Myth for Bachofen was "nothing other than a picture of the national experience in the light of religious faith." He felt that to trace myths was to find the history of human interaction and migration. In myth is the essence of cults, religions, moralities, and societal differences.

Perhaps, as some religious believe, we are all part of the same dream.

BODY LANGUAGE

Body language seems a far more reliable indicator than, say phrenology (studying bumps on the head), physiognomy (criminal types identifiable by their faces, ears, and so on), and other nineteenth-century pseudosciences. Coleridge believed in body language and believed where people place their hands "when lost in thought or vacant, and what is their commonest posture in sleep was an indicator of many a man's secret harms."

Do you sleep in a fetal position, on your back, on your stomach, or what? Does the position in which you sleep affect your dreams or *vice versa*?

DREAMING IT UP

Some people can make their unconscious work for them while asleep, and "dream up" scientific inventions or creative writing. But trying to learn something while you sleep is probably not good for you. People try to learn foreign languages this way, but it interferes with healthy sleep, as does the use of hallucinatory drugs.

I do not approve of learning foreign languages while asleep. I suggest that they be learned in waking interaction with native speakers. If that is not possible, I prefer they be learned in the traditional manner, in the classroom, at least half-awake.

DREAMING OF THE FUTURE

There hasn't been nearly as much serious scientific interest in the divination by interpretation of dreams—the Greeks called it oneiromancy—as you might think. For one thing, parapsychology does not have much of a reputation among respected scientists. For another, if we are to believe our dreams, the future—as they say—sucks. People's dreams are often full of threats and disasters. Nonetheless, many people stand like the Old Norse character Skull (English word *shall*), staring at the future.

If you think you have had a dream about some disaster yet to happen, go right out and have a notary public put his stamp on your full description of the dream.

PHANTASMS OF THE LIVING

(1886)

BY

EDMUND GURNEY

FREDERIC W. H. MYERS

AND

FRANK PODMORE

A FACSIMILE REPRODUCTION
WITH AN INTRODUCTION

BY

LEONARD R. N. ASHLEY
Brooklyn College

VOLUME I

"The president was assassinated on a Wednesday morning by a woman in a pink overcoat and a Gucci scarf", "an American Airlines plane from Europe burst into flames just before crashing at Kennedy," and so on.

No use telling us *afterwards* that you saw it coming! No use either telling the unfortunates who are going to be embroiled in the disaster you foresee, because if it is going to happen warnings won't stop it. In fact, knowing the future, *if it is set*, is not a lot of use—unless you can find out what the Dow or NASDAQ is going to be a few weeks from now. If indeed people could know what the stock market would do next week, or which horse will win this afternoon's race, or which numbers will come up in the lottery, there would be no such thing as prophets who are not very rich.

PRIVATE DREAMS

Your dreams are private. No, despite all the movies with this plot gimmick, no one can get into your dreams. Science can detect when you are dreaming but cannot see the movie in your head. It is also interesting to note that while there is some evidence that people can read minds when they are awake—maybe they are reading subtle body language, for all I know—there is no evidence that mind readers can look at a sleeping person and tell what they are dreaming.

Quit worrying about spoon-bending tricks, folks, and look into this.

DREAMING YOUR PRESCRIPTION

John Aubrey was an inveterate collector of gossip and trifles. In his *Miscellanies* he reports what he heard about the dream in which the great architect Sir Christopher Wren found a cure for his kidney condition:

> When Sir Christopher Wren was at Paris about 1671, he was Ill and Feverish, made but little Water, had a pain in his Reins [kidneys]. He sent for a Physitian, who advis'd him to be let Blood [to permit bad humours to escape], thinking he had a Pleurisy: But Bleeding much disagreeing with his Constitution, he would defer it a Day longer: That Night he dreamt, that he was in a place where Palm-Trees grew (suppose Egypt), and that a woman in a Romantick Habit, reach'd him Dates. The next Day he sent for Dates, which cured him of the pain in his Reins.

Is it possible that in our subconscious we know how to medicate ourselves and only need to find out in our dreams what our conscious mind cannot tell us? Do our bodies tell us what they need awake and asleep? Do you experience, for instance, unexplained cravings for certain foods?

IS SCIENCE THE ONLY WAY TO TRUTH?

William James in *The Will to Believe* (1897) wrote that "a public no less large [than the academic establishment] keeps and transmits from generation to generation the traditions and practices of the occult; but academic science cares as little for its beliefs...as you, gentle reader, care for those of the readers of the *Waverley* novels and the *Fireside Companion* [cheap popular magazines]."

I cannot agree with James that those who are superstitious are to be regarded on par with the scientific, but I agree with James' next sentence: "To no one type of mind is it given to discern the totality of truth."

Let me repeat that: "To no one type of mind is it given to discern the totality of truth." Religious fundamentalists should read this paragraph several times.

Just because the folk have believed something for a long time is no compelling reason to accept it as true. People have believed many idiocies for many centuries. Science at least admits that it is always wrong, or inaccurate, and keeps on searching for truth, resisting dogma.

CRITERIA FOR VERIDICAL DREAMS

Some people claim to have dreams that are true. The authors of *Phantasms of the Living* examined hundreds of reports of relatives arriving in dreams to announce their deaths and say goodbye. I have a friend who claims that her sister appeared in a dream to announce she had lost her virginity, but these days she might just have used a cell phone.

The *Phantasm* authors tried to be very scientific and set out these criteria for deciding whether a case was a "dream-coincidence" or clairvoyance and would be included in what they call the "sifted survival" of cases presented in the book. They insisted each dream worth noting be "distinct, unexpected, and unusual." Further:

If it combine all three characteristics in a high degree, its evidential value may be very considerable; in proportion as the degree falls short, or the combination fails, the evidential value sinks; and none of the characteristics taken alone, even though present in a high degree, would lead us to include a dream in the present collection. Thus, the dream-content must be neither a vague impression of calamity or happiness; nor a catastrophe on which the sleeper's mind is already fixed; nor some such ordinary event as has frequently occurred in waking experience. It may, indeed, be not the less significant for being trivial; but in that case it must not be of a bizarre or unlikely kind. Then again, amount of detail, and the number of connected events, are of immense importance, as each subsequently verified detail tells with ever-mounting strength against the hypothesis of accidental coincidence. Once more, dream-content must be considered to some extent in relation to the dream-habits of the particular dreamer. Before estimating the value of the fact [allegation] that a person has dreamt of the sudden death of a friend on the night when the death took place, we should have to ascertain that that person is not in the habit of dreaming of horrible events.

PRECOGNITION

Can we tell the future by ESP while awake and see the future in dreams?

Joseph Banks Rhine (1895–1980) devoted his scientific life to the study of parapsychology. He wrote the impressive *Extra-Sensory Perception* (1934). His colleague, K.E. Zenner devised the five Zenner cards with symbols that tested whether some people have the power to predict which cards will turn up. Neither Rhine nor Zenner was able to create convincing repeatable experiments.

Nonetheless, many people persist in believing in *psi* precognition and that sometimes dreams can actually foretell the future.

I presented *Phantasms of the Living* as a reprint with an introduction in the twentieth-century. Thirty years later I am unconvinced that there is evidence future events can be foretold in dreams.

What is your opinion? Have you ever had a dream that accurately foretold the future? Have you ever had dreams that did not come true? Ty Cobb became the greatest baseball player of all-time with a batting average of .367. When it comes to dream predictions, what is your batting average? You do not have to hit a home run every time at bat.

Remember: the unlikely *possibility* that the future can be predicted is not absolutely to be ignored and, as Nietzsche said, "Even a thought, even a possibility, can shatter and transform us."

Keep an open mind about shut-eye.

QUALITY TIME

You need both deep sleep and dreams. The old superstition that deep sleep is salutary (probably because Puritans thought it was the fullest necessary rest, preparation for getting up to do a hard day's work) and dreaming is not (Puritans tended to think it was usually goofing off, like watching television) is wrong.

If you fall behind in your dreaming, you will be distressed. If you are kept awake long enough, you will die. Young people like to "pull an all-nighter" and have the energy for it. Druggies may go a long time without sleep, but are only compounding the damage.

Sleep is nice. It is restful and relaxing; it is R&R time. Dreams can be useful escapes from everyday stresses and strains. Kierkegaard said at one point that his waking life was so miserable that dreamtime was his sole delight, a pleasant vacation. Of course retreating into sleep is a sign of depression.

FROM CHARLES DICKENS'
THE UNCOMMERCIAL TRAVELLER

Are not the sane and the insane equal at night as the sane lie adreaming? Are not all of us outside this [mental] hospital, who dream, more or less in the same condition of those inside it, every night of our lives? Are we not nightly persuaded, as they daily are, that we associate preposterously with kings and queens, emperors and empresses, and nobilities of all sorts? Do we not nightly jumble events and personages and times and places, as they do daily? Are we not sometimes troubled by our own sleeping inconsistencies; and do we not vexedly try to account for them or excuse them, just as these do sometimes in respect of their waking delusions?... I wonder that the great who knew everything [Shakespeare], when he called Sleep the death of each day's life, did not call Dreams the insanity of each days sanity.

LONG DREAMS AND SHORT DREAMS

Ever since science has been able to measure REM (Rapid Eye Movement) it has been possible to discover when a person is dreaming. You may be able to see REM yourself as you look at a dreamer, and all dreamers lose muscle tone in the neck while dreaming so you can see your pet's ears droop, head loll, etc., as it dreams long dreams of (say) hunting or short dreams of (say) being hunted.

Most human dreamers seem to dream longer as each night progresses. However, whether the dream lasts a short time or more than an hour, it may seem long to the dreamer. It is alleged that in some cases, when you are about to die, your whole life flashes before you, so the brain may be able to run the film very fast! See Coleridge's story on page XXX about composing 200 or 300 lines of poetry in a dream that couldn't have lasted more than half an hour.

Some people claim, though it would be impossible to test, that they are aware that they are dreaming and deliberately extend the dream to enjoy the experience. I believe I do this, but I may be dreaming that too.

We do seem to have some power to end a dream: think how often we manage to wake-up before the monster chasing us, or some other peril, catches up! I cannot recall ever having died in a dream, can you? If you die in your dream, do you ever wake up? What does science have to say about that?

NOCTURNAL ADMISSIONS

There are those go-getters who think that time spent sleeping is time wasted. At least one part of males, anyway, is right up to snuff while sleeping. What do they think about the fact that males have erections most of the time they are in deep sleep and often when they are in the vague state between snoozing and drowsing?

These days, science can offer a number of treatments for impotence, but to determine whether the problem has any physical cause requires only a very simple experiment. If the male finds upon waking up that a band of postage stamps sealed around his penis before he went to sleep has broken, then he has experienced erections while asleep that he may not be able to achieve while awake. Don't use the self-stick kind.

If always limp, a male may have to move from the bed to the couch.

IT'S *DÉJÀ VU* ALL OVER AGAIN

I happen to think that this common experience comes from the unconscious mind taking in information, presented as a memory faster than the conscious mind grasps it. But some people think it is a waking recollection something experienced when asleep. On occasion, the experience seems connected to intuition, which Descartes thought was a sort of sudden illumination.

See Vernon M. Neppe's *The Psychology of Déjà Vu* (1993).

TO BE CONTINUED

Occasionally people dream episodes in serial form, like the cliffhangers of Buck Rogers, Hopalong Cassidy and other heroes of the movie serials of my youth.

Speaking of movies, what do you think they do to the public perception of science in regard to dreaming? In twentieth-century art and architecture, for instance, we witnessed considerable impact of science and technology. I think it would be interesting to study the impact of art on science, especially in film and broadcast media. If that has already got off to a small start, I hope it will be continued.

THE BENZENE RING

Freidrich August von Kekulé von Stradonitz (1829–1896), was a university professor at Ghent. One day in 1865 he was writing a textbook on chemistry when he fell asleep in his armchair by the fire. Or it was at least what he called "a half sleep." In this state one of the problems solved itself for him.

Later he recorded:

> Again the atoms flitted before my eyes. This time the smaller groups kept modestly in the background. My mental eye, made more acute by repeated visions of this sort, could now make out larger structures, of manifold conformation; long rows, sometimes more closely bunched together, wriggling and turning like snakes. But, see, what was that? One of the snakes seized its own tail and the image whirled scornfully before my eyes. As though from a flash of lightning I awoke. I spent the rest of the night in working out the consequences of the hypothesis.

Years later, addressing a scientific conference in 1890, Kekulé recalled how the trimethyl benzene ring was discovered to be six carbon atoms closed in a ring. (His early training in architecture, before he turned to chemistry, may have assisted him in guessing how the benzene ring might be structured). His discoveries founded the science of aromatic chemistry and organized all organic chemistry known up until that time. They also made Germany preeminent in the dyeing business of the nineteenth-century. This was the chemist who urged his audience of scholars "to dream, gentlemen!"

Today scientists in many fields from cosmology to the search for a Unified Theory, from computer technology and chemistry to biochemistry and mathematics and physics and beyond, are attempting to dream up solutions to difficult problems. Some even try to put their sleeping hours to work.

See Albert Rothenberg's "Creative Cognitive Processes in Kekulé's Discovery of the Structure of the Benzene Molecule," *American Journal of Psychology* 108 (Fall 1995), 419–438.

THE SEWING MACHINE

The first practical sewing machine was also the result of a dream. Isaac Merrit Singer (1811–1875) is often considered the inventor of the sewing machine but another American was actually the first to produce a practical machine. Elias B. Howe (1819–1867), however, really invented the eye-pointed needle and lock stitch (in 1846). Howe sued Singer in 1854 and won.

This did not stop Singer from selling his machines; by 1860 he was the largest producer of sewing machines worldwide. Singer founded the Singer Sewing Machine Company with Edward Clark in 1863. Singer retired to England.

Now the name of Singer is synonymous with sewing machines as Hoover's is with vacuum cleaners. But we must not forget Howe.

Here is the tale of Howe's nightmare that solved the problem of the sewing machine's continuous stitching. The story is from Jacob M. Braude's *Speaker's and Toastmaster's Handbook of Anecdotes by and about Famous Personalities* (1971):

> A major problem in the development of Howe's sewing machine was the location of the eye of the needle. The inventor was rapidly running out of money and ideas when one night he had

a peculiar dream. He was being led to his execution for failing to design a sewing machine for the king of a strange country.

But here is the kicker: the guards carried spears with holes in the spearheads. In Howe's mind something clicked. He woke up and found that needles with holes in the sharp end were the solution to the problem of continuous stitching.

NIKOLA TESLA (1856–1943)

This Yugoslavian genius is still not fully appreciated. He was the inventor of the Tesla coil, the induction motor, the first radio-controlled boat, and (perhaps) even the "Death Ray" (indicative of a desire to create more than a Strategic Defense Initiative, but to make war impossible by permitting every nation the means to protect itself). "I prefer," he said, "to be remembered as the inventor who abolished war," but of course he did not succeed in that.

He did succeed, however, in laying the foundations for radio and television transmission, and perceived the possibilities of the ionosphere to transmit electrical power through the air around the globe. Marconi got the credit for inventing radio, but Marconi appears to have stolen Tesla's basic patents to do so.

Where did Tesla get the fundamental ideas for wireless communication? He got it in a dream!

Tesla recorded a dream in which he saw "a cloud," and winged creatures flying around. One had the face of his mother. He believed that she was providing him with insights to transmit messages through the air from a broadcaster to a receiver, if both were tuned to the same frequency. People thought he was weird and impractical, particularly when he started to talk of telepathic communication between people on the "same wavelength."

He got involved with psychics and swamis such as Vivikenanda. He was also greeted with laughter when he claimed to receive a message from aliens in outer space, "from another world." I'll tell you the complete message: it was "one, two, three." That's all.

Tesla's employers, such as Westinghouse, did him little good personally. Tesla's financial backers, including J. P. Morgan, left him in the lurch and a tragic fire destroyed his New York City laboratory and all his equipment. Yet before the turn of the twentieth-century Tesla had laid the groundwork for wireless broadcasting.

He lost his patents—Marconi gained one in 1904 for radio—and Tesla was too poor to fight effectively in the courts, though eventually Marconi lost the patent because it was proved that Tesla got there first with the essential ideas—ideas from a dream.

His dream of world peace derived from the ultimate weapon has not come true. Much of the rest of what he did accomplish has transformed the world. He died broke and alone in a New York hotel room and the "terrible weapon" he said he had in a box there, along with many of his papers, seems to have got into the hands of the FBI the day he died and just disappeared.

DREAMING IS NORMAL. ARE YOU?

In the course of eight hours of sleep you dream a total of an hour and a half, on or off. You know that this is healthful and normal. Not to dream at all would be unnatural and unhealthy. Even if you think you have passed a dreamless night in deep sleep, you have not. Whether or not you can recall dreams, you dream every night.

As Freud might say, if you cannot remember dreams you may be repressing. What are you trying to hide? You know that with Freudians you can't win. If you refuse to see an analyst they say you're crazy. If you come early to your appointment, you're anxious; on time and you're compulsive. Did you come late? You're antagonistic. The joke is that even if you kill yourself, strict Freudians will bill you for all the sessions you miss.

The existence of jokes such as these is (as a German pedant might phrase it) *not without significance*. Freudian analysis uses the reported dream as a mere jumping off point for interpretation, and assumes that the dreamer has encoded rather than straightforwardly expressed things in the dream. There is also a preference for assuming that a dream may express the exact opposite of what is intended, which is getting pretty tricky. It can be suggested that Jung tends to believe dreams, Freud is suspicious of them, or so some would agree. (In these matters never expect easy agreement on anything.) When the analyst and the analysand disagree over what a given dream may mean, the naïve dreamer is apt to say, "Well, it's my dream and I know what it means, even if you don't, Doctor." Is he right?

It is normal for people to take things more at face value than subtle analysis likes to do. And many people honestly believe that Freud is far less reliable when it comes to standard dream symbolism than the tatty little "gypsy" dream-book you can buy in an occult bookshop or on the newsstand and read for yourself. Certainly more people consult such books, even rely on them, than ever crack C. S. Hall's "A Cognitive Theory of Dream Symbols" in the source book *Psychopathology* (ed. C. F. Reed *et al.*, 1958).

CAN DREAMING AFFECT UNBORN CHILDREN?

Laodice was said to have been visited in a dream (353 BC) by the god Apollo. He presented her in the dream with a precious stone, engraved in intaglio with an anchor, set in a ring, and he instructed her to give the jewel to the son she would bear nine months after. When she awoke there was such a ring beside her. When her son Seleucis was born he had a birthmark in the shape of an anchor on his thigh, and so, it was claimed, had all his successors in the Seleucid dynasty. Seleucid and his successors wore the ring at all times.

It is possible that dreams can so affect a pregnant woman that they can produce certain birthmarks or other effects on the child?

I think listening to Mozart during pregnancy can be good for the child but when it comes to effects produced by being frightened by a rabbit I am skeptical.

DREAMS UNDER HYPNOSIS

Early scientific investigation of dreams and dreaming coincided in the nineteenth-century with a great interest in what Mesmer called "animal magnetism" and hypnosis. Scientists attempted to understand dreaming by placing a subject under hypnosis and then telling them to dream, perhaps touching them or letting them smell some odor or otherwise attempting to affect the dream (because, you know, dreams will process stimuli in the oddest ways). When the dream was over, the subject, still under hypnosis, could be instructed to report all the details of the dream, including many details that might not be remembered by a dreamer returning to wakefulness after regular sleep.

It was not well established precisely how dreams under hypnosis differed from the dreams of ordinary sleepers. In the nineteenth century modern methods of measuring changes in brain function over time were not available. It was only with the invention of the electroencephalogram that brain waves could be examined. They were found to be different between waking and sleeping persons but not so different between dreamers in ordinary sleep and dreamers under hypnosis. There is still a lot we do not know about consciousness and about brain

The term *hypnosis* suggests a sleeping state but this altered mind state differs from *sleep*. Franz (or Friedrich) Anton Mesmer (1734-1815) popularized what people called *mesmerism* by the use of what he called *animal magnetism*, inducing a trancelike state. The police drove him out of Vienna but he was the toast of Paris in 1778. Denounced as a charlatan (1785), he nevertheless was onto something, and hypnotism is now more than a vaudeville or parlor trick. It is still employed, for instance, in dentistry and weight loss.

activity, though we are far beyond the phrenology of the nineteenth-century, which examined bumps on the skull and attempted a rough map of localization of function. Deep within the brain where surgical instruments cannot reach, as you already have been told, there are still things going on about which we would like to know more.

The study of dreams under hypnosis may now be less pursued than previously and C. S. Moss' *The Hypnotic Investigation of Dreams* (1967) may be basically the last word on the subject though not the latest word.

The French used to be fascinated by hypnosis and sonambulism, even before Charcot. In the twenties, for instance, there were Grasset's *L'Hynotisme et la Suggestion*, Pieron's *Le Problème psyilolgique du sommeil*, and Hesnard's *L'Inconscient* , and much more.

THE PINEAL GLAND

This gland deep in the brain has been said to be a third eye, and Colin Wilson in *The Occult* (1971) tells us that "occult tradition declares [it] to be the doorway to 'other' states of being." Wilson refers to C. D. Broad's article in *Occult Review* (1929) in which one Oliver Fox is described as learning how to become aware he is dreaming and then to control his dreams by pushing through that "doorway" into another world, in effect escaping from the dreaming body.

> He also discovered that once he was "in control" of the dream, he could float through brick walls, levitate and so on. What was happening was, in fact, the reverse of a nightmare, where your legs refuse to run. He gradually became fairly expert at inducing these dreams....

Can you induce dreams of this sort? Do you dream you are in charge of your dream and capable of pushing beyond the "doorway?" Do you believe you can get through into "other states of being" beyond dreaming? As stated in *The Complete Book of Werewolves*, it was believed that while the body lay in sleep a man's spirit could go out and inhabit the body of a wolf.

THE DREAM ENCYCLOPEDIA

James R. Lewis is the author of a big book (1995) of that title. It addresses much of the same material discussed here. All the dictionaries and encyclopedias of dreams get into the psychological and even theological aspects of dreams and dreaming but I recommend Spence's book especially in terms of the anthropological aspect. It presents a great deal of information about primitive peoples of Africa, the Pacific, and South America. They are subjects about which most of writers on dreams know far too little. There are useful references to specialized works by anthropologists who have studied the ways that tribes have used dreams, feared dreams, and incorporated them into their religious and social dynamics.

"PROPHECY, MAGIC, REINCARNATION, PAST LIFE REGRESSIONS, THE TAROT AND STAR TREK SCIENCE"

Another book recommendation ends this chapter—the heading is what Daniel Cohen, former editor of *Science Digest*, liked in D.H. Robinson's

D. H. Robinson's *1999: Apocalypse Maybe.*

1999: Apocalypse Maybe (1995, 1997). The novel recounts the adventure of Harper Raye, a female history professor troubled by nightmares "that could only come from Nostradamus himself." It combines quantum physics and the paranormal in a heady mix.

Is this the end prophesied? The puzzle had to be solved by July 1999, and Y2R brought no cosmic crisis, but the book remains interesting. The author is a Chicago playwright who writes under the name D. H. Robinson. His first effort full-length novel produced a riveting read.

Nostradamus' maddeningly obscure prophecies on the basis of his confessed "habitual, nocturnal watchings" have appeared in countless books, but in a manner that has seldom been this gripping. On top of that, "relativistic mechanics" is analogized to getting members of your family to fix your car, so there is humor appeal as well as detective story suspense. Not a bad deal....

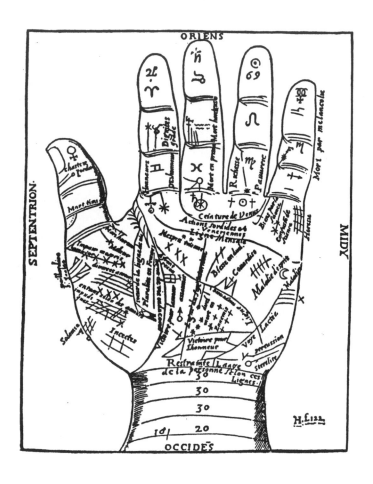

"And he [Jacob] dreamed, and behold a ladder set up on the earth, and the top of it reached to heaven: and behold the angels of God ascending and descending on it."

—*Genesis* 28: 12

3

Religion, Magic, and Dreams

Religion is the dream of the human mind. But even in dreams we do not find ourselves in emptiness or in heaven, but on earth, in the realm of reality; we only see real things in the entrancing splendor of imagination and caprice, instead of in the simple daylight of reality and necessity.
—Ludwig Feuerbach, *The Essence of Christianity*

A SIMPLE PRAYER

Because people who clung to the Manichean heresy equated light with good and darkness with evil, they feared the forces that might be abroad at night. So they prayed before going to bed (as well as taking other precautions to protect the sleeper such as a cross above the bed, etc.). Here is an anonymous prayer at least as old as the eighteenth-century:

> Now I lay me down to sleep;
> I pray the Lord my soul to keep.
> If I should die before I wake,
> I pray the Lord my soul to take.

Inevitably, there was a parody:

> Now I lay me down to sleep,
> My brand new boots are off my feet.
> If I should die before I wake,
> Give them to my brother, Jake.

95

GREEK PERSONIFICATIONS

Among the minor Greek gods were Hypnos, god of sleep, and Oneiros, god of dreams. Morpheus was said to be one of the sons of Hypnos; from him we get the word *morphine* and the expression "in the arms of Morpheus," meaning safely asleep.

THE DREAMING

The aborigines of Australia have a religion that considers "The Dreaming" to have begun the world as we know it, the time when out of chaos came the first human beings. Every culture has its own creation myth, but the aborigines of Australia base Creation on a dream. One might say it was a dream in the mind of God.

The aborigines of Australia, as most people know, speak of dream lines on the earth. They say that each time a new person is born, a spirit comes to inhabit the body, and when that spirit leaves the body is dead. During life, rituals can call upon other spirits, both the gods and the dead. Mircea Eliade's *Australian Religions* (1973) tells us about the relationships between The Dreaming and the living, and about how the art of the Australian aborigines relates to The Dreaming. In primitive religions such as The Dreaming the connection that Freud saw between the unconscious and the conscious mind are expressed in what we might call creation myths, or even in everyday activities.

See: Baldwin Spencer & F. J. Gillen, *The Northern Tribes of Central Australia* (1899) and Géza Róheim, *The Gates of the Dream* (1952), and Christopher Finch, "Aboriginal Dream Paintings," *Architectural Digest* 55:5 (May 1998), 174 *ff.*

DEUTERONOMY XVIII. 10–12

Neither let there be found among you any one…that consulteth soothsayers, or observeth dreams and omens, neither let there be any wizard, or charmer, nor any one that consulteth pythonic spirits, or fortunetellers, or that seeketh the truth from the dead. For the lord abhorreth all these things.

DREAMS AND VISIONS

Joel 2:28 says "your old men shall dream dreams, your young men shall see visions" and this suggests that all of Israel shall be involved in prophecy. In *Acts* II 14:21 St. Peter says that Pentecost has fulfilled this prophecy for Christians. One of Sir Francis Bacon's *Essays* ("Of Youth and Age") points out that in the view of the rabbis youth was superior to senior citizens, in that visions are better than mere dreams, that "young men are admitted nearer to God than old, because vision is clearer revelation than a dream."

The prophets of old, however, were not youthful. In any case, I am not obliged to pay attention to rabbinical interpretations, though I often find them entertaining.

According to The Bible, God's communications are usually verbal and do not involve apparitions, but the Jews regarded dreams, disembodied voices, and apparitions in the same category. The word for *visions* includes visitations without apparitions.

Would you rather have a dream or a vision?

If you want to interpret your dream or vision according to someone's idea of the scriptures, you can turn to books like these:

Castro, David A. *Understanding Supernatural Dreams according to The Bible* (1994).
Klemp, Harold. *The Art of Spiritual Dreaming* (1999).

Personally, I do not believe we have supernatural dreams. We have a conscious and an unconscious mind, and to me that is miracle enough.

A TRANCE ORACLE

In Tibet, there has been a Nechung Oracle since the eighth-century, each considered to be the reincarnation of the former one. The present Nechung Oracle goes into trances some 20 or 25 times a year to bring prophecies, warnings, etc. He advised the present Dalai Lama on the exact time and route by which to leave Tibet in 1959. His trances are by no means dreams. He goes into a trance and then fitted with a 20-kilo golden helmet and a sword, after which he vigorously performs a violent dance and utters the message purportedly conveyed through him, quite unlike the calm trance mediums at séances who do, indeed, appear to be sleeping.

MASTERS' THESES ON DIVINATORY DREAMS

Dissertation Abstracts International makes easily available facts about what scholarship there is in doctoral dissertations, but too often forgotten are the hard working women who took masters' degrees and wrote useful M.A. theses in earlier times when few women went past that to the Ph.D. Here are half a dozen sample M.A. theses on dreams and foretelling the future:

Wanda D. Cade, "Prophecies, Omens, and Premonitions in Shakespeare Tragedies," University of Alabama 1935.

Mary Margaret Cannell, "Signs, Omens, and Portents in Nebraska Folklore," University of Nebraska 1932.

Henrietta Carroll, "The Treatment of Omens and Portents in Latin Epic," University of Pittsburgh 1926.

Mary Beth Stoner Croft, "The Role of Ghosts, Superstitions, and Dreams in Seventeenth-Century French Tragedy and Tragi-Comedy," University of Alabama 1948.

Wilhelmina Henrietta De Feyter, "The Prodigies, Omens, and Oracles in Virgil's *Aeneid*," University of Chicago 1918.

Esther June Hand, "A Study of Divination and Kindred Subjects in Suetonius' *Lives of the Caesars*," Columbia University 1946.

GENESIS 41:14–41

Then Pharaoh sent and called Joseph, and they brought him hastily out of the dungeon; and he shaved himself, and changed his raiment, and came in to Pharaoh.

And Pharaoh said unto Joseph, 'I have dreamed a dream, and *there is* none that can interpret it: and I have heard say of thee, *that* thou canst understand a dream to interpret it.'

And Joseph answered Pharaoh, saying, 'It is not in me: God shall give Pharaoh an answer of peace.'

And Pharaoh said unto Joseph, 'In my dream, behold, I stood upon the bank of the river:

And, behold, there came up out of the river seven kine [cattle], fat-fleshed and well-favored; and they fed in a meadow:

And, behold, seven other kine came up after them, poor and very ill-favored and lean-fleshed, such as I never saw in all the land of Egypt for badness:

And the lean and ill-favored kine did eat up the first seven fat kine:

And when they had eaten them up it could not be known that they had eaten them; but they *were* still ill-favored, as at the beginning. So I awoke.

And I saw in my [other] dream, and, behold, seven ears come up on one stalk, full and good:

And, behold, seven ears, withered thin *and* blasted with the east wind, sprung up after them:

And the thin ears devoured the seven good ears: and I told *this* unto the magicians; but *there was* none that could declare it [the meaning] to me.'

And Joseph said unto Pharaoh, 'The dream of Pharaoh *is* one: God hath showed Pharaoh what he [God] *is* about to do.

The seven good kine *are* seven years: and the seven good ears *are* seven years: the dream *is* one.

And the seven thin and ill-favored kine that came up after them *are* seven years; and the seven empty ears blasted with the east wind shall be seven years of famine.

This is the thing which I have spoken unto Pharaoh: What God *is* about to do he showeth unto Pharaoh.

Behold, there come seven years of great plenty throughout all the land of Egypt:

And there shall arise after them seven years of famine; and all the plenty shall be forgotten in the land of Egypt; and the famine shall consume the land;

And the plenty shall not be known in the land by reason of that famine following; for it *shall be* very grievous.

Joseph interprets the dream of Pharoah in this painting by Jean-Adrrien Guignet.

And for that the dream was doubled unto Pharaoh twice; *it is* because the thing *is* established by God, and God will shortly bring it to pass.

Now therefore let Pharaoh look out a man discrete and wise, and set him over the land of Egypt.

Let Pharaoh *do this*, and let him appoint officers over the land, and take up the fifth part of the land of Egypt in the seven plenteous years.

And let them gather all the food of those good years that come, and lay up corn [grain] under the hand of Pharaoh, and let them keep food in the cities.

And that food shall be for store to the land against the seven years of famine, which shall be in the land of Egypt; that the land perish not through the famine.'

And the thing was good in the eyes of Pharaoh, and in the eyes of all his servants.

And Pharaoh said unto his servants, 'Can we find *such a one* as *this is*, a man in whom the Spirit of God *is?*'

And Pharaoh said unto Joseph, 'Forasmuch as God hath showed thee all this, *there is* none so discreet and wise as thou *art*:

Thou shalt be over my house, and according unto thy word shall all my people be ruled: only in the throne will I be greater than thou.'

And Pharaoh said unto Joseph, 'See, I have set thee over all the land of Egypt.'

NEWS FROM GOD

According to Hebrew scriptures, God communicates with mankind in various ways. This of course includes signs and portents. The other ways involve God speaking directly, if sometimes symbolically, in dreams (*Genesis* and I *Kings*), and while pagans also have dreams they cannot well interpret them without consulting a prophet of the God of the Jews (as in *Daniel* and elsewhere). In this, also, the Jews are the chosen people.

God can also speak through visions and interlocutors. The visions of prophets are to be interpreted by God or an angel (*Amos* and *Zachariah*) and taken as instructions for political actions, war, regulating the rulers of Israel, and so on. After King David's time, the prophet replaced the priestly oracles and both the temple and the court retained resident prophets.

A second way of prophesying involves the *urim* and *thurim*. If you look at a picture of the High Priest of the Jews you will see he wears a breastplate adorned with jewels. Each has long been believed to correspond to one of the tribes of Israel, but when I was writing about magic and witchcraft I noticed that the jewels were arranged in the wrong order if gem magic was involved, so I consulted a number of learned rabbis. This arrangement, I suggested, could not be to work magic and yet the breastplate was said to be magical.

What could it be? None of the rabbis I consulted was able to answer my questions. They were astonished when I discovered that the real purpose of the breastplate, attached to a ceremonial garment called the *ephod*, was fortune-telling.

Behind the breastplate were kept the *urim* and *thurim*. These were apparently magical lots cast to get a yes or no answer to questions put by the High Priest. This is stated in *Numbers*.

The post-Davidic religion appears to have relied upon other methods, and by the time of *Ezra*, if not earlier, the use of magical lots had been abandoned as a way of learning God's will, although Jewish magic continues to be a concern of the *Mishna* and the *Gemara*.

Today, as everyone knows, there is no High Priest of the Jews nor will there be until a third temple is erected and the ancient temple ceremonies resumed. Meanwhile the temple is really just a *shul* (school), a place for prayer and study but not priestly ritual. The rabbi is learned in The Torah. He is considered a teacher, not a priest. Religions differ; in Mormonism all adult males are priests, while in Judaism there are now no priests at all.

The prophets were not priests but spoke for God and called "men of God," of whom Moses was an important one. They conveyed God's messages to men. The term "men of God" seems to indicate some sort of shaman in pre-Mosaic religion. Moses, an Egyptian, may have been using powerful Egyptian magic to counter the magic of the pharaoh's magicians. Moses says in *Deuteronomy*:

> Let no one be found among you who consigns his son or daughter to the fire [sacrifices humans], or who performs auguries or a soothsayer, a diviner, a sorcerer, or one who casts spells, or who consults ghosts or familiar spirits, or one who inquires of the dead [necromancer]. For anyone who does such [magical] things is abhorrent to God.

The Jews relied upon prophets, not magicians (although King Saul famously consulted the dead Samuel through the Witch of Endor). Sometimes the prophets could transfer prophesying powers to followers, but only if God ordained it: Elijah could not confer his power on Elisha in II *Kings*. He could simply give Elisha a way of recognizing the authentic voice of God if God deigned to speak through him.

False prophets and false interpretations of messages, naturally, are to be avoided at all costs. God chooses what He will communicate and to whom; any attempt to force communication by, for example, music or ecstasy or magical means is roundly condemned. Only pagans, heathens, the enemies of the God of the Jews, the opponents of Yaweh, Jehovah, or Adonai, practice it.

Of all the ways in which divinity communicates to humanity in the religion of the Jews, dreams appear to be the most common but can also be the most misleading. It was considered black magic to dream omens and auguries. I suppose it must have been forbidden to attempt to incur such dreams through magic.

THE NIGHT JOURNEY

Mohammed, The Prophet, dictated revelations in what became The Koran, the sacred scripture of Islam, the standard version set in the seventh-century of the common era. The Prophet's messages began with a dream in which his mission and first revelations were made known to him. He had had many dreams before but in this one Mohammed dreamed that he was transported to Jerusalem and there conversed with earlier prophets (Abraham, Moses, and Jesus) who assured him he would be a prophet.

After that revelations came to him while awake and asleep. Both were regarded valid and form the 114 *suras* or sections of The Koran. The orthodox of Islam believe that The Koran must not be translated, so throughout the world followers of the religion (whose name means Surrender, to the will of God) read the holy book in Arabic.

A convert to Islam, Mohammed Marmaduke Pickthall, translated The Koran into English, but the act was considered blasphemous by fundamentalists. It also offends some to print The Koran, rather than copy it in manuscript, like The Torah of the Jews. In Europe in the early sixteenth-century an attempt was made to print The Koran but the Roman Catholic Church burned the books.

It was at last printed in Europe in the second half of the seventeenth-century and of course has been reprinted ever since, in Muslim and non-

Muslim countries. It is the most significant Book of Dreams in the history of revelation, unless you count *Revelations* as dream material.

See Marcia K. Hermansen, "Introduction to the Study of Dreams and Visions in Islam," *Religion* 27 (January 1997), 1–5.

THE ANGELS FIND THE DEVIL TEMPTING EVE

From John Milton's *Paradise Lost* IV:

> ...him there they found
> Squat like a toad, close at the ear of Eve;
> Assaying by his devilish art to reach
> The organs of her fancy, and with them forge
> Illusions as he list, phantoms and dreams;
> Or if, inspiring venom, he might taint
> Th'animal spirits that from pure blood arise
> Like gentle breaths from rivers pure, thence raise
> At least distempered, discontented thoughts,
> Vain hopes, vain aims, inordinate desires
> Blown up with high conceits, engend'ring pride.

See Jane M. Petty, "The Voice's at Eve's Ear in *Paradise Lost*," *Milton Quarterly* 19 (May 1985), 42–47.

FROM *THE HOLY KABBALAH*

A. E. Waite is the leading, if perhaps clumsiest, writer on the mystic books of the ancient Hebrew sages. He has this to say about dreams:

Having regard to the consideration allotted to the interpretation of dreams by the Old Testament, if would surpass expectation if the ZOHAR rejected the possibility, more especially with the authority of the TALMUD to support the affirmative view. It does something, however, to reduce the rank of dreams. They are the gross form of that which the soul sees when it is separated from the body. The soul then discerns things as they actually are, while the body perceives them only in a form corresponding to its own degree. Every dream is regarded as an admixture of truth and falsehood; but the most curious thesis of all is that a dream is realised according to the interpretation placed upon it: should this be favourable, favours will overwhelm the man, but in the contrary case he will be weighed down by adversity. The reason is that the word governs, and it follows that no dream must be disclosed to anyone by whom the dreamer is not loved. There are in all three degrees—dream, vision, and prophecy: the greatest of these is prophecy.

You may wish to point out to anyone psychoanalyzing you that "no dream must be disclosed to anyone by whom the dreamer is not loved". We are not talking about transference here—love.

If you happen to love difficult texts, here is a stunning example: Sheldon Brivic, "The Mind Factory: *Kabbalah* in *Finnegans Wake*," *James Joyce Quarterly* 21 (Fall 1983), 7–30.

DREAM INTERPRETATION IN ANCIENT HEBREW LITERATURE

Gutheil, Emil A. *"Traumdeutung im Talmud," Psychoanalytische Praxis* 3 (1933), 89–91.

Lauer, C. *"Das Wesen des Trasumen in der Beurteilung der talmudischen und rabbinischen Literatur," Internationale Zeitscrift für Psychoanalyse* (1913), 459–469.

Unfortunately for most of us, a great deal of the material involved in the *Zohar* (Splendor), The Talmud and similar sources are only in Hebrew. Some folks say that even A. E. Waite could not read that. On top of that, as you see from a few examples listed above, the modern scholarly writing about dream psychology from early Talmudic and rabbinical writings is almost exclusively in German. But Freud and many of his colleagues have been translated and with that some of the talmudic and rabbinical tradition continues, with the occasional appearance out of left field of something like the orgone box or something from the buffet of eastern mysticism, whose spice we seem to like to perk up modern theories and new syncretic or synthetic religions.

For "the occult in Torah perspective," see Ya'akov Mosheh Hillel's *Faith and Folly* (1990). Also see C. von Orelli, *Alttestamentliche Weissagungen* (Old Testament Prophecy, 1855) and E. Clodd, *Myths and Dreams* (1885).

THE MOON GODDESS

Many religions have a moon goddess. Even The Blessed Virgin is often depicted standing on the crescent moon. Some scholars have suggested that the moon goddesses in all religions come from the fact that dreams can be predictive. That is why the moon goddess is so often the patroness of magical cults, which one writer says are engaged in "drawing down the moon." The Moon Goddess is not to be confused with the Mother Goddess of New Age beliefs.

THE ORPHIC CULT

In the sixth century BC the Orphic cult was powerful in Greece. It preached resurrection from the dead, as in the cult of Dionysus, the religions of Mithras or Christ, or the *soma sema* (body as tomb) belief.

In Albrecht Dürer's Madonna of the Crescent moon, pagan and Christian iconography are both used.

Duality was not only seen in the good and evil in man, derived, said the Orphic cult, from the origin of man in the remains of Zagreus (who was a son of Zeus, and the evil Titans) but in the separate identities of body and soul, the material and the spiritual. There are still those who fear for the wandering spirit if harm comes to the sleeping body.

WET DREAMS

Judaism, which endorses sex for procreation chiefly, to expand the remnant of Israel, and Christianity, founded as an end-of-the-world religion emphasizing chastity and preparation for The End rather than procreation, look rather askance at sex. This includes sex in dreams. Freud takes up the subject of wet dreams, and in the Teutonic stiffness of an English translation, informs us that

> the apparatus of sex, at varying intervals, which, however are not ungoverned by rules, discharges the sexual substance during the night to the accompaniment of pleasurable feeling and in the course of a dream which hallucinates the act of sex.

Celibate holy persons in Christianity have trouble with this, but you will be glad to know that both St. Jerome and St. John Crysostom let us all off the hook. They declare that we are not responsible for our dreams, and what the Victorians used to call "self-pollution" is no sin, just messy.

Tertullian, mentioned earlier, wrote a number of chapters in his treatise on the soul about dreams but does not consider it sinful to have sexual dreams. Dream on—sexual dreams release tensions, offer compensatory thrills, and assist wish fulfillment to protect us against physical and mental ill health. Wilhelm Reich and others suggest that orgasm is not only fun but also healthy. It is nice to find a pleasure that, as the saying goes, is not immoral, illegal, or fattening.

FROM *RELIGIOUS CULTS OF THE CARIBBEAN* (1980) BY GEORGE EATON SIMPSON

Among the Yoruba, dreams are believed to portray future events and distant happenings. A juice or a powder may be placed in or near the eyes at night to stimulate the power of occult sight. Diviners determine which dreams are transparently clear and will come true, and which are symbolical or go by opposites and require interpretation (Parrinder 1951:191). Leaders of the *shango* cult in Trinidad say that some dreams are perfectly clear, (*e.g.* an order from a power to move his flag from one side of the house to the front yard) but others have to be interpreted. One may receive healing remedies through a dream-experience, or a power may give one a message or a warning to pass on to another person. If one dreams that he is "keeping a feast," or that he has been sent to the river to perform a ritual, he is supposed to carry out such acts later.

A voodoo *drapeau* (flag to honor or summon spirits) depicting the Haitian goddess of love, Erzulie Freda, as The Blessed Virgin Mary.

Amombahs are often asked to interpret the dreams of their clients. Mainly the dreamer is told whether the portent of his dreams is good or bad. Dream subjects which are interpreted favorably include: flying (prosperity); drizzling rain; birds; and certain fruits, especially mangoes and grains, especially corn. Among the unfavorable omens in dreams are: falling (trouble, sickness); dog eating food (trouble); death (dreamer or relative will die soon). Some *shango* leaders, like their opposite numbers in the Shouters church, use the Bible to interpret their clients' dreams. The officiant prays, opens the Bible at random and reads three or four lines where his left hand rests. The meaning of the devotee's dream is found in the words of these verses.

Dream-experiences and visions are of great importance to some leaders in the *shango* cult of Trinidad. They take their own dreams seriously and they interest themselves, for "spiritual" or practical reasons, in their clients' dreams. The dreams of these leaders tend to be elaborate and narrating them enhances their reputations . While other leaders and the rank and file of shangoists attach much less importance to these experiences, the general attitude is that "dreams do not lie." Dreams and visions serve to reinforce traditional beliefs concerning illnesses, the hazards of everyday life, wrong living, good fortune, and the desires of the powers and the dead. In addition, the dreams of shangoists, together with possession, establish a two-way communication with the gods. These dreams, like Haitian peasant dreams (E. E. Bourguignon, "Dreams and Dream Interpretation in Haiti," *American Anthropologist*, April 1954, 262-268) encourage idiosyncratic modes of worship and give support to such mythology, mainly Catholic hagiography, as still exists. As Bourguignon points out, the mythological material, "in turn, furnishes the basis for dream interpretation and for the manner in which dreams are experienced."

ORACLES

The ancient world was full of oracles. As their name implies, they *speak*. Sometimes they were supposed to speak through a priestess in a trance but often all you had to do to get the answer to your question (an answer which, by the way, could be as riddling as a dream) was to sleep, naturally or drugged, in the sacred precincts.

The most famous Greek oracle was that of Apollo, at Delphi, thought to be the navel of the earth. There was another in Didima in Turkey. The most famous Roman oracle was the goddess Fortuna at Præneste, where you drew inscribed sticks for an answer in much the same way as a bird picked a piece of paper with your fortune on it in the streets of modern cities. Dreaming could get you the answer to your question, whether the answer came to you at home in your own bed or, supposedly more reliably, in the sacred precincts of the shrine to some god or goddess.

Home was more convenient, if only because the *pithia* or priestess of Apollo, like an academic, worked only nine months each year. She also prophesied only on the seventh day (the day Apollo was born) of each month. Most of all, there was no fee for home visits in dreams.

THE BOOK OF JOB

Poor Job. It truly is, as the *Epistle to the Hebrews* would say, "a fearful thing to fall into the hands of the living God," especially the rather nasty God of the Old Testament, Who is quite capable of making a nice guy like Job suffer. Job is well aware of being picked on. *Job* 7, demands of God that He stop tormenting him:

Ruins of the Temple of Apollo at Delphi.

When I say, My bed shall comfort me, my couch shall ease my complaint;

Then thou scarest me with dreams, and terrifiest me through visions:

So that my soul chooseth strangling, *and* death rather than my life.

I loathe *it*; I would not live always: let me alone; for my days *are* vanity.

What *is* man, that thou shouldest magnify him? and that thou shouldest set thine heart upon him?

And *that* thou shouldest visit him every morning, *and* try him every moment?

A number of modern thinkers are of the opinion, rightly or wrongly, that The Creator set the whole thing in motion but afterwards kept His hands off. Some despair that He has died. Others joke that He doesn't care and lives in South American under an assumed name. The people of the Old Testament were certain God was involved in everyday affairs, and Jewish politics in particular. They believed Providence was both watchful and proactive (if not always pro-Man).

In *Job* 33 the subject of communication in dreams continues:

For God speaketh once, yea twice, *yet man* perceiveth it not.
In a dream, in a vision of the night, when deep sleep falleth
Upon men, in slumberings upon the bed;
Then he openeth the ears of men, and sealeth their instruction,
That he may withdraw man *from his* purpose, and hide pride
    from man.
He keepeth back his soul from the pit, and his life from perish-
    ing by the sword.

So all is for the best in the best of all possible worlds, and
Providence is everywhere, not just in Rhode Island.

THE BOOK OF DANIEL

From *Daniel* 4:

Nebuchadnezzar the king, unto all people, nations, and languages, that dwell in all the earth; Peace be multiplied unto you.

I thought it good to show the signs and wonders that the
high God hath wrought toward me.

How great *are* his signs! and how mighty *are* his wonders!
His kingdom *is* an everlasting kingdom, and his dominion *is*
from generation to generation.

I Nebuchadnezzar was at rest in mine house, and flourish-
ing in my palace:

I saw a dream which made me afraid, and the thoughts upon
my bed and the visions of my head troubled me.

Therefore I made a decree to bring in all the wise *men* of
Babylon before me, that they might make known unto me the
interpretation of the dream.

Then came in the magicians, the astrologers, the Chaldeans,
and the soothsayers: and I told the dream before them; but they
did not make known unto me the interpretation thereof.

But at the last Daniel came in before me, whose name *was*
Belteshazzar, according to the name of my god, and in whom
is the spirit of the holy gods: and before him I told the dream,
saying,

O Belteshazzar, master of the magicians, because I know
that the spirit of the holy gods *is* in thee, and no secret troubleth
thee [to disclose], tell me the visions of my dream that I have
seen, and the interpretation thereof.

These *were* the visions of mine head in my bed; I saw, and behold a tree

In the midst of the earth, and the height thereof *was* great.

The tree grew, and was strong, and the height thereof reached unto Heaven, and the sight thereof to the end of all the earth:

The leaves thereof *were* fair, and the fruit thereof much, and in it *was* meat [food] for all: the beasts of the field had shadow under it, and the fowls of the heaven dwelt in the boughs thereof, and all flesh was fed of it.

I saw in the visions of my head upon my bed, and, behold, a watcher and a holy one came down from heaven;

He cried out, and said thus, Hew down the tree, and cut off his branches, shake off his leaves, and scatter his fruit: let the beasts get away from under it, and let the fowls from his branches:

Nevertheless, leave the stump of the roots in the earth, even with a band of iron and brass, in the tender grass of the field: and let it be wet with the dew of heaven, and *let* his portion *be* with the beasts in the grass of the earth:

Let his heart be changed from man's, and *let* a beast's heart be given unto him; and let seven times pass over him.

Job with his accusers, by William Blake

The Jews believed, as you know, that as Chosen People they alone could correctly interpret the messages from God. Daniel interpreted the dream for the king, who is the tree, his empire so powerful that it grew up to heaven. (God was jealous of the Tower of Babel built to reach up to heaven, and destroyed the project. God must have felt threatened.)

Daniel told Nebuchadnezzar that the dream was "to them that hate thee, and the interpretation thereof to thine enemies." As it happened Nebuchadnezzar went mad and grazed upon grass for seven years, like a beast of the field. Then his reason returned and he recognized, as he says at the end of this chapter, that God "is able to debase" for the correction of mankind. Theirs was a god that was jealous and to be held in awe.

In the next chapter of *Daniel*, during a feast given by the king, there appeared four characters, writ large: MENE, TEKEL, UPHARSIN.

Daniel read these to mean that Nebuchadnezzar's kingdom was finished, and would be divided between the Medes and the Persians. For this bad news the king rewarded Daniel with a gold chain and a robe of scarlet. Apparently the king had not read *Leviticus*, in which robes of scarlet are expressly forbidden to the Jews, but his gratitude was at least real.

That night Nebuchadnezzar, king of the Chaldeans, was slain and Darius the Persian and Median the Mede divvied up his kingdom. The prophecies given in dream and written on the wall had come true, as Daniel had said they would.

OLD ENGLISH RELIGIOUS VERSE

Naturally, because only churchmen could read and write in those days, there is a great deal of religious verse in Old English. One of these poems retells the story of Daniel, although he Anglo-Saxon version brought Nebuchadnezzar, not Daniel, to the fore. The drama is not in the Jewish prophet's ability to read the future but in the plight of the Chaldean king. The poem of 764 lines and six fits (sections) occurs at the end of what is called the Junius Ms. (G.P. Krapp, ed., 1930).

The Renaissance bibliophile Cotton family kept their treasures (now in the British Library) in bookcases identified by busts of Roman dignitaries on top of each, so this poem's Ms. is called Junius xi. George K. Anderson's standard *Literature of the Anglo-Saxons* (1949) notes *Daniel*'s treatment not of dreams but of landscape...some relevant lines

I translate:

> O God Almighty! summer bright
> Praise the Savior day and night.
> The frost and snow, the winter sky,
> The clouds that pass in praise on high,
> O mighty Lord, the earth so fair
> And all the plains and mountains there,
> The salty waves, the surf and flood,
> The gushing springs, declare Thy good.
> Eternal Lord and righteous God.

Of course Anglo-Saxon verse did not use rhyme, obtaining its decoration and regulation from alliteration. The Old English poem is not as superstitious, one might say, as The Bible, playing down the magic of Daniel reading the future.

See Antonina Harbus, "Nebuchadnezzer's Dreams in the Old English *Daniel*," *English Studies* 75 (1994), 489–508. More dream material is to be found in *Ezekiel, Jeremiah, Zacharias* and elsewhere, in the scriptures, the *Apocrypha*, and in patristic literature both Greek and Latin as well as in later Christian theology.

Dreams today are individual—anger and fear, sadness and sex, etc. Still, religion says we must dream, presumably about holy things, and the rabbinical tradition says that "a dreamless life is a sinful life," even though most people ascribe dreamless sleep to peace of mind.

THE THREE WISE MEN

The Magi dreamed about this great event of the birth of Christ that would shatter forever their old ways. Their gifts were to the king of the new world. T. S. Eliot has a poem in which he has one of these magi at the end of his life reflecting on the visit to the holy child: "I should be glad of another death."

The French writer A. Boucher-Leclerque wrote a history of divination in the ancient world (1871–1889) that, translated, would contribute to our history of dream divination.

Even without divining, however, the Magi received dream messages to lead them to Christ and a dream warning not to return to King Herod, whose motives were not of the best. Instead, they were to honor the infant to which the star led them.

DIVINATION

Divination means dealing with the divine. When we engage in divination we are supposedly turning to gods and goddesses, or God, or other superior forces who know more about the past, present, and (especially) the future than humans.

When we gaze into crystal balls, magic mirrors, or a blot of ink we are trying to evoke in waking visions what we think we encounter in dreams. Even physical methods of fortune-telling, such as reading tea leaves or the *I Ching* or The Tarot, demand interpretation. Similarly, you can simply look at the palms of your hands, but if you really want to get into palmistry you have to read an expert like Cheiro.

In passing, I have to tell you that researching lots of books over lots of years I have had my horoscope cast by a number of so-called experts and no two results are alike. My palms have been read often and the results are remarkably similar, at least among so-called professionals. Today literary criticism tends to emphasize that it is the reader who gives meaning to the text. It was the interpreter who gave meaning to old methods of sortilege or divination such as when a finger was placed at random into The Bible or a poet such as Virgil was dipped into for advice. Even if deities, saints, the dead or other personages come to us in dreams what they say and mean calls for interpretation, just as necessarily as the messing about in entrails of sacrificed animals—haruscpication—ever did.

Whether we seek knowledge in how arrows fall or how the planets move, in connection with dreams, working out a hidden meaning is required of divination. We may be presented with omens but what do they *mean*? In our dreams divination is just as mysterious, as they speak in what psychologist Erich Fromm called *The Forgotten Language* (1951).

Dream books translate the symbolic language of dreams, but, as in astrology, we must always ask: *Who says* that is what it means? How do they *know*?

Remember that most Christian denominations forbid fortune telling in all forms. If you are a follower of Islam, the whole script of your life is already written; you cannot change it, so why would you want to skip ahead?

DREAMS IN THE BIBLE

Jacob dreams about a ladder that climbs to heaven in The Bible. Saul turns to necromancy after "the Lord did not answer him, either by dreams, or by *urim*, or through prophets." Daniel was able to interpret dreams and so was Joseph in Egypt.

Joseph the carpenter had no need to interpret the message an angel gave him in a dream: his wife was pregnant with the Christ Child. The Magi are warned in dreams not to return to King Herod. Joseph is told by another angel in a dream to flee with his family to Egypt. Later another angel tells him to return to Israel, not to Judea but to Galilee. St. Paul has "a vision in the night."

The Lord spoke to some of the prophets in dreams. *Obadiah, Nahum* and *Habakuk* claim to contain visions. *Genesis, Ezekiel,* and *Job* all counted on visions and dreams, but one of the prophets (Jeremiah) warned that a rival might be peddling what his own narcissistic dreams were telling him as the word of God. So be careful when you think you have received The Word, by omens, portents, visions, intuitions, clairvoyance, fortune telling, or dreams. In fact, be wary of thinking you have been singled out for divine communication. Better try a little humility: "Lord, I am not worthy that Thou should'st enter under my roof...." And remember that there are other scriptures of other religions.

ALARMING EFFORTS TO RECALL DREAMS

Because of what science has discovered about dreaming, some people set alarm clocks to go off every hour and a half, hoping to wake up while a dream is occurring and recall it better. However, science says you are more likely to recall your dream if you do not wake suddenly. However, religious people say dreams that are authentic communications from God can always be recalled clearly. God doesn't want you to have to resort to psychoanalysis for translation or to receive partial faxes of faith.

HOLY WAKEFULNESS, BATMAN!

Christ Himself complained that His apostles could not stay awake in the Garden of Gethsemane. There was no garden there, but it was an important night, certainly, and they might have spent more time conscious of Him.

Wakefulness has traditionally been perceived as a sign of holiness. Stories are told about certain saints not sleeping, though I must say I do not believe all of them. St. Colette limited herself to an hour's sleep every eight days. St. Agatha of the Cross, stayed awake the last eight years prior to her final sleep, death. St. Lidwine was said to have slept only three hours in 30 years, which would have given her just about enough time for one dream.

This cannot have been good for these holy women. Science tells us that if one goes without sleep for two weeks serious and permanent mental damage ensues. If saints really did go without sleep and dreams there must have been miracles. It should have killed them.

DEEP SLEEP

Women generally have deeper sleep than men but mothers will awake at the slightest signal that their babies are in trouble, sounds to which men would not react.

It is argued that holy persons are more alert to messages from the divine. As parapsychological talents are merely inherent human talents heightened, receiving messages from the divine is a more developed talent in some persons than in others; however, they are inherent in us all.

TAIPING TIEN KUO

The rebellion of the Celestial Kingdom of Universal Peace, which is what that Chinese phrase means, started with a dream of Hung Hsiu-chu'an in nineteenth-century China. He conceived a violent hatred of the Manchu dynasty when he failed the civil service examinations, which were, in fact constructed to discourage southerners from becoming mandarins. This hatred shaped the rest of his life.

He fell ill, and in 1837 strange figures began to occupy his feverish dreams. A gentle man with a beard appeared, cleansed him of evil and gave him a sense of being chosen. But chosen for what? Hung came upon some literature from Christian missionaries and decided that the wise man of his dreams was Jesus Christ. By the mid-thirties he embraced Christianity and gathered other "God Worshippers" determined to overthrow the Chinese emperor and the ancient Chinese religion.

From 1850 on, Hung led a successful Taiping Rebellion. His forces captured Nanking, where Hung declared himself Celestial Ruler in opposition to the Manchu emperor. Rebellions raged in China for decades thereafter.

Before he died by his own hand in 1864, Hung saw his forces defeated by the Manchus and the British general "Chinese" Gordon—who also planned his campaigns with a Bible in hand. Later, native rebellions brought down the centuries-old Manchu dynasty without foreign-devil intervention. But of the colorful figures in the story Hung alone saw Jesus Christ in a dream.

TURNING TO MAGIC FOR USEFUL DREAMS

Magic and religion are closely allied, and if you do not want to wait for divinity to contact you, here is a recipe. If you insist on trying to peer into your future—I do not recommend any such effort—"To Produce Prophetic Dreams" here is a recipe (*Complete Book of Magic and Witchcraft*, 1995):

> Get up between 3 and 4 AM any morning in June, go out silently, and pick one full-blown red rose. Take it back to your room and "fumigate" it over a brazier in which you are burning sulfur and brimstone; let it have at least five full minutes of this. Write the name of the person you love and your own name on a clean sheet of paper and fold the rose in it. Seal the paper with three wax seals and bury it under a tree from which the rose was gathered. Over the spot trace the letter *A* (for *Amor*).
>
> On July 6 at midnight, dig up the rose wrapped in paper, take it to your room, and put it under your pillow. Sleep on it for three successive nights. "You will enjoy dreams of great portent."
>
> The resulting visions may not be prophetic, only revelatory. After all this autosuggestion, you're fairly likely to get something.

DREAMS PREGNANT WITH MEANING

Pregnant women naturally have concerns about the baby and these worries often appear in dreams. Hagiography tells us that women about to bring a saint into the world have on occasion dreamed about it.

The Order of Friars Preacher, founded by St. Dominic (who lived *c.* 1170-1221 and was canonized in 1234), was nicknamed *cani Domini* (dogs of the Lord). St. Dominic's mother, before he was born in Old Castille, dreamed of a small dog, it was said, "which she was to bear in her womb from which it would issue forth bearing in its jaws a flaming torch seeming to set the world on fire."

The mother of St. Thomas (not the doubting apostle but St. Thomas of Canterbury) dreamed that "the water of the Thames entered her womb" and made her pregnant. The result of this conception was to be the martyred Archbishop Thomas à Becket (1118-1170, canonized 1172).

The mother of St. Bernard of Clairvaux (1090-1153, canonized in 1174) is said to have dreamed of a dog in her womb, presaging the "bark" of this fierce opponent of heresy. The mother of Pius II went one better and dreamt that the little Piccolomini on the way would become pope: the baby appeared in her dream wearing the triple tiara. The mother of Nicholas V received similar assurances.

Sometimes The Blessed Virgin would appear in dreams to promise success to the baby about to be born or to ask it be dedicated to her service. The Blessed Virgin could also bring magical powers to mothers or babies in dreams.

If the Holy Mother did not appear in your dreams perhaps the fairies would. Appollonia Madizza, in the 1580s, in a dream received what she called "certain prayers" from the fairies, by which she meant words of power, magical incantations. It was thought that the fairies "can hurt, or help" and, as with trolls, leprechauns, and "good companions" in general, it was best to be on the good side of them. They could, like the saints, heal or harm, bring good fortune or bad, curse or cure disease, bless or curse you or your offspring. Dreams could tell you where you stood and what the future would bring. Wise women or other supposedly gifted persons could tell you what would follow if you dreamed of a hare or some other creature, or anything else.

MEDIUMISTIC ACTION IN SLEEP, NOT TRANCE

Usually people communicate in trance from The Other Side, as mediums, not as sleepers. But it was reported that after the death of Bishop Pike's son, a boy who had bad drug experiences and committed suicide in 1966 in a New York hotel room, the bishop sat up in bed and, still asleep, delivered a lecture from the dead son.

The bishop consulted a London medium, Ena Twigg, who brought him more messages from his dead son or, skeptics accused, read the bishop's mind for intimate details.

The bishop's widow consulted her again when Pike was lost in a desert the Holy Land in 1969. The widow had left the bishop in the desert when he was too exhausted to go on and went for help, then could not lead the rescuers back. Ms. Twigg provided the information about where the body could be found. Was she reading the widow's mind?

Here we have a medium in trance *and* a sleeper through whom the dead were supposed to speak.

"AT NIGHT, WHEN YOU'RE ASLEEP...."

In sleep you may have to worry about something far worse than the Sheik of Araby creeping into your tent; you may be visited by demons. As I have noted in an earlier book, Orthodox Judaism states that a man must not sleep alone in a house lest demons come to assail him.

There were two kinds: *incubi* for men and *succubi* for women. I suppose homosexuals might have to deal with same-sex horrors. Many learned theologians were of the opinion that half-demonic offspring could be born from sexual connections in sleep. Roman Catholics claimed Martin Luther was such a product.

I do not know if modern Roman Catholics are bound to believe in these demonic personalities, as they are bound under pain of excommunication to believe that The Devil is a real person; however, one papal bull, Giovanni Baptista Cibò, successor of Peter as Pope Innocent VIII, believed in the possibility of Catholics having sex in their sleep with demons. What he said is so weird we had best get it right:

> *Sane ad Nostrum, non sine ingenti molestia, peruenit auditum quod...complures utriusque sexus personæ, propriæ salutis immemores et a fide catholica deuiantes, cum dæmonibus incubis et succubis abuti.*

Innocent VIII's statement can be translated like this:

> It has in fact come to Our knowledge and deeply sad are We to hear it that many persons of both sexes utterly forgetful of the salvation of their souls and straying from the Catholic faith have had [intercourse] with demons, both incubi and succubi.

Those of us who consider ourselves less superstitious may blame sex in dreams on the relaxation of the censors that keep us in check while we are awake and out in society. The idea of a governor of the uncon-

In this detail from a fresco by Maso di Bianco in the Capella Bardi di Vernio (Church of Santa Croce, Florence) St. Silvester is shown healing two magicians. Notice that while their bodies lie supine their spirits sit up miraculously. In dream states, some people believed, we could have out-of-body experience.

scious that holds us to our culture's standards is central to Freud's concept of the human mind and Freud is our new religion.

Demons in dreams, however, were central to the early Christian faith. St. Augustine said that all disease Christians suffer, of body or mind, comes from demons. So your wet dream was a demonic attack. Diabolical possession indeed!

It was supposedly pleasurable to "pollute" yourself with a demon. Brignoli, in his *Alexicacon*, relates that when he was at Bergamo in 1650, a young man, twenty-two years of age, sought him out and made a long and ample confession. This youth avowed that some months before, when he was in bed, the chamber door opened and a maiden, Teresa, whom he loved, stealthily entered the room.

To his surprise she informed him that she had been driven from home and came to him for refuge. Although he suspected delusion, he consented to her solicitations and passed a night of unbounded indulgence in her arms. Before dawn, the visitant revealed the true nature of the deceit, and the young man realized he had lain with a succubus.

Nonetheless, such was his doting folly, the same debauchery was repeated night after night, until struck with terror and remorse, he sought the priest to confess and be delivered of this abomination.

"This monstrous connection lasted several months," reported the priest; "but at last God delivered him by my humble means, and he was truly penitent for his sins."

If you are in your loft and some girl appears in the night and wants to share your futon, check her credentials.

CONSCIENCE

Shakespeare is only one, albeit the most famous, of the many authors that have written about the conscience and nightmares (Hamlet complains of "bad dreams"). Such villains as Macbeth cannot sleep peacefully, having waded eye-deep in blood, and near his end Richard III is haunted in dreams by the victims of his crimes. In writings aimed at the superstitious, guilty dreams drive murderers to confess, for, as Macbeth tells us, "murder will out," betrayed by conscience if nothing else. Uneasy lies the head that wears a crown but uneasier lies the head full of gnawing guilt.

An example from the popular broadside ballads (peddled in the streets in the old days) is *The Midwife's Maid's Lamentation in Newgate* (1693). Newgate was a prison, where the ghosts of babies she had let die haunted a midwife. People liked to know that criminals would be wracked by conscience and brought to justice.

An addendum to that seventeenth-century ballad is this unusual eighteenth-century tale of a guilty conscience in dreams. The *Ipswitch Journal* for 29 July 1721 reported the sensational story of a man who turned himself in because, as he said, "I am not able to conceal my dreams any longer, my sleep departs from me, and I am pressed and troubled." This man was not a murderer—murderers turning themselves in was common—but the witness to a murder. He had seen his neighbor killed and could no longer rest easy with the knowledge. He knew the awful truth and felt obliged to unburden himself of it. The murderer was tried, convicted, and executed on this sleepless man's evidence.

Malcolm Gaskill in *Crime and Mentalities in Early Modern England* (2000) says that sometimes a witness who claimed knowledge from a dream was actually implicated in some other way but unwilling to confess. The dream alibi gave him a way to accuse without being implicated. Dream witnesses came forward long after Roman Catholicism had been replaced by the allegedly less superstitious Protestant religion in the sixteenth-century.

Some recent murderers have been convicted after coming forward to "assist" the police in their inquiries.

DREAM INCENSE

Maybe you think aromatherapy stinks. But incense is required for many operations of ritual magic and some people even recommend it for good dreams. Here is one recipe for dream incense: sandalwood, rose petals, camphor, and a drop or two of tuberose oil and jasmine oil. As is the case in so much magic, it works fabulously—if you believe in it.

Obverse   *Reverse*

Talisman of Jupiter

SPIRITUALISM

While we are on superstition, let us turn to the delicate matter of spiritualism. This is dangerous ground, for spiritualism is a religion to some. Tempers can run high on this topic, but I'll attempt to be honest without insulting anyone else's beliefs. So often the desire to "prove" an afterlife is equally strong in spiritualism and in dreams. I think both deal in hope.

In our Judeo-Christian tradition there has always been an urge for communicating with the dear departed. Contacting the dead, who were supposed to rest in peace, was a black art, and called just that: necromancy. The Witch of Endor may have done it for King Saul, but we were not supposed to deal in it. It is heresy and witchcraft.

Established religions could not say it was impossible to contact the dead but they could say it was absolutely forbidden. And they did. This, of course, did not stop attempts. In fact, the thrill of the forbidden often creates the heightened emotional states demanded of high magic.

Then, in the mid-nineteenth-century, some young girls in a farmhouse in Upstate New York, the Fox Sisters, said they communicated with the dead in séances. They did not care for any religious denomination and would accept no control by clergy over their mediumistic powers. One of the great appeals of table-rapping was that you could do it yourself if you were a gifted medium or, if you had no gift, you could fake it.

But the mediums were in trance, not asleep. Spiritualism became one of the new American religions of the nineteenth-century, which spread, like Mormonism, around the world. This could not but have some effect on the long tradition of the dead speaking to the living in dreams. The cruel wars of the nineteenth and twentieth-centuries left many people without loved ones. They had good reason to want to communicate with them across the divide that separates this world from the next. But while mediums could hold a séance at will, dreamers could never control the visitations of the dead in dreams. Women mediums could much improve the position of women in the social hierarchy, but feminists have to admit that leading psychoanalysts and dream interpreters have all too seldom been women. Since the mid-nineteenth-century spiritualism has perhaps shiefly involved women. Since the mid-twentieth-century spiritualism has been in decline and so, to a lesser extent, has been Freudian dream analysis, once a kind of secular religion.

You could not make a religion out of dreaming the dead—though that certainly bolstered one of the basic tenets of religion, that there is a life after this one.

WITCHCRAFT

In his *History of Witchcraft*, the "Rev." Montague Summers gives an example that may well be more disturbing than he intended. He cites the case of a woman who only imagined—dreamed—she was a witch engaged in forbidden practices, practices to which many thousands of deluded women confessed under vile tortures and were put to death.

We recoil in horror to think how many people believed themselves in league with The Devil and attended black masses and sabbats. Presumably, rationalists will say, they only dreamed such things, sometimes because of the hallucinogens arising from the burning of substances at magical ceremonies, or from the flying ointment's ingredients, or sometimes from ritual drinks. Moreover, in their dreams they may have seen friends and identified them to the authorities, who then sent the confessors to their deaths in the interest of saving their souls.

The history of mankind is full of horrors arising from our inability to tell the real from the imagined. It is nightmarish to consider the number of people murdered, or murdering, in the name of God. One wonders how many were misled by their dreams.

DREAMS AND THE PROTESTANT MINISTRY

Reverend John A. Sanford, while rector of St. Paul's Episcopal Church in San Diego, wrote *Dreams: God's Forgotten Language* (1968) "to show, in as clear and simple a manner as possible, the relationship of dreams to religious experience." Here is a dream from a middle-aged woman he counseled.

Hypnos, by Scopas (?), fourth century BC. The British Museum.

This dream occurred on December nine, nineteen hundred and forty-four. Our baby had died suddenly on November twenty-ninth, nineteen hundred and forty-two, at the age of four months. In my dream...I saw a young woman of about thirty grasping the hand of a small boy, just learning to walk. I knew instantly that the boy was ours although both figures faced away from me. I noticed his sturdy little legs particularly. They were running freely and happily up a gentle slope of greensward dotted with flowers—the color[s] of these latter were indescribable—they were not of this world.

The young woman wore a loose dress of indeterminate color, with a girdle at the waist. I felt very close to her. I thought that she was someone very near to me.

I awakened my husband to tell him of my dream because it was so vivid, and I got such great comfort from it. I said, "I believe that was my grandmother [she means the baby's grandmother, her own mother] with our baby, because I felt so close to her and he is all right because she is taking care of him." I felt very happy. My husband noted the time—one-thirty AM.

The next morning I received a telegram that my mother had died at one-thirty AM. Having had that dream, I went through the funeral with never a thought of grief. I have never grieved for my mother or baby since.

Father Sanford added:

Let us avoid a tendency to metaphysical explanations of the dream symbols. We simply do not know how to interpret the symbols of the hill, the flowers, and the age of the little boy in the dream. They point to the continuance of life in another reality, but beyond that we can say little. But we can point to two indisputable facts: first, that the dream occurred at the same time as the death of the dreamer's mother; second, that it brought an irrational but profound reassurance. The first fact demonstrates that the unconscious source of our dreams is not necessarily limited by space and time in our conscious mind. The second fact manifests that real religion is not based, as some would have it, on fabrications of man's conscious mind, or a desire to prolong a childish dependence on parental figures, but upon our innate recognition that our space-time reality is affected by another kind of reality, that the words "visible and invisible" of the Nicene Creed actually exist.

The words of the creed of the Council of Nicæa do exist; the question is whether what they assert is true. But you see what the Episcopal priest means.

This woman's dream is a great challenge to Christian dogma. If at The End we will all come back "with the same bodies that we had in this life"—as my own creed and the good father's states— at what age(s) will we have been hanging about in the afterlife and what age(s) will we assume for eternity? I would settle for anything between 25 and 45 but if I am to be among the blessed I wish I could have a more splendid appearance the next time around, more Brad Pitt than William Pitt, if you please.

RECIPE FOR DREAMY SMELLS

Rose petals, lemon balm, costmary, mint, and cloves. What, no poppy? What incense have various religions used in connection with transcendental states?

ON THE LAST FRONTIER

Science now promises to bring us the answers to questions that only religions used to undertake to answer, or tell us to leave unanswered, and the last frontier of discovery is the human mind. You may think that a comic novel by David Lodge, *Thinks*, is an odd place to get reliable information on the nature of human consciousness, but at least consider what the character called Messenger ("Media Dong" Messenger) offers as a message about the origin of religion:

> The homo sapien was the first and only living being in evolutionary history to discover he was mortal. So how does he respond? He makes up stories about how he got into this fix and how he might get out of it. He invents religion, he develops bridal customs, he makes up stories, about the after-life, and the immortality of the soul. As times goes on these stories become more and more elaborate.

After a while some people lose faith in these stories and turn to science for truth about the world and the human condition. A new breed of priests and new dogmas emerge. Science becomes a religion, but all superstitions are too comforting to let go of. As Messenger goes on to say:

> Not many intelligent people believe the religious story any more, but they still cling to some of its consoling concepts, like the soul, life after death and so on.

Why not be meat-eating vegetarians, I say. Does either religion *or* science seem to you to have exclusive truth? Why choose one only? I think we need all the help we can get and also that we suspect the answers are not simple.

A dreamscape (with Marius Goring as a French dandy) in *Stairway to Heaven* (1946).

The Sleep of Reason Begets Monsters
by Francisco Goya

From Earl Wilson's *Show Business Laid Bare* (1974) this about Marilyn Monroe:

> She remembered a friend showing her Goya's hobgoblins at the Metropolitan Museum of Art. "I understand Goya!" she exclaimed to her friend. "He understands me. I see ghosts and goblins in my dreams every night." She shuddered.

4
Dreams in Art, Literature and Folklore

The eye
of man hath not heard, the ear of man hath not
seen, man's hand is not able to taste, his tongue
to conceive, nor his heart to report, what my dream
was.
　—William Shakespeare, *A Midsummer Night's Dream*

WRITING IN YOUR SLEEP

You do not just make up stories in your sleep that you can interpret. You may also be able to write fiction, poetry, and plays.

William Archer (1856–1924) was a famous drama critic in his day. He was the inveterate champion of *le pièce bien fait* (the well-constructed play), and translator and promoter of Henrik Ibsen. Archer's own play, *The Green Goddess*, had some success as a melodrama. But this story is about a play William Archer wrote in a dream.

The incomparable Sir Max Beerbohm tells about it:

Did you know that Archer, who always wished to demonstrate that, though a drama critic, he could write a play, had one night of triumph when he felt he had achieved a beautiful play? He told me this himself. One night, between sleeping and waking, it seemed to him that he had evolved a perfect plot, saw the whole thing from beginning to end. He saw that it only remained to write it—like that...! Then he fell into a blissful sleep. When he wakened he went over the whole plot again in his mind. He had a disillusioning, a frightful revelation. What he had dreamt was [Ibsen's] *Hedda Gabler.*

Archer had better luck composing in dreams. He says in his *Memoirs,* "the objects which had occupied my attention during the day often reappeared at night in connected dreams. On awakening, a new composition, or a portion of one I had already begun, presented itself to my mind."

You can also do mathematics, write music, or think through politics (as did Condorcet and Benjamin Franklin) in dreams. You can even straighten out law cases or figure out the original uses of archeological finds. Cockburn is quoted as saying of Francis, Lord Jeffrey (1773–1850), a Scottish jurist:

He had a fancy that though he went to bed with his head stuffed with the names, dates, and other details of various causes [at law], they were all in order in the morning; which he accounted for by saying that during sleep they all crystallized round their proper centres.

DANTE'S DREAM

From Marina Warner, "Demons to the Life," *Times Literary Supplement* 30 March 2001, p. 16:

One of the earliest illustrated manuscripts of the *Divine Comedy* (Ms. Egerton 943, *c.* 1320–50, in the British Library) opens with an illumination of Dante asleep in a four-poster bed under appatterned coverlet; to the right of this delightful domestic vignette,the poet is stepping forth into the dark wood, at the start of a momentous journey.

Dante's is arguably the most famous of dream poems.

FINDING THE RIGHT TITLE

William Makepeace Thackeray told the story of how the title of his novel *Vanity Fair* came to him in the middle of the night: "I jumped out of bed and ran three times around the room, uttering as I went, Vanity Fair! Vanity Fair! Vanity Fair!"

ALLEGEDLY WRITTEN IN A DREAM

Samuel Taylor Coleridge (1772–1834) said that one of the greatest poems of all time, *Kubla Khan*, was written in an opium dream. Lowndes (*The Road to Xanadu*) and other critics have written at great length about sources from which the poems were derived. But no one has been able to explain how the poem was assembled through what Coleridge calls "the esemplastic power of the imagination."

Certainly there is doubt whether the romantic story of the poem's origin is true. For many it smacks too much of the kind of fakery that Edgar Allen Poe attempted to perpetrate when he said he had written *The Raven* wide-awake but on half a dozen bottles of beer. In any case, here is Coleridge's story on his own words:

In the summer of 1797, the author, then in ill health, had retired to a lonely farmhouse between Porlock and Linton, on the Exmoor confines of Somerset and Devonshire. In consequence of a slight indisposition, an anodyne [laudanum, an extract of opium] had been prescribed, from the effects of which he fell asleep in his chair at the moment of reading the following sentence, or words of the same substance, in Purchas' *Pilgrimage* [*or, Relations of the World and the Religions Observed in All Ages*, 1613]: "here the Khan Kubla commanded a palace to be built, and a stately garden thereunto. And thus ten miles of fertile ground were enclosed with a wall." The author [Coleridge] continued for about three hours in a profound sleep, at least of the external senses, during which time he has the most vivid confidence that he could not have composed less than two or three hundred lines; if that indeed can be called composition in which all the images rose up before him as *things*, with a parallel production of the correspondent expressions, without any sensation or consciousness of effort. On awakening he appeared to himself to have a distinct recollection of the whole, and taking his pen, ink, and paper, instantly and eagerly wrote down the lines that are here preserved [which he published as a "fragment" of "a vision"]. At this moment he was unfortunately called out by a person on business from Porlock, and detained by him above an hour, and on his return to his room, found, to his no small surprise and mortification, that though he still retained some vague and dim recollection of the general purport of the vision, yet, with the exception of some eight or ten scattered lines and images, all the rest had passed away like the images on the surface of a stream unto which a stone has been cast, but alas! without the restoration of the latter.

If he slept for three hours, it would have provided him with time in which his unconscious presented him a travelogue with a voice-over reciting the poem for him. I do not doubt that authors can write in a dream.

I am well aware of the need to get it down as soon as possible on waking, and I know that one often seems to have "lost" some part of the work. But I really doubt Coleridge ever derived from any dream anymore than what we read in *Kubla Khan*.

Others have reported writing under the influence of drugs, especially opium, which even some twentieth-century authors of note have taken, but never anything as good as *Kubla Khan*.

Have you ever experienced the feeling that you have written something extraordinary in a dream and, on awaking, cannot remember it? I think such a thing is common because dreams so often deal in wish fulfillment.

Dreams also frequently deal in frustrations: Homer in *The Simpsons* dreamed he had created a wonderful invention that would make him rich and famous, but in the dream, whenever he tried to get a look at it, something got in the way.

For "Coleridge on Dreaming," see Micheal O'Neill in *Times Literary Supplement* for 18 September 1998, p. 14.

WORKING NIGHTS

That Coleridge claim posits aural composition in dreams. Though dreams are basically visual, a number of composers have worked in their sleep. J. Bryan, III, claims that Mozart wrote *The Magic Flute* in a dream, which, to my mind, explains the confused plot. It is a piece in which audiences that cannot understand German have a tremendous advantage.

Mozart seems to have composed a lot in his head, and his rival Salieri was said to have been furious at the ease with which Mozart took "dictation from God". Did Mozart compose while asleep as well as awake? It is possible that the mysterious figure in black that drove him to write his great *Requiem* arrived in a dream? Inspiration of that sort in sleep is not uncommon, but to write great music asleep! Some of us at the opera simply sleep through great music!

SOME THEORY AND PRACTICE

Bernard, Catherine A. "Dickens and Victorian Dream Theory" in *Victorian Science and Victorian Values: Literary Perspectives* (1981, ed. James Paradis & Thomas Posstlewait), New York: New York Academy of Sciences, pp. 197–216.

Hall, Calvin S. "Slang and Dream Symbols," *Psychoanalytic Review* 51 (1964), 38–48.

McCurdy, Harold H. "The History of Dream Theory," *Psychological Review* 53 (1948), 225–233.

Ullman, Montague. "The Social Roots of the Dream," *American Journal of Psychoanalysis* 20 (1960), 180–189.

Wolff, Reinhold. "*Baudelaires 'Chant d'automne'*" in *Psychoanalytische und Psychopathologische Literaturinterpretation.* Darmstadt (1981), pp. 47–72, and on Goethe's *Triumph der Empfindsamkeit* and *Proserpina*, pp. 125–152.

A MYSTERY PLAY

In the Middle Ages, the public was entertained and instructed by series of brief plays presented in the streets on pageant wagons, which told about the Bible. Some people say these plays were named for the mysteries of the Christian religion and others say that the mysteries came from the *métiers* of the artisans whose guilds took on the presentation of these plays after the Church stopped doing them.

The group of such plays surviving from civic presentations in the city of York runs to 50 plays. One of them is worth noting in connection with dreams: *The Dream of Pilate's Wife.*

In this playlet, Satan approaches the wife of Pilate, procurator of Judea, and tries to influence the next day's verdict regarding Jesus. If Pilate were to pardon Jesus, His sacrifice on the cross (and our redemption) would be derailed.

Pilate's wife's dream occurs before midnight. That, according to St. Thomas Aquinas in *De veritate* (On Truth), means the dream is false. On what basis Aquinas and many others are so sure that false dreams come

before midnight and true dreams come after I cannot for the life of me discover. So revered were these authorities, however, that in medieval times what they said was never questioned.

A FALSE DREAM

In Edmund Spenser's *The Faerie Queene*'s first canto the Red Cross Knight is sent a false dream obtained from the god of sleep. The idea is to seduce the knight by sending him a Duessa rather than his true Lady. If you find one stanza hard to read, imagine tackling half a dozen or more "bookes" of this kind of thing:

> Now when that ydle dream was to him brought
> Vnto that Elfin knight he bad him fly,
> Where he slept soundly void of euill thought
> And with false shewes abuse his fantasy,
> In sort as he him schoolèd priuilly:
> And that new creature borne without her dew
> Full of the makers guile, with vsage sly
> He taught to imitate that Lady trew,
> Whose semblance she did carrie vnder feignèd hew.

A MIDSUMMER NIGHT'S DREAM

> If we shadows have offended,
> Think but this, and all is mended,
> That you have but slumbered here
> While these visions did appear.
> (V, ii, 54)

The dream in Shakespeare, in *A Midsummer Night's Dream* and elsewhere, is usually very sensibly used in contrast to the way it is used in some modern dramas such as movies, where "it was all a dream" chick-

Bottom's dream in Shakespeare's *A Midsummer Night's Dream*, a painting by Henry Fuseli.

ens out on the ending. Adversity not only makes strange bedfellows (as The Bard says) but desperation creates some weird script shifts, too.

THE DREAM VISION

This is a major genre of our literature. Medieval writers picked up the format of a vision in a dream from the ancients (Cicero's *Somnium Scipionis* and Macrobius' commentary on this *Dream of Scipio*). It helped to structure didactic allegories and so the writers used the dream vision for both serious and satirical effect. The Middle Ages' delight in the supernatural and grotesque is well satisfied in this first-person, surreal presentation. On top of that, the imaginative journey of the dreamer can be likened to the journey of life or the process of learning.

René d'Anjou's *The Book of the Love Smitten Heart* (edited by Stephanie Gibbs & Kathryn Karczenska in 2001) combines the dream vision with two other medieval favorites, the autobiographical epistle and the quest romance. The heart unites desire, writing and the self.

What looks like some ordinary peasant taking a nap is supposed to be the biblical Jacob having his wonderful dream. The painting (in The Prado) is by "Lo Spagnoletto" (The Little Spaniard), as they called him in Italy, José Ribera (1591-1652). *Jacob's Dream* is dated 1639.

The first important appearance of the dream vision in English literature came along when Chaucer adapted from the *Romaunt of the Rose* (if indeed that translation is his work) of Guillaume de Lorris and Jacques de Meun. Chaucer certainly used the dream vision approach in a number of works that were unquestionably his. See Michael St. John's *Chaucer's Dream Visions* (2000).

William Langland produced the allegorical poem in which Piers (Peter) the Ploughman has a dream vision in alliterative verse. It contains rather scanty biblical knowledge of the Fathers, considering it is the fourteenth-century. *Piers the Ploughman* tackles social issues and seeks a Christianity of integrity despite the sins of the regular clergy and the evils attributed to the mendicant orders. Franciscans, among others, competed with the parish priests for the pennies of the pious; they were thus mightily resented. Langland's poem echoes the disturbing new ideas of the Lollards and John Wyclif. The work presages the Reformation.

The revival of medievalism in the nineteenth-century revitalized social concerns in dream visions such as *News from Nowhere* (1890), "A Utopian Romance." William Morris dreams of waking up in the twenty-first century. Many of us will live to see at least the beginnings of the changes in central government and daily life that Morris predicted—if, in fact, he was right.

See David Mills, "The Dreams of Bunyan and Langland," in *The Pilgrim's Progress: Critical and Historical Views*, New York: Barnes & Noble (1980), pp. 154–181. See if you can recall modern works in which dream visions occur.

The following are examples of other literature connected with sleep and dreaming. We will start with the exceptionally politically incorrect work of Giovanni Boccaccio, whose big mouth—that is what his surname means—spoke the prejudices of his time.

A character in his famous *Decameron* calls women "fickle, quarrelsome, suspicious, cowardly and easily frightened," which is precisely some Englishmen still say of Italians of both sexes. Prejudice still exists everywhere.

IL CORBACCIO

This was Boccaccio's final work of fiction. He gives us a dream vision of a man visited by a ghost from Purgatory at the urging of the Blessed Virgin, to talk him out of his lust for a nasty widow. The ghost ought to know about the widow; she was his wife. He cautions that her beauty trapped him and he describes the extreme measures to which she went to stay young.

He mocks her painting herself up to lure some poor unfortunate into her sensual clutches. The ex-husband spews misogynist comments from Juvenal, Theophrastus, St. Jerome, and various contemporaries of Boccaccio. Here we get no impressive women, as in *Decameron*. Instead it is a frontal attack on the female sex, wherein women are described as vindictive birds of prey.

If man is made in the image of God, then, says Boccaccio, woman is an imperfect copy of man. She is a toy, fun but fatal, with which to play. The work is a calumny that some men may find uproariously funny but feminists may want to burn, along with the writer, if they could get a hold of him.

Is the dreamer simply trying to express passion in dream for a woman he cannot take on in reality? There is some kind of driving force behind such an adamant denunciation of the sex that holds up its half of the world, and without whom no male would exist.

John Bunyan's *The Pilgrim's Progress* was still very much in the public mind in Victorian England, as this political cartoon (suggesting the difficulty of establishing Home Rule for British-held Ireland) by Swain, for *Punch*, testifies.

DREAM CHILDREN

Dream Children (1864) is by Horace Elijah Scudder (1838–1902), who wrote biographies, adult and children's books. It is one work you probably never heard of, the tale of a fantasy world in which strange things happen to children, similar to *The Wizard of Oz*. It is a world where fact and fantasy are confused in the same way they are when we dream. He also edited juvenile magazines and the *Atlantic Monthly*, etc. You could look him up.

THE DREAM LIFE OF BALSO SNELL

This is a tyro novel in rather surrealist form by Nathaniel West (Nathan Weinstein), written in Paris after he graduated from Brown University and stoked up on Joycean experimental techniques. There is something in its scatology of the uncensored (or what appears to be uncensored) aspect of dreaming, as well as something of the confused organization of dreams and daydreams. It has some of the power of later, nightmarish works like *The Day of the Locust*.

THE DREAM OF EUGENE ARAM

This is a poem somewhat influenced by art ballads such as *The Rime of the Ancient Mariner* (Coleridge) and even more influenced by the popular broadside ballads it imitated, bearing a cover decorated by deliberately crude woodcuts. It is by the talented Thomas Hood (1799–1845), who wrote in disparate genres, from horror to social satire. He claimed he was "a lively Hood for his livelihood."

THE DREAM OF GERONTIUS

One of the most important oratorios of the twentieth-century was written right at the start of it (1900) by Sir Edward Elgar. Elgar wanted to set John Henry, Cardinal Newman's poem *The Dream of Gerontius* to music. The poem (1866) is a dramatic monologue that is the triumphant expression of a just soul as it leaves the body at death, released to greater glory.

It is based on the Office of Requiem. The Victorian era was a time when religion

A drawing by G. Richmond of John Henry Newman, author of *The Dream of Gerontius*, before he became Cardinal Newman.

warred with science and nostalgic medievalism conflicted with modern progress. This poem was immensely moving and consoling to a disenchanted people. Sir Edward found it both an inspiring religious theme and an impetus for organizing what was referred to as "wayward" music.

> Now that the hour is come, my fear is fled;
> And at this balance of my destiny,
> Now close upon me, I can forward look
> With a serenest joy.

A DREAM OF JOHN BALL

William Morris first published this socialist fantasy in the journal *Commonweal* in late 1886 and early 1887. It became a book in 1888. A dreamer goes back to the time of The Peasants' Revolt (1381) and meets John Ball, a socially conscious priest. With him the dreamer conducts a dialogue that is more a satire of his time and its politics than historical.

Morris, a progressive thinker, hopes that in the future mankind will discover social justice, seeing "things as they verily are." Morris may complain that he is a dreamer stuck with the problems of a world he never made but he was the kind of man, like the peasants of old, who wanted to revolt against injustice and oppression.

THE DREAMPLAY

Strange symbols proliferate in this romantic drama by August Strindberg (1901, prologue 1906, produced 1907) who preaches that "at the heart of happiness sprouts the seed of disaster." The whole play is somewhat like a nightmare. Despite huge problems of stage presentation of this episodic and demanding drama, Max Reinhardt and Alfred Jarry both put it on the boards and Ingmar Bergman put it on television. Lately Robert Wilson has staged it effectively and it has become an opera.

There are many dramas that make use of dream and nightmare, but this may be the *locus classicus*. Like a terrifying dream it haunts us and demands that we puzzle over its meaning, as it touches on archetypal issues such as misogyny and guilt. The play is drenched in mystery and misery but does suggest that after all misery must have some purpose behind it. Strindberg called the play "my most beloved drama, the child of my greatest suffering."

THE DREAM OF RHONABWY

This is a very stylized and elaborate story in the tradition of the Welsh *Mabinogion*, written in Powys in Wales during the thirteenth-century by an anonymous successor of the old bards. The descriptive passages and plot are quite complicated. It is, however, one of the typical dream stories of the Middle Ages. It appears later in the section of short narratives.

THE DREAM OF THE RED CHAMBER

This is not in the western dream vision tradition at all but must be included because it may well be the greatest work in any language with the word *dream* in its title. In its English title, I should say, because this is a masterpiece of Chinese literature. It imitates a dream only in that real-life situations are employed, an unusual device for Chinese fiction of that time, but given new meanings and relationships.

It was written by T'sao Chan (1715?–1763), better known by the courtesy title of Hsueh-Ch'in. In Chinese transliterated, it is called *Hung Lou Meng*. The author circulated some of this long work in manuscript during his lifetime, and when he died 80 chapters were known. In 1791 another Chinese printed 120 chapters claiming he had found, not invented, the ending of the long novel. Wang Chi-chen's English translation (1958) buoyed the work's fame in the west.

For more on Chinese literature and dreams see the likes of Dell R. Hales, "Dreams and the Demonic in Traditional Chinese Short Stories" in *Critical Essays on Chinese Literature* (1976, ed. W. H. Nienhauser); Hong Kong: Chinese University of Hong Kong, 71-88; and Pia Skogemann, "Chuang Tzu and the Butterfly Dream," *Journal of Analytic Psychology* 31 (1986), 75–90.

In our little short story anthology in Chapter 6, you will not only find a ninth-century Chinese short story but a much later Japanese version of it. There are better stories in Chinese and Japanese literature in which dreams are prominent, but they are too long for our purposes. These two brief stories, however, you will enjoy.

Anthony C. Yu has a book on *The Dream of the Red Chamber*, reviewed by W.L. Idema in the *Journal of the American Oriental Society* 119:2 (April/June 1999), 368-369.

THE DREAM OF THE ROOD

Rood is the cross on which Christ was crucified. This Old English poem in three parts and a little over 150 lines is by an anonymous religious poet in a tenth-century, probably Vercelli, manuscript. The manuscript exhibits the puzzling imagery of Anglo-Saxon riddles and everyday dreams. The cross itself appears in the vision, surrounded by angels, and delivers a sermon to the dreamer who envisions it.

Presumably it was considered more credible for the cross to speak to a person in a dream than in waking life, but in a sense the cross did speak to the faithful in the Middle Ages and make them more appreciative of the sacrifice of Calvary.

The church, in liturgy, vestments, stained-glass windows, statues, and so on, used iconography to reinforce the ideals of Christianity. Shapes, colors and symbols often function in dream imagery to convey deep meaning.

DREAM SONGS

Although these poems by John Berryman are largely autobiographical (problems with his parents, problems with his own addictions and shortcomings), these meditations on modern life and literature are introduced as the dreams of a character named Henry. *Dream Songs* (1969) combined two earlier books, 77 *Dream Songs* (1964) and *His Toy, His Dream, His Rest* (1968). John Berryman killed himself in 1972.

For a good article on these poems, see "The Significance of Dreams in *The Dream Songs*," *Literature and Psychology* 25 (1975), 93–107.

FINNEGANS WAKE

This extraordinary and experimental novel ends in an incomplete sentence, just as it began, suggesting an endless cycle. It was published in 1939 by James Joyce (1882–1941), and constitutes one of the most remarkable if not most influential fictions of the twentieth century. It is supposed to be the stream of consciousness of the dreamers H[umphrey] C[himpden] Earwicker, a tavern-keeper of Dublin, his wife Anna [Livia Plurabelle] and two sons, Shem and Shaun.

Freud's psychology of dreams is mixed with theories of cyclical motion, fragmentation of experience, myth and legend, and unbridled wordplay. Joyce began the novel in 1923 and published it in a dozen pieces as *Work in Progress* (1928–1937). The wordplay especially uses the playfulness and encoding of dreams as a vehicle to imitate their narrative style. If you think decoding dreams is difficult, try this story, with or without the several "keys" scholars have provided.

Finnegans Wake may well be the most significant artifact of a century whose art became increasingly narcissistic, self-absorbed, idiosyncratic, obscure, and even absurd. Artists were almost proud to communicate nothing to the average person, or to have put one over on the public and sucker the baffled critics. Critics were discouraged from declaring that any artist had failed in their purpose because they could not fathom what the purpose, if any, may have been.

JOURNEY TO THE BORDER

This novel with a neurotic protagonist characteristic of the work of Edward Upward (b. 1903), is an example of the fictional use of fantasies and daydreams in a work that definitely tried to get something across. A tutor resents his position in a wealthy family and fantasizes while he is in between waking and sleeping. Upward says we are not facing reality by having his protagonist escape to the races for the day, until he snaps out of his hallucinatory state and realizes that his kind of evasion is just as empty as the materialist world of his capitalist employer. Socialist Upward ends the novel with the protagonist ditching his job and joining a workers' movement.

KINGIS QUAIR

James I of Scotland (1394–1437) was detained in England for 19 years, where he married (1424) Lady Jane Beaufort, the granddaughter of John of Gaunt. Well educated, James translated *The Consolations of Philosophy* from the Latin of Annius Manlius Severinus Boethius (*c.* AD 480–524). It was a work of major importance in the medieval west.

James called his book the *Kingis Quair*. In the original by Boethius, the dialogue between the narrator and Lady Philosophy is not actually a dream vision, but in James' version it is. Lady Jane becomes the heroine of the piece.

Some critics have doubted that this Scottish monarch was the author of the *Kingis Quair.* Why should a monarch be thought incapable? I don't doubt James' authorship of this dream vision.

Elizabeth I undoubtedly translated Boethius, and her works are now considered serious literature. Not all monarchs are dull and semiliterate nor devote their time (as a cynic said at the Silver Jubilee of George V) to twenty-five years of stamp-collecting.

OF THE FARM

John Updike (b. 1932) is known as a realistic writer, but this 1965 novel's contemporary Joseph cannot effectively interpret his many dreams. You will recall that in the Old Testament the favorite son of Jacob, Joseph, was sold into slavery in Egypt and there rose to high rank because he was a good organizer, constant under duress, and able to resist the advances of Potiphar's wife, but it was really because he could interpret dreams for the pharaoh.

The correct interpretation of dreams permitted the Egyptians to store up in seven fat years the food they would need for the seven lean, so dreams proved useful. In fact, John Updike in his memoir, *Self Consciousness* (1989), asserts, "Dreams come true; without that possibility nature would not incite us to have them."

It must be stressed that Joseph, the dream interpreter, was an extremely practical (and therefore successful) man. He even knew when it was to his advantage to leave his coat of many colors in the hands of the harlot and get right out of there. Ralph Waldo Emerson advised anyone who would be self-reliant to "leave your theory, as Joseph his coat in the hand of the harlot, and flee."

From Joseph descended the tribes (or half-tribes) of Ephraim and Mannaseh. The most noted modern representations of this Christ-like figure of the Old Testament are in Thomas Mann's *Joseph and His Bretheren* and in the popular *Joseph and the Amazing Technicolor Dreamcoat*, an early musical by Sir Andrew Lloyd Webber.

Joseph can represent the man who is practical, down to earth, not a dreamer, but able to interpret dreams and turn the information to practical use.

PALIS OF HONOUR

A palace of crystal and ivory, silver and gold "anamalit all colouris," appears in a dream vision to the central character in Bishop Gavin Douglas' poem (1501) in aureate nine-line stanzas with only two rhymes per, a great feat if at times a great bore. It is, however, a serious poem, treating the conflict between life and art much as Chaucer does in *The House of Fame*. Douglas' is a major piece of Scottish literature of the Renaissance, and a very good example of the dream vision school of poetry, followed also by William Dunbar (particularly in *The Goldyn Targe*[t]) and other Scottish Chaucerians. The dream-vision poem is a genre that the Renaissance inherited from the medieval period with all its didacticism and delight in profusion of detail.

LA PÈLERINAGE DE LA VIE HUMAINE

This medieval "Pilgrimage of Human Life" by the French poet Guillaume de Guillville resembles the "journey" of Dante in the *Divine Comedy*. The poet in a dream sees the *speculum humanæ salvationis* and learns of man's redemption by Christ. Like *The Dream of the Rood, Divine Comedy, Romaunt de la Rose, Wynnere and Waster,* and many other dream visions of the Middle Ages, famous and obscure, the dreamer has a series of experiences that are allegorical and didactic. As with the medieval *Pearl* poet, and much later in John Bunyan's *Pilgrim's Progress,* all these dream vision frameworks are designed to turn fiction into evangelism. Bunyan's story of Christian and his travails are supposed to be a dream experienced in prison where, in fact, Bunyan spent time. For quite a while if any English-speaking household had two books they were The Bible and Bunyan's *The Pilgrim's Progress.* Both remain the most praised and unfortunately to a great extent the least really read books available in our language.

LE RÊVE D'ALEMBERT

"I put my ideas," wrote Denis Diderot of *The Dream of d'Alembert,* "into the mouth of the man who dreams." He wrote it in 1769 but it was deemed too inflammatory for print. He melodramatically threw the manuscript into the fire, but kept another copy, the sly rogue. It did not actually see print until 1830.

Diderot argues philosophy with d'Alembert in his own person. Then d'Alembert, exhausted, goes to sleep, watched by his Platonic mistress (Mlle. de Lespinasse) and Dr. Théophile Bordeu. They chat about a wild dream d'Alembert has had, at one point start to make out (d'Alembert wakes up, is told to go back to sleep—and does), and the conversation goes on about the dream. At one point, the doctor, a verbose man, gets going on the subject of sleep:

d'Alembert (1727-1783)

Sleep is a state in which unity [of the senses] is no more. All concerted action, all discipline, ceases. The master is abandoned to the discretion of his vassals.... Is the optic thread irritated? Then the origin of the [brain's nervous] network sees. If the auditory thread so dictates, it hears. Action and reaction are the only things which exist between them. This is a result of the law of continuity and habit. If the action begins by the voluptuous end which nature has designed for love's pleasure and the propagation of the species....

Well, then sex rears its head. Throughout the piece Diderot makes strong statements but hides behind his characters, sidestepping responsibility. However, when I say that he hides behind his characters I am not being exact. In fact, as in the flawed plays he wrote, Diderot cannot resist pushing the characters out of the way and presenting his personal opinions.

The work is challenging to read and difficult to translate. It is worth the trouble in the long run because Diderot the encyclopedist contributes almost everything—except God. Being a Deist, Diderot is only to be expected to pass on that subject, despite the fact that much of what he has to say touches on religion. Diderot comes very close to modern ideas about the conscious and the unconscious mind. He even suggests some elements of later theories of evolution and ecology, perhaps more correctly than he dreamed.

For more on Diderot and dreams, you can consult extensive French bibliographies and this German source on psychology, sociology, and the interpretation of dreams: Hans-Jörg Neuschäfer, "*Die Methode der Traumdeutung* (The Method of Dream Interpretation)" in *Psychoanalytische Literaturwissenschaft und Literatursoziologie* (1982, eds. Henning Krauss & Reinhold Wolff), Frankurt: Peter Lang, pp. 29–38.

RIP VAN WINKLE

Washington Irving's tale of a sleeper from the Old Dutch period of New England affected Americans not only in book form but also on the stage. For a long time, starting with the nineteenth-century, rips such as Charles Burke and the indefatigable Joseph Jefferson brought to audiences all over the country the vivid image of the man who fell asleep, slept for a long time, and emerged into an unfamiliar world. Nothing like that will be experienced again until the world ends and the famous Seven Sleepers come out of their cave again.

Washington Irving's story has a list of predecessors. The earliest I can find is the story of Epimenides of Athens. He was said to have fallen asleep in a cave only to awake in 40 or 47 years. Pliny says 57. Naturally, the sleeper found things so changed he hardly recognized them. Epimenides was supposed to have lived until 596 BC, a life of 289 years. The supposedly true and the made up stories of sleepers continue. See the entry about Woody Allen's *Sleepers*.

ST. PATRICK'S PURGATORY

This *visio spirituale* is, according to legend, from St. Patrick himself and is called *St. Patrick's Purgatory* to suggest winning Heaven through suffering. Like Dante, this anonymous author makes use of Virgil, discussing Hell and Heaven and eventual bliss. There is a real place in Ireland called St. Patrick's Purgatory.

THE VISION OF SIR LAUNFAL

James Russell Lowell (1819–1891) established his poetic reputation with the shrewd Yankee wit of *The Biglow Papers*, the direct satire of *A Fable for Critics*, and *The Vision of Sir Launfal* (1848). The latter was in the nineteenth-century medievalist mode and whistled tunefully in the dark, attractive to an age of growing disbelief.

Somehow Lowell contrives to make the medieval knight's quest analogous to Lowell's desire to see American democracy reach perfection. "Slowly Sir Launfal's eyes grew dim/Slumber fell like a cloud on him."

VISIONS OF THE DAUGHTERS OF ALBION

William Blake (1757–1827) was a mystic and visionary. Blake believed, according to his character, in *Jerusalem*, "I must create a System, or be enslav'd by another Man's." He did this with the help of a sensitive social consciousness, an unfailingly rebellious spirit, a wonderful imagination (both poetic and pictorial), and visitation from angels, one of whom, he said, taught him to draw. If you look at his drawings, which he could hardly sell for a penny apiece, it is difficult to doubt Blake's story.

Visions of the Daughters of Albion (1793, Albion being an old name for Britain) is one of many poems in which dreams and visions appear. Allen Ginsberg claimed that when he was a student at Columbia University he had a visitation from William Blake, which inspired him to become a poet of social reform. He was reading *Ah, Sunflower!* and masturbating at the time of the auditory visitation. He was not asleep.

SOME AUTHORS ON THE SUBJECT OF DREAMS

"Time for a little something," as Winnie-the-Pooh would say, in brief snippets from literature. The poets and prose writers have much discussed our subject, from the Spanish playwright who said "Life is a dream" to the English one whose Hamlet worried about "what dreams may come" to us in the sleep of death.

The lyrical Thomas Moore wrote that "There's nothing half so sweet in life/As love's young dream" and the dreams of lovers have produced a great deal of verse, good and bad, innumerable novels, etc. But love is not the sole subject of commentary on dreams. Here are some of the ideas expressed by various writers on the broad subject of dreams, and there are many more that could be cited from orators ("I have a dream" declared the Reverend Dr. Martin Luther King, Jr.).

Peter DeVries would say that those who dream instead of facing the real issues of life are guilty of Noël Cowardice.

In one of the most bitingly satirical letters written to a patron, Dr. Samuel Johnson wrote that he had "awakened from that dream of hope" that the Earl of Chesterfield would help him with his career. He said he was angered to find Chesterfield watching calmly while Johnson struggled, drowning. When Johnson struggled to shore, Chesterfield *encumbered* him with help.

Some have even warned of unrealistic expectations while others cannot live without hopes and dreams, even if they are of the pipe variety. Sir Peter Ustinov is one of many who have noticed how much our American Republic depends upon dreams of conquest, expansion, and success. He once said, "Unfortunately the balance of nature decrees that a superabundance of dreams is paid for by a growing potential for nightmares." Still others praise Americans not for nightmares but for dreaming big; even for walking off the tops of buildings, as characters do in the cartoons, and not falling until confidence wanes and they look down.

Certain artists simply accepted the gifts of dreams and made paintings, music, sculpture, or stories like Henry James' "The Jolly Corner" out of them.

Some useful comments on dreams and dreamers, starting with that very prolific and popular author, Anonymous:

To dream of the person you would like to be is to waste the person you are.

—Anonymous

Your old men shall dream dreams,
your young men shall see visions.
—*Joel* 2: 28

He who regards dreams is like him
that grasps at a shadow and chases
after the wind.
—*Ecclesiastics* 34:2

Thou shalt make castels thanne in
  Spayne
And dreme of joy, al but in vayne.
—Geoffrey Chauncer, *The Romaunt
of the Rose*

Be assured that there are other remedies needed rather than dreaming, a
weak contention of art against nature.
—Michel de Montaigne, *Essais*

We are such stuff as dreams are made on,
our little life is rounded with a sleep.
—William Shakespeare, *The Tempest*

That children dream not the first half-year; that men dream not
in some countries, with many more, are unto me sick men's
dreams; dreams out of the ivory gate [of lies], and visions before
midnight.
—Sir Thomas Browne, *Of Dreams*

Old men commonly dream oftener, and have their dreams more
painful, than young.
—Thomas Hobbes, *The Deceitfulness of the Heart*

Dreams, books, are each a world; and books, we know, are a substantial world, both pure and good.
—William Wordsworth, *Personal Talk*

How wonderful is Death,
Death and his brother Sleep.
—Percy Bysshe Shelley, *Queen Mab*

I confess an occasional nightmare; but I do not, as in early
youth, keep a stud of them.
—Charles Lamb, *Witches and Other Night Fears*

How troublesome is day!
It calls us from our sleep away;
It bids us from our pleasant dreams awake,
It sends us forth to keep or break
Our promises to pay.
                    —Thomas Love Peacock, *How Troublesome is Day*

All that we see or seem
Is but a dream within a dream.
                    —Edgar Allen Poe, *A Dream within a Dream*

Dreams are the touchstones of our characters.
                    —Henry David Thoreau

Dreams are the bright creatures of poem and legend, who sport
on earth in the night season, and melt away in the first beam of
the sun, which lights grim care and stern reality on their daily
pilgrimage through the world.
                    —Charles Dickens, *Nicholas Nickleby*

And dreaming through the twilight
That doth not rise nor set,
Haply I may remember,
And haply may forget.
                    —Dante Gabriel Rosetti, *When I Am Dead*

I have put my days and dreams out of mind,
Days that are over, dreams that are done.
                    —Algernon Charles Swinburne, *The Triumph of Time*

A dreamer is one who can only find his way by moonlight, and
his punishment is that he sees the dawn before the rest of the
world.
                    —Oscar Wilde, *The Critic as Artist*

They are not long, the days of wine and roses:
Out of a misty dream
Our path emerges for a while, then closes
Within a dream.
                    —Ernest Dowson, *Vitæ Summa Brevis*

If you can dream—and not make dreams your master...you'll be
    a Man, my Son.
                    —Rudyard Kipling, "If"

A man that is born falls into a dream like a man who falls into the sea. If he tries to climb out into the air as inexperienced people endeavour to do, he drowns.

—Joseph Conrad, *Lord Jim*

I dream, therefore I exist.

—August Strindberg, *A Madman's Defense*

In bed my real love has always been the sleep that rescued me by allowing me to dream.

—Luigi Pirandello, *The Rules of the Game*

But I, being poor, have only my dreams;
I have spread my dreams under your feet;
Tread softly, for you tread on my dreams.

—William Butler Yeats, *The Cloths of Heaven*

Our dreams are tales
Told in dim Eden
By Eve's nightingales.

—Walter de la Mare, *All that's Best*

His life was a sort of dream, as are most lives with the mainspring left out.

—F. Scott Fitzgerald, *Notebooks*

Surrealism is based in a belief in the omnipotence of the dream.

—André Breton

For one person who dreams of making fifty thousand pounds, a hundred people dream of being left fifty thousand pounds.

—A. A. Milne, *If I May*

I dream quite a bit, myself. Only when I'm asleep, of course. Curious thing is it's always the same dream....Not that I mind, of course, I'm not one to hanker after change the whole time.

—Henry Reed, *The Primal Scene*

He's out there in the blue, ridin' on a smile and a shoeshine....A salesman has got to dream, boys.

—Arthur Miller, *Death of a Salesman*

I was at the University of Edinburgh myself, but in the dream
I'm the Devil and Cambridge.
> —Muriel Spark, *The Ballad of Peckham Rye*

Shelley dreamt it. Now the dream decays
The props crumble.
> —R. S. Thomas, *Song at the Year's Turning*

We do not really feel grateful toward those who make our
dreams come true; they ruin our dreams.
> —Eric Hoffer, *The Passionate State of Mind*

In a dream you are never eighty.
> —Anne Sexton, *Old*

Is a dream a lie if it doesn't come true,
Or is it something worse?
> —Bruce Springsteen, *The River*

A BOY'S DREAM OF GOD

Laurette Howard printed in a newspaper compilation of "Young-'Un's
Visions" when I was a boy of about eight. I'll never forget this:

> I had a dream that God was walking down my street. I raised my
> hat and said, "Hello." He patted my head and then softly faded
> up into the sky.

SLEEPING IN A FAIRYTALE

There are many legends about important persons who stayed asleep for
a long time. The Emperor Charlemagne is the subject of one of these
legends. The giant (eight-foot tall) Charles the Great has yet to reap-
pear, but legend says that when The Antichrist comes, this great warrior will arise to fight for the Christian faith. The final triumph of
Christ and the blessed will not take place until The Antichrist has
reigned for 33 years, and then been defeated by The Second Coming of
The Savior.

SLEEPING BEAUTY

You may not have heard that old tale but you do know *Sleeping Beauty*.
Charles Perrault (1628–1703) gave this fairytale to generations of
children. He wrote *La Belle au Bois Dormant* in his tales of Mother

Goose in 1697. You recall the curse, the 100 years of sleep, and the happy ending. I do not think the average child, even today, sees any sexual symbolism in the tale, from the prick of the needle that puts her to sleep to the brambles that grow around her coffin, and the kiss of Prince Charming. However, there is more sex and violence in fairytales, Perrault's as well as the more obvious Brothers Grimm, than we admit to ourselves. In my opinion, some are not suitable for impressionable children!

They do, however, well suit the ballet. Tchaikovsky's *Sleeping Beauty* (choreography by Marius Petipa) contains a lovely dance. Some corny miming narrates acts out the story of the king and queen whose chamberlain invites the fairies to the christening of the royal daughter but forgets the wicked Carabosse, played by a man in drag. Carabosse crashes the party and vengefully says that the princess will die at the age of 20 by a finger prick. (Don't get started on sexual innuendo.) The Lilac Fairy, however, arranges that the princess will not die but fall into a coma—for 100 years. Then she will be awakened by the kiss of a handsome prince.

The time passes, the twentieth birthday arrives, and the princess pricks her finger on a spindle presented by the evil Carabosse, and falls asleep. In the fullness of time a handsome prince dreams of this ideal beauty, seeks her out, wakes her with a kiss, and it all ends happily, except for the king and queen, of course, who are long gone. It can be read as a dream of sexual awakening. Supple dancers prove the rule that Diaglieff confessed: "ballet is sex."

THE NUTCRACKER

No sex, despite the title of this Tchaikovsky ballet. But it is all a dream. It was infused with life in a Seattle production designed by children's book illustrator Maurice Sendak. Nancy Dalva said in *Harper's* in 2000:

> No one in all of children's literature better understands the dark fascination with things that go bump on the night, and no one better illustrates the peculiar and disturbing power of dreams that are realer than real. Always with Sendak one has the creepy sense that the land of nightmares exists in the continuous now— past, present, and future are one and the same. He knows just the color and clarity of a night spent wandering in the subconscious. Therefore, unlike some *Nutcrackers*, this production makes clear that the little girl who is the heroine is indeed dreaming and is not in some sweet yet scary alternate universe. On Christmas Eve, Sendak shows us, everyone is a child, and everyone dreams.

TO SLEEP, BY JOHN KEATS (1819)

O soft embalmer of the still midnight,
Shutting, with careful fingers and
    benign,
Our gloom-pleas'd eyes, embower'd
    from the light,
Enshadèd in forgetfulness divine!
O soothest Sleep! If so it please thee,
    close
In midst of this thine hymn my willing
    eyes,
Or wait the amen, ere thy poppy
    throws
Around my bed its lulling charities,
Then save me, or the past will shine
Upon my pillow, breeding many
    woes,—
Save me from curious conscience, that still lords
In strength from darkness, burrowing like a mole;
Turn the key deftly in the oilèd wards,
And seal the hushèd casket of my soul.

ADVENTURES IN INNER SPACE

Robert Silverberg wrote of science-fiction writers: "We take all the universe as our province, and there are many ways of exploring that universe, from the bang-bang space opera to the abstruse excursion into inner space." Although sci-fi deals in fantasy, it usually tries to pass itself off as realistic and seldom involves dreams or dreamers.

Folklore offers magical routes to inner space. For instance, on the burning question of whom you should marry. My advice: someone with more money than yourself but fewer problems, although I confess to difficulties with this search.

You can eat a salt herring before bedtime or try the more elaborate dumb cake. (This was named by folklore, not by me.) Fast all day, make and eat the cake in complete silence (which explains the name) and immediately walk backwards to your bed without a word.

This is said to work not only on St. Agnes' Eve, January 20th, and on Christmas Eve, when not a creature is stirring.

Between January and December you are on your own if you want to find a mate. Just do not pick one with the same surname as yourself, a custom that may be derive from fear of incest.

The simplest folklore method for dreaming of the person you will marry is to place a piece of someone else's wedding cake under your pillow.

HAVING A LOOK AT REALITY

Islam believes that the soul can leave the living body in sleep, and travel around, perceiving reality in proportion to the soul's purity. Followers of Islam believe that in daydreaming the soul may be out of the body but stays close to it. Naturally, Islam believes that Allah sends true dreams but it is difficult, say the faithful, to distinguish between truth that Allah sends and evil dreams that come from bad *djinn* (genies).

THE VULGATE

While translating The Bible into Latin, St. Jerome occasionally rendered the Hebrew for *witchcraft* as *observo somnia* (observation of dreams), which gave dream interpretation a heretical flavor. Today religious orthodoxy would permit the interpretation of personal dreams but not attempts thereby to divine the future. That is superstitious.

CICERO ON DREAMS

Cicero was learned in the ancient arts of dream interpretation or at least found out a lot about the tradition, but he was unwavering in his condemnation of dream interpretation as superstition. He included *The Dream of Scipio* in his *De Republica*, with its prediction of Scipio's own fate and a description of the afterlife, but seems to have regarded the whole thing as a mere literary device. Perhaps at the very end he changed his mind, because he had dreamed repeatedly that Octavius would achieve imperial power. When Octavius did, one of his first hit lists contained the name Marcus Tullius Cicero.

THE SLEEPER'S SOUL IN FOLKLORE

Folklore in many cultures says that in sleep, as well as death, the soul can leave the body. It can even fly out of the body when you sneeze, which is why people say "God bless you!" to protect you from The Devil.

If you wake up tired, your soul may have traveled a great deal. Maybe you really did all that work you dreamed about. Maybe your bones ache (as A. B. Ellis records in *The Ewe-Speaking Peoples of the Slave Coast of West Africa*, 1890) because that dream of a fight was really your soul tussling with another.

Among the Dyaks, according to Sir James Frazer's *The Golden Bough* (1890), if you dream you have fallen into the water, on awaking you must send "for a wizard, who fishes for the spirit with a hand-net in a basin of water till he catches it and restores it to its owner."

Sir James also tells us that primitive opinion is completely against moving or altering the appearance of a sleeping person. The soul may not recognize the body when it is ready to return. W. W. Rockhill in *American Anthropologist* 4 (1891) reports that Koreans believe that even a piece of paper put over the face of a sleeping person can kill the person because the soul will not recognize the body and will be unable to return after sleep.

If you want to kill someone—say, a witch—change the person's appearance while they sleep, or just reverse their position in the bed. They will never wake up. The whole point of the Egyptians mummifying the dead was so the body would be recognizable when the departed soul wanted to return for a visit. Many religions promise the soul either oblivion or, more often, a final resting place free of the body, so the preservation is not terribly important to them.

According to them, we need the body in dreams; in death, it is superfluous. Our souls are added back into the Oversoul, from which we are temporarily apart.

Meanwhile, take care of the body (which the Roman Catholics call The Temple of the Holy Spirit). When waking a sleeper, do it slowly and gently, giving the soul warning and opportunity to return. See A.C. Hollis, *The Massai* (1905) and other sources for this belief.

In dreams, they say, our souls voyage. This is another way in which sleep resembles death.

> I sent my soul into the Invisible,
> Some letter of the afterlife to spell....

DYING IN A DREAM

Folklore says that if the pursuing monster really does get you, or if you don't wake up before something else fatal happens, you will actually die. Many people, however, dream not only of dying but of attending their own funerals, and live to talk about it. If you dream your own funeral, check who is in attendance. On waking, you may wish to alter your will to exclude non-attendees.

DYING OF A DREAM

The lovely heroine of Tang Xianzu's romantic comedy *The Peony Pavilion*, a Chinese masterpiece of 1598, dies of a desire conceived in a dream. See Judith T. Zeitlin's "Shared Dreams: The Story of the Three Wives' Commentary on *The Peony Pavilion*" in *Harvard Journal of Asiatic Studies* 54 (June 1994), 127–179.

BEOWULF

This great Anglo-Saxon epic, created in Northumberland but full of Anglo-Saxon ideas from The Continent, includes a monster that wreaks havoc at night in Heorot, the great hall of Hrothgar, king of the Danes. Hrothgar has a dream in the story and an important ally in the hero Beowulf, who goes after the monster Grendel, Grendel's mother, a fiery dragon, and perhaps even the world, the flesh, and The Devil.

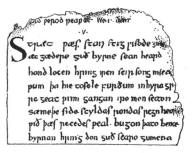

C. L. Wrenn reminds us that though Beowulf is presented as a superman, his character is (like King Arthur's) rooted in some truth among the mists of history. Margaret E. Goldsmith summed up *Beowulf* neatly as the tragedy "first and foremost [of] a just man who nobly fought a losing battle against the evil powers." Beowulf (as the poem ends with the sad note of his death) is said to be "of kings of the world the mildest of men and the gentlest, the kindest to his people, and the most eager for fame." Fame, at least, he won.

NIGHTMARES IN ART

Francisco Goya's *Los Caprichos* (The Caprices) declare that the dream of reason produces monsters. You have seen Goya's picture. Many painters paint what they see in terrifying and surreal dreams, just as Kafka made short stories and novels out of his nightmares. On that note, Walter S. Gibson has a sensitive and scholarly discussion of "Bosch's Dreams: Responses to Bosch's Imagery in the Sixteenth-Century" in *Art Bulletin* 74 (June 1992), 205–218.

It is clear that Bosch—whose work Philip II thought perfect decoration for his bedroom in the gloomy Escurial—created an iconography that was partly derivative and partly personal nightmare. Bosch also challenged his contemporaries to work out the meaning of his dream symbolism.

Van Gogh said, "I dream my paintings, and then I paint my dream." Fuseli painted nightmares. When I was writing books about demons and vampires and werewolves and such, I came across a great many horrific pictures of nightmarish creatures of the imagination. Some of the imaginative, surreal art is Bosch and some of it just bosh.

Some people rather like the *frissons* (thrills) these horrors produce, as you well know from horror movies and the gothic novel and such. Ancient Greeks had harpies and other horrors that flew by night. Christians had the incubus and the succubus who sexually attacked dreamers. English had the nightmare (taking *mara* from Old Norse) that sat on top of the sleeper and crushed him or her (in French a *cauchemar*, that tramples) and worse. "The Nightmare Life-in-Death was she/Who thicks man's blood with cold."

Some people retain a sense of humor about all this. Stravinsky was quoted in 1969 as saying, "I had a dream the other day about music critics. They were small and rodent-like with padlocked ears, as if they stepped out of a painting by Goya."

ARISTOTLE ON PREDICTIVE DREAMS

Aristotle took an unusually skeptical approach, considering his time, as to whether dreams could predict the future. He was sure they could not. For him, all dreams were the result of human conditions, not divine messages; they mirrored the past or present, not the future. If a dream prediction came true, Aristotle deemed it sheer coincidence. Needless to say, his skepticism was ignored by subsequent generations of professional and amateur interpreters of dreams. They said Aristotle eschewed dreams for the same reason he didn't like fiction and poetry— they provided escape from reality.

HENRY FUSELI

This was the name adopted by Johann Heinrich Fuseli (1741–1825), born in Zurich, when he went to England. There the president of The Royal Academy, Sir Joshua Reynolds, encouraged him to paint (1767). Fuseli exhibited *The Nightmare* at The Royal Academy exhibition of 1782. He was professor of painting there from 1799 until his death. He is probably the leading English painter of nightmare scenes.

Modern art has tried to keep up with the nightmarish history of the twentieth-century. It was perhaps the most horrendous in the history of humanity (or inhumanity), but Fuseli appears to hold the title to the depiction of nightmares. His intentions are blatant, which is not always the case with modern artists. They require as sensitive an interpretation as dreams and nightmares do.

DR. JOHNSON

Ursa Major (Great Bear) was more certain of almost everything than most people are about almost anything. His *Prayers and Meditations* (1767) records his nightly prayer: "Preserve me from unseasonable and immoderate sleep." If I asked him about them, however, I suppose I might get a reply along these lines: "Sir, in order to be scholarly, it is not necessary to be prying. I understand that you, Sir, are an American. I could comment on that, but I shall not."

THE NOVELISTS AND DREAMS

A great deal of fiction is inspired by real life, and as such literary criticism and psychological investigation arise from novels, for fiction records and comments on society, bringing about change. The articles in the literary bibliographies are overwhelmingly numerous when it comes to dreams and dreaming, but here are some from the smaller (and, some may think, more useful, usually less consulted) number of citations in the psychological literature. They supplement what you can more easily find online in the bibliography of The Modern Language Association, etc.

Bemporad, Jules R. "Franz Kafka: A Literary Prototype of the Depressive Character" in *Severe and Mild Depression* (1978, ed. Silvano, Arieti & Bemporad), New York: Basic Books.

Cohn, Dorrit. "A Triad of Dream Narratives: *Der Tod George, Das Märchen A der 672. Nacht, Traumnovelle*" in *Focus on Vienna 1900* (1982, ed. Erika Nielsen), Munich: Fink, pp. 58–71.

Field, Trevor. "The Literary Significance of Dreams in the Novels of Julien Green," *Modern Language Review* 75 (1980), 291–300.

Hirschbach, Frank D. "*Traum und Vision bei Hermann Hesse,*" *Monatshefte für deutschen Unterricht* 51 (1959), 157–168.

Katz, Michael R. "Dreams in Pushkin," *California Slavic Studies* 11 (1980), 71–103.

Lowin, Joseph G. "The Dream-Frame in [Théophile] Gautier's *Contes fantastiques,*" *Nineteenth-Century French Studies* 9 (1980 – 1981), 28–36.

Martin, Jay. "Three Stages of Dreaming: A Clinical Study of Henry Miller's *Dream Book,*" *Journal of the American Academy of Psychoanalysis* 12 (1986), 1–22.

For original research, in addition to other standard sources, always check on any topic the specialized but often fact-packed doctoral dissertations summarized in *Dissertation Abstracts International.* In connection with dreams you will find such useful writers as Clara Stuyver (on psychology and symbol in Ibsen's plays, University of Utrecht 1942,

Dutch) and Marilyn Ann Dyrud (on dreams in five novels by Virginia Woolf, *DAI* 42, 1981, 224A) and Dutta Ramesh Thippavajjala (on Arthur Miller's flawed heroes, *DAI* 36, 1975, 290–311). Some of the learned journals are reader-friendly for the non-specialist and have useful articles and special issues on dreams and dreaming. For instance, *Psychoanalysis and History* 31 (Winter 2001) is entirely devoted to dreams, their cultural context and interpretation, nineteenth-century theories in Germany, "Freud and Jewish Dreaming" (Stephan Frosh), "Dreaming & Cinematographic Consciousness" (Laura Marcus), etc.

ENGLISH FOLKLORE METHOD TO SEE WHOM YOU WILL MARRY

If a girl puts a leaf of the ash tree under her pillow she will dream of her future husband.

> Even-ash, even-ash, I pluck thee
> This night my own true love to see,
> Neither in his rick nor in his rare
> But in the clothes he everyday wear.

"Even-ash" is a leaf with an even number of leaflets. The best time for seeing the lover in dreams was St. Thomas' Eve (substitute an onion for the ash leaf with nine pins stuck in it) and St. Agnes' Eve, as you may know from the Keats poem. Dreamlore on this topic is abundant and keeps cropping up. Are you seeking a dreamboat? Are you already in love with someone you have not yet met?

YARROW

Another plant useful, say the folk, for divination in dreams, as well as in witchcraft, is yarrow. Sew an ounce of yarrow in a piece of flannel and put it under your pillow with this invocation:

> Thou pretty herb of Venus' tree,
> Thy true name it is yarrow.
> Now, who my bosom friend must be
> Pray tell me thou tomorrow.

PROVERBS ON DREAMS AND SLEEP

The proverb is the wit of one that becomes the patrimony of all. Among many proverbs regarding sleep and dreams:

Morning dreams are true dreams. (Latin)
Sleep upstairs and live long. (French)
In sleep we are all equal. (Spanish)
In a dream one gets what one covets awake. (German)
Dreams are a sixtieth part of prophecy. (Hebrew)
Sleep makes all men pashas. (Turkish)
Dreams go by contraries. (English)
The beginning of health is sleep. (Irish)
You can make your dreams come true if you wake up and work.
  (American)
Where there is no vision, the people perish. (*Proverbs* 29:18)
Even the one-eyed man has to sleep. (Yiddish)

POLITICAL ORATORY

One of the most renowned American political speeches speaks of "a dream" in the typical sense of a vision of the future. At a rally in Washington, D.C., in 1963, the Reverend Dr. Martin Luther King, Jr., said:

> I still have a dream. It is a dream deeply rooted in the American dream. I have a dream that one day this nation will rise up and live out the true meaning of its creed: "We hold these truths to be self-evident: that all me are created equal...." I have a dream that one day on the red hills of Georgia the sons of former slaves and the sons of former slave owners will be able to sit down together at the table of brotherhood. I have a dream that my four little children will one day live in a nation where they will not be judged by the color of their skin but by the content of their character.

From ancient times it has been believed that divinity communicates with humanity through dreams and visions. Religious men speak solemnly of dreams for the future and political men created the American Dream. Although ridiculed by writers such as Arthur Miller and Edward Albee, the American Dream has shaped the American mind and destiny.

A DISTURBING DREAM

We often dream about our worries. In *Devotion*, Ida Lupino dreamed that Death came to her on a white horse. Thomas Babington, Lord

Macaulay, author of the famous history of England, tells of a dream he had in a letter to a friend:

> so vivid that I must retell it. She [Alice, a young niece] came to me with a penitential face, and told me that she had a great sin to confess; Pepy's Diary was all a forgery, and that she had forged it. I was in the greatest dismay. 'What! I have been quoting in reviews, and in my *History*, a forgery of yours as a book of the highest authority. How shall I ever hold up my head again?' I awoke with the fright, poor Alice's supplicating voice still in my ears.

AGRIMONY

Old verses from England tell of this plant's reputation in folklore:

> If it be leyd under mann's head,
> He shall sleepyn as he were dead.
> He shall never drede ne wakyn
> Till fro under his head it be takyn.

WAS IT A DREAM?

George Guy Greville, the fourth earl of Warwick, had an odd experience that Charles, third earl of Somers repeated to Lady Waterford. She handed it on to Augustus Hare and he repeated it in his autobiography, *My Solitary Life*. A lot of name-dropping, but it's a good story:

> ...I want to tell you such an odd thing that has happened to me. Last night I was in bed, and the room was quite dark (this old-fashioned room of the inn at Lymington which you now see). Suddenly at the foot of the bed there appeared a great light, and in the middle of the light the figure of Death just as it is seen in the Dance of Death and other old pictures—a ghastly skeleton with a scythe and a dart; and Death balanced the dart, and it flew past me, just above my shoulder, close to my head, and it seemed to go into the wall; and then the light went out and the figure vanished.
>
> I was as wide awake then as I am now, for I pinched myself hard to see, and I lay awake for a long tome, but at last I fell

asleep. When my servant came to call me in the morning, he had a very scared expression of face, and he said, "A dreadful thing has happened in the night, and the whole household of the inn is in the greatest confusion and grief, for the landlady's daughter, who slept in the next room, and the head of whose bed is against the wall against which your head now rests, has been found dead in her bed."

It seems to me that the earl may have dreamed about Death, awoke in fear, and then pinched himself, as it was not until after "the figure vanished." I also am a little skeptical about the "wall against which your head now rests," a detail that the servant, it seems to me, would not have included in the announcement of the death in the adjoining room. Was it a dream in which Death came for the earl—and missed?

ANOTHER STORY FROM AUGUSTUS HARE

This one I have had occasion to tell before, because I have written about ghosts. I repeat it here as an example of the belief in astral projection: the woman who was dreaming was taken for a ghost! Here is the tale:

A few years ago [Hare's autobiography was printed about the turn of the twentieth century] there was a lady living in Ireland—a Mrs. Butler—clever, handsome, popular, prosperous, and perfectly happy. One morning she said to her husband, and to anyone who was staying there, "Last night I had the most wonderful night. I seemed to be spending hours in the most delightful place, in the most enchanting house I ever saw—not large, you know, but just the sort of house one might live in oneself, and oh! so perfectly, so deliciously comfortable. Then there was the loveliest conservatory, and the garden was so enchanting! I wonder if anything half so perfect can really exist.

She kept having the dream, and enjoyed pleasant visits to the dream house, but, to make the long story short, "the district [in Ireland] was wild and disturbed" and "the people were insolent and ungrateful" and the Butlers took off for London. They engaged real estate agents to find them a house and visited one in Hampshire, which Mrs. Butler immediately claimed was the house of her dreams, exact in every detail. Well, not every detail: there was one door she did not "remember." The housemaid assured "that door has only been there six weeks."

The house was cheap because it had a reputation of being haunted. The real estate agent heard the story of her dreams and said to her, "you are yourself the ghost!"

"On the nights when Mrs. Butler dreamt she was the ghost, she—her 'astral body,'" says Augustus Hare, "had been seen there."

Is it possible that when we dream of visiting distant places our spirit actually goes there, by astral projection, and may even be detected by psychics or even seen by waking persons?

If nothing else, it makes for a good story to perk up an autobiography and might well serve as a movie scenario.

TALANO D'IMOLE HAS A DREAM, AND SO DOES ELISABETTA

In the seventh story of the next to last day of the ten days of *The Decameron* by Giovanni Boccaccio (1313–1375) occurs the tale of one Talano d'Imole. It is very instructive.

Talano's wife, Margherita, had a foul temper. Their marriage was not a pleasant one, but when Talano dreamed she would be attacked by a wolf in the woods he could not but warn her. She sharply replied that evil wishes create such evil dreams, but she promised to stay out of the woods.

Suspicious as she always was, she worried that her husband might be planning some romp in the woods with a mistress, so as soon as her husband went out that day, she went into the woods.

In the thickest part of the woods she was seized by the throat by a giant wolf and would have perished had not some shepherds rescued her.

She was taken home and she recovered, but was horribly scarred. She often cried about her foolishness in not believing her husband's dream or heeding his warning that there was a dangerous wolf in the woods.

It's a little dated, for the wife is regarded as foolish for not obeying her husband and indeed (though there are some exceptional women in the tales) the *Decameron* is generally misogynistic, and that stands out more than the idea of prophetic dreams.

Perhaps the most famous story of the lot is earlier, the fifth story on the fourth day. It concerns Elisabetta, who has a lover. Her brothers do not approve and kill the lover. The lover appears to Elisabetta in a dream and tells her where his body has been buried.

She goes to his grave, unearths his head and puts it in a pot of basil, which she waters with her tears. When her brothers discover the gruesome secret of the pot of basil on her windowsill, they take the head away from her and she dies of grief.

LA VIDA ES SUEÑO

This is probably the best work of the hundreds of plays by the leading Spanish dramatist, Pedro Calderón de la Barca (1600–1681). In English translations (such as that by Roy Campbell) the title is *Life is a Dream.* The harsh father of Calderón himself may be reflected in this play, a departure from this dramatist's usual "cape and sword" swashbucklers.

Segismundo, prince of Poland, has been prophesied to usurp the throne, so his father the king has kept him imprisoned in a tower all his life. As Basilio grows old he becomes concerned with the succession. Astolfo, duke of Moscow, suggests that Basilio leave his throne to a nephew, but Basilio decides to put the prophecy about Segismundo to the test.

Segismundo is brought, unconscious, from the tower to the court. On awakening, he finds himself given all the courtesies afforded a prince and his anger at having been treated badly all his life causes him to act outrageously; he assaults people, throws one out of the window, even threatens the life of his father. This is enough for Basilio, who has Segismundo put back to sleep and returned to his tower before he can cause anymore trouble.

When he awakes, Segismundo regards the episode at court as just a dream. Meanwhile, the populace now hears rumors of the existence of this hidden prince and chooses him to lead an opposition to Basilio and the hated duke of Moscow. Segismundo manages to triumph over Basilio's forces, and is made king.

To Basilio's surprise, Segismundo does not then become the terrible tyrant of the prophecy. He magnanimously forgives his father and restores harmony and tranquility to the kingdom. From his experience Segismundo has learned that one can exert one's own will to counteract prophecies of disaster in a life in which no one can be certain what is real and what is just a dream.

Grillparzer's *Der Traum ein Leben* (Dream is a Life) was intended as comedy, as were Martyn's *The Dream Physician* and Rice's *Dream Girl.* There are fewer plays about dreams and sleepers than you might expect and titles can be misleading. For instance, Lennox Robertson's *The Dreamers* (1915) is an historical drama about Robert Emmet (1778-1803)'s dream of liberty in Ireland, which ended in his being hanged by the British.

PRINZ FRIEDRICH VON HOMBURG

This romantic play was written in the year of its playwright's suicide but not published until a decade later. The prince is warned by the Elector of Brandenburg not to be rash in combat but at the battle of Fehrbellin he takes a gamble and wins. The elector accuses the prince of risking the German forces and sentences him to death. The elector asks the prince if this sentence is just, and the prince agrees but insists his dream of winning the battle and securing the hand of his beloved Natalia, who has interceded for him, drove him on—and he did, after all, win. The elector reprieves the prince, who marries Natalia in a fairytale ending.

Dreams of glory are common. Occasionally they get people into trouble, but most people do not have to fight huge military battles such as playwright Kleist, the descendant of Prussian generals, described.

PREMONITIONS OF DEATH

An effective dramatic device, dreams can create expectations and can foreshadow. Shakespeare has an ecclesiastic foresee the death of the king in one of the *Henry VI* plays, which prepares the audience if not the king.

NIGHTMARE PREVENTION

Iron was always a good shield against evil spirits, so it is no surprise that putting an iron or steel knife in your bed is supposed to keep nightmares at bay. You could try it. As with most superstition, if you really believe it, it really works.

THE VISION OF VASAVADATTA AND SOME OTHER DREAM PLAYS

Pandit Ganapati Shastri first edited and published 13 plays in Sanskrit that may date from the third-century BC and have been written by Bhasa. Shastri found them in Trivandrum, in southern India. These plays include one about Udayana, semi-historical ruler of Vatsas.

It is called *The Vision of Vasavadatta* in the English translation by H. C. Woolner & Lakshman Sarup (1930). Henry W. Wells in Gassner & Quinn's *Reader's Encyclopedia of World Drama* (1969) says that it is "as its title suggests…a dream play with metaphysical connotations, [and] successfully combines love scenes of tender pathos with scenes of super ingenious political intrigue."

This is an arcane example of the dramatic vision. I might as easily

have cited a Hungarian masterpiece that went unstaged for a generation. *Az ember tragédiajá* (The Tragedy of Man), by Imre Madách.

Let us pause a moment to speak of the ambitious and impressive
play called *The Tragedy of Man*, in which Adam and Eve and Lucifer
dreams the past and the future. As in a dream, Adam participates personally in each period piece while Eve is a new character in each period. Lucifer, as the embodiment of evil, battles light with darkness, but
Adam persists in the struggle, which the conclusion of the play states is
the meaning of it all. This reminds me very much of a nightmare that
Aldous Huxley once had. He found himself hanging from a huge cross
suspended high above the stone floor of a vast cathedral and was terrified of falling. He was given the message—in Latin—"Hold on, and
pray!" I mention that dream often. Good advice.

You can contribute a host of more familiar dream plays (and some
musicals with dream sequences) to prove the point that this kind of
thing has had a very long life onstage. In fact, all our dreams are dramas
and all plays are a kind of dream, aren't they?

DON JUAN IN HELL

Don Juan in Hell is the leading dream play of the twentieth-century. It
is actually the long third act of George Bernard Shaw's magnificent
Man and Superman. It is a dream sequence that is often omitted or
staged on its own.

TRAVEL IN A MEXICAN NEIGHBORHOOD

On the subject of dreamlike surrealism in modern art, the names of
Dalí, Giorgio DeChirico, René Magritte, and so on, are well known,
but you ought to consider Remedios Varo (1908–1963).

Born in Spain, she fled to Mexico during World War II, where she
spent the rest of her life. She began to paint full-time in 1953, the year
she married a second husband, Walter Gruen.

Many of her pictures, says Peter Engel in "The Traveler"
(*Connoisseur*, February 1988), resemble imagination in dreams and
share qualities of Surrealism, "fantastic imagery, perceptual illusion,
humor, and the unusual juxtaposition of ordinary objects to achieve
extraordinary effect."

To compete with Dalí's melting timepieces or DeChirico's ominous-
ly empty plazas, her central figure, in pseudo-medieval dress, in "The
Troubadour" (1959) rides through a wood where birds are about as large

as he, and a pan-pipe playing woman is encased in a tree. He rides in a boat that is woman in front and fish's tail behind. He plays on the woman's hair with a bow as on a stringed instrument.

PERSONAL DREAMS, PUBLIC FICTIONS

Dreams can provide forgotten facts, a narrative architecture, fantastic events, and valuable insights. Alma Villanueva's third novel, *Dreams*, was inspired by dreams and thoughts of her Mexican grandmother. See *Ms.* 4 (May/June 1994), 70–73.

William Burroughs, granddaddy of The Beats, in *Grand Street* 13 (Winter 1995), 194–201, writes "My Education: A Book of Dreams" and asserts that dreams can be dull because they have no context but goes on to repeat and comment on some of his dreams. He notes images of dogs and people, real and fictional, who pop up in those dreams.

I myself appeared in Burroughs' nighttime ruminations. I met him when I looked at a loft for rent over his, in New York. He showed it to me but warned me that the roof leaked. The next day I got a call from him telling me that I had "scared the hell" out of him in a nightmare that "went on all night." He said, "I know it's not your fault. You must have reminded me of someone." We can make use of strangers we meet in a dream or a nightmare and then discard them.

SOME CURIOUS IDEAS ABOUT THE BRAIN

Feminists are scouring the records to unearth female writers of the past who have been neglected. They could take a look at the seventeenth-century Duchess of Newcastle born in 1738. Samuel Pepys said "all she does is romantic." One of things she did was write poetry:

> The brain is like an oven, hot and dry,
> Which bakes all sorts of fancies, low and high;
> The thoughts are wood, which motion sets on fire;
> The tongue a peel[e], which draws forth the desire;
> But thinking much the brain too hot will grow,
> And burns it up; if cold, the thoughts are dough.

The duchess kept a servant by her bed all night every night in case she should get an idea like this, awake or asleep, and it needed recording. She was obsessive about this, the way Hans Christian Andersen was about his fear of premature burial. (When he stayed in hotels he always left a note on the dresser reading "I am not really dead.")

DREAMS IN WOMEN'S LITERATURE IN AFRICA

Some unfamiliar names that deserve recognition are African women authors such as Ama Ata Aidoo, Tsitsi Dangarembga, Buchi Emecheta, Bessie Head, and Flora Nwapa. These African women deal in stories of dreams and dreaming, and are studied by M. Phillips in "Engaging Dreams...," *Research in African Literatures* 25 (Winter 1994), 89–103.

The thousands of African cultures exhibit a wide variety of attitudes toward dreams and dreamers. Some African cultures fear them, and some turn to the talented to interpret dreams or even to dream for them.

LITERARY PROPHECY

In the vision of *Piers Ploughman*, William Langland foretold destruction of the monasteries by an English king. People had to wait a long time until this prophecy came true at the hands of Henry VIII (whose dying words are said to have been "Monks! Monks! Monks!"). This was just the foresight of a student of politics and author of a dream vision, however, not a true prophecy. Usually we are, as the wise Solon lamented, "ignorant of futurity" but sometimes we feel we are granted visions of what is to come, in our dreams. Sometimes the future is foretold in the works of writers. Art guesses forward.

THE LOTTERY PLAYERS

For the symbolism of dreams put to the use not of science but of superstition, see the studies of dreams used (along with names and places) to give so-called lucky numbers. I could cite a lot of dream books and similar publications but here are two classic Italian lottery-winner guides. The Italians specialize in dream books of this sort, though they are surely not alone in their interest. I add an obscure discussion of African-Americans playing the numbers.

> Luigi Chiurazzi, *Smorfia napoletana* (1876)
> Anonymous, *Libro di Sogni* (7th edition 1882)
> George J. McCall, "Symbiosis: The Case of Hoodoo and the Numbers Racket," *Social Problems* 10 (1963), 361–371.

Do you pay the tax on superstition, playing the lottery? Try dream numbers. "Hey, you never know!" If you win, why not send me material thanks for this advice? If you do not win, serves you right for playing against such impossible odds.

AFRICAN-AMERICAN FOLKLORE AND DREAMS

Arthur Huff Fauset, *Folklore from Nova Scotia* (1931, "the majority told by Negroes").

Leon R. Harris *et al.*, *The Black Book* (1974).

Margaret Jackson, "Folklore in Slave Narratives before the Civil War," *New York Folklore Quarterly* 11 (1955), 5–19.

Marilyn Powe, "Black 'Isms'," *Mississippi Folklore Register* 6 (1972), 76–82.

Susan Showers, "Alabama Folk-lore," *Southern Workman* 29 (1900), 179–180.

ANOTHER WAY TO SEE WHOM YOU WILL MARRY

If prayers and visits to soothsayers and sticking pins in statues of saints or otherwise threatening them does not get their cooperation, if sleeping with a spade or rubbing your naked belly against menhirs (standing stones) or other phallic objects does not work for you, folklore suggests you try this trick from Guernsey: stick 27 pins in a tallow candle, put it in a candlestick made from clay from a churchyard, light the wrong end of it (for this is witchcraft, which works with reverses), place it on the left side of the fireplace (sinister is for The Devil), and then beside your bed as you go to sleep. Your intended should appear in your dream. There are two awkward things about this particular procedure. First, it only works on 29 February, which is rare. And the graveyard clay must come from the grave of a virgin, perhaps rare as well.

"AN INTRODUCTION TO THE SCIENCE OF FOLKLORE AND LITERATURE"

That is the subtitle of Munro S. Edmonson's *Lore* (1971) where he writes on style:

Perhaps the most direct information we can acquire on the formation of personal style and the influences that bear on it can be obtained from the study of dreams. If anywhere, in the pattern of dreams we may find purely personal metaphors. The study of dreams is somewhat similar to the study of a foreign literature in a language one does not understand. We require an interpreter (the dreamer) and a denotative translation (his associations to the dream symbols). Any account of a dream is, of course, a verbal description of an experience that may or may not have been importantly verbal, and some distortion is inevitable on this account. In a favorable case, however, dream metaphors can be reliably reported and translated, and we can then specify their meaning even when they are personal....

AUTOMATIC WRITING

There is a way of getting in touch with something like the world of dreams called "automatic writing." It dates back at least as far as ghosts rapping in a kind of Morse code (one knock for *yes*, two for *no*) and the Ouija board, fashions of the nineteenth-century. In that century the talented Mrs. Verrall was one of many who turned to automatic writing, scribbling as fast as possible without looking, without controlling the hand consciously, trying to see what the spirits (or the unconscious) would produce. It was a version of the mediums' trick of placing a piece of chalk in a package with a slate and coming up with what "the spirits" wrote down. It was another way of taking dictation from the dead who, in that century and even later, on occasion sent us whole books, musical compositions, all sorts of information. Pierre Janet, a French psychologist, called automatic writing evidence of "mental automatism." The societies for psychical research in the U.S. (William James) and in Britain (F. W. H. Meyers, Edmund Gurney, Frank Podmore and others) studied automatic writing, and Meyers saw in it proof of the existence of what he called the "co-conscious," what Freud and others were to call the "unconscious" mind. To this Jung was to add the "collective unconscious." What we had in automatic writing was some kind of clue to the existence of activities of the mind different from normal, waking consciousness.

What automatic writing produced (and, if they were not faking, what mediums were producing in trance states) came not from the dear departed or any spirit world but from the issuer's deepest mind. Not from Beyond, from Deep Inside. Sometimes it was strikingly coherent, sometimes not. Gertrude Stein once put her arm in a sling and wrote automatically. I do not know if her "to write is to write is to write is to write is to write" was achieved this way, or if any of her other work was produced in this way, but her prose does greatly resemble a lot of automatic writing. Stein's writing may be somewhere between automatic and conscious writing. I think most creative writing may fall more or less into this category. Even the most controlling writers often find that they have put down something that surprises them. They call it inspiration, which originally meant the gods speaking through people.

Even so-called thoughtless writing calls for thoughtful analysis. Of course we may find that there was more than he imagined in Professor Morris Zapp (of the State University of Euphoria) in the novel *Small World* saying, as this comic creation did in his talks at literary conferences, that "every decoding is another encoding." Intrepretation of other people's writing, or even one's own, as with other people's dreams or one's own, is challenging.

As you look over what automatic writing produces, just as when you recount what you have dreamt, you inevitably succumb to the human desire to find meanings and patterns. You even try to do this with accidents produced by flinging paint at a canvas or tossing objects together to form assemblages, or combining found objects at random. Is anything like this really random?

What you have to do with automatic writing, as with the accounts of dreams, is to read out, not read in. At least with dreams you are assured that it was you yourself, at the unconscious level, who produced the result, not some passing ghost. James Merrill and his boyfriend wrote poetry with the aid of a Ouija board and claimed that someone was dictating it to them. The results look to me a lot like what James Merrill consciously wrote. I hear his voice repeatedly in what he claims someone Out There said. Painters and sculptors may go with the flow and see what eventuates. They, too, may be in touch with their unconscious and work by intuition as much as by intention. Whatever art is produced, it takes art to interpret art.

Automatic writing got its name about 1850. Even earlier, in 1823, Karl Ludwig Börne wrote in German an amusing and interesting essay whose title is translated as "How to Become an Original Writer in Three Days." He seems to have presaged Jack Kerouac. Börne advised on how to get everything you have crammed into your head out on paper and to force the emergence of some new, original work:

> Take a ream of paper and write down everything that passes through your head for three days, without stopping or correcting yourself. Write what you think of your wife, of the war against the Turk, of Goethe...and after three days you will be astounded at how many new and unheard-of thoughts you have come up with.

Paul Labarge, in "Stop Making Sense" (*Village Voice*, 17 April 2001, where I found the Börne quotation) reports that in Oakland (CA) in November 2000, to celebrate National Novel Writing Month, Chris Baty got 140 participants involved in a scheme to write 140 novels of 50,000 words each in 28 days. Not so batty as it appears. Writing as fast as they could and maybe as badly as they could some were amazed at how much good stuff was found among the trash. Write fast, but don't forget to edit. Don't give me the Beat argument that today you are not the person who wrote that yesterday "so who am I to fool with someone else's creation." And sleep faster. We need the dreams.

HALF A DOZEN AMERICAN PROVERBS

To dream is to see beyond.
Dreams are wishes your heart makes.
Dreams are what you hope for; reality is what you plan for.
Dreams retain the infirmities of our characters.
In dreams, and in love, nothing is impossible.
I'm a dreamer—aren't we all?

AND, CONCERNING SLEEP

Long sleep makes a bare back.
One hour's sleep before midnight is worth three hours after.
He sleeps well who doesn't know he is sleeping.
There will be sleeping enough in the grave.
Some sleep five hours; nature requires seven; laziness needs nine;
    and wickedness exacts eleven.

DISSATISFACTION

Dreams frequently deal in dissatisfactions of the sort that the old rhyme tells of:

> O that I were where I would be
> Then I would be where I am not;
> But where I am there I must be,
> And where I would be cannot.

It seems only logical that people who tend to believe in pie in the sky (that they will get in heaven what they were denied in life) should also produce in dreams the illusion of having what everyday waking life stubbornly refuses to give them.

THE SHREWDNESS OF THE FRENCH

Ring down the curtain—the farce is over.
> —Attributed to François Rabelais, dying.

Life is a dream; when we sleep we are awake, and when awake
we are asleep.
> —Michel de Montaigne, *Essais*

If a little dreaming is dangerous, the cure for it is not to dream
less but to dream more, to dream constantly.
> —Marcel Proust, *Remembrance of Things Past*

Someone who may be in me, more myself than I.
> —Paul Claudel, "Toward the Exit"

Like all dreamers, I mistook disenchantment for truth.
> —Jean-Paul Sartre, *Words*

One of the characteristics of the dream is that nothing in it surprises us. Without regret, we agree to live in it with strangers,
completely divorced from our habits and our friends.
> —Jean Cocteau, "Of Dreaming"

A WARNING IN A DREAM

Once a man from Lancashire started to reclaim some thousands of acres
of Dartmoor. A local man came to him and said:

> I valled asleep, and then I saw the gurt old sperit of the moors,
> Old Crockern hisself, grey as granite, and his eyebrows hanging
> down over his glimmering eyes like sedge, and his eyes deep as
> peat-water pools....Sez he to me, "Bear Muster Vowler a mes-
> sage from me. Tell Muster Vowler if he scratches my back I'll
> tear out his pocket."

Well, Mr. Fowler went right ahead with his steam ploughs and
steam threshers and scarred the land but, sure enough, he ran out of
money.

There are many stories of persons who had, or claimed to have,
dreams that encouraged or discouraged actions. Some consider it foolish to ignore a dream. Perhaps the commonest story involves a warning
dream, or a sudden disinclination to board a plane or a ship.

DON'T TELL YOUR DREAMS

Warren S. Walker & Ahmet E. Uysal's *Tales Alive in Turkey* (1966) give us a folktale also found in Armenian, Greek, and other languages. It concerns a boy who stayed asleep longer than usual; he wanted to finish a dream. When he awoke he explained his long sleep but refused to tell what the dream was. Angered, his father put him out of the house. He got into the house of a wealthy man but was tossed into a pit when it came out that he had a dream he would not reveal. However, he was rescued and ran off with the rich man's daughter, whom he married. He also married the daughter of a king, whose dreams he interpreted and whose riddles he solved. But he steadfastly refused to tell his own dream.

THE TAILOR'S DREAM

A tailor dreamed that he died and went to Hell where he was confronted by The Devil, who accused him of theft. The Devil showed him a large patchwork quilt made up of all the pieces of cloth the tailor had filched over the years. When he woke up, the tailor told his dream to a fellow worker. The worker later spied the tailor stealing a piece of scarlet cloth. "It's alright," the tailor explained, "there was no piece of this color in that patchwork quilt."

I DREAMED I DIED AND WENT TO HEAVEN

There is an old Mexican tale whose title translates *The Priests are All in Hell*. In English-speaking countries it is sometimes called *The Parson's Meeting*. In the German version (see Kurt Ranke's *Folktales of Germany* translated by Lotte Baumann) the story involves a priest who berated a parishioner for non-attendance at church. The parishioner later had a dream he went to Heaven but was stopped at the gate by St. Peter who wouldn't let him in because he had not partaken of holy communion. "Is there no priest in Heaven who can give me communion?" the man asked. "No," said St. Peter, "the priests are all in Hell."

DREAMS OF AVARICE

The Grimms' *German Legends* (No. 433) and other books (such as Dorson's *Folktales around the World* and Seki's *Folktales of Japan*) all retell the story of the man who dreamed that he found a treasure in a mound and, waking, went to such a mound and dug up wealth. But the best dream of wealth being found and the dream coming true is that of the man who dreamed that if he went to Constantinople he would find great wealth. I've told the tale before and will tell it again now. The dreamer decided to go to Constantinople but when he got there he had no idea of what to do and in fact got thrown into jail. When he was brought before the authority he was asked what he was doing in the city and he told of his dream. The magistrate berated him saying, "To come all the way to Constantinople because you had a dream is foolish. I myself have often dreamed of a garden in a far-off city where great treasure is buried but I would not for a moment think of setting off to journey there." The visitor to Constantinople, however, recognized the description of the garden: it was his own garden back home. He rushed back to his own home and dug up the treasure that was in his own backyard all along.

35 FAIRYTALES, LEGENDS AND MYTHS CONCERNING DREAMS

Chin and Yi
The Death of Balder
Ed Grant Has Dream
The Fairies in the White Mountains
The Fortunate Shoemaker
The Golden Horse with the Silver Mane
Haku's Power
How Coyote Brought Back People after the Flood
The White Stone Canoe
Itsayaya and the Chokeberries
Kantjil Interprets a Dream
The King's True Dream
The Little Shepherd's Dream
Maimonides and the King's Dream
Menaseh's Dream
The Mighty Hunter

Mr. Frog's Dream
The Pedlar of Swatham
The Phoenix and the Falcon
The Piece of Straw
The Russian and the Tatar
St. Michael and the Idle Husband
The Secretive Little Boy and His Little Sword
The Seller of Dreams
The Silver Ship
The Snake and the Dreams
The Spring
The Strange Dream of Chanticleer
A Town in a Snuff Box
The Weight of the Cart
The Wise Man's Pillow
Wynken, Blynken, and Nod

These are chosen from Norma Olin Ireland's *The Red King and the Green King Index to Fairy Tales, 1949–1972 (1973).*

SCIENCE FICTION DREAMS

Dreams have been a large factor in fantasy literature from *Arabian Nights* to the sci-fi movie epics and novels. Here are but two representative examples of dreams and dreaming in unusual older science fiction:

S(ydney). Fowler Wright, *Dream; or, The Simian Maid* (1931). "A depressed socialite seeks distraction in hypnotically sharing the experiences of individuals long dead."

Roger Zelazny, *The Dream Master* (1966). A somewhat mad doctor of the psychiatric persuasion links minds with highly disturbed patients in attempts to construct therapeutic dream experiences. This does not turn out well.

Both before and after this, in various formats, the idea of literally getting in someone's dreams has been a staple of a certain kind of sci-fi narrative. Ordinarily science fiction puts its faith in technological and scientific progress, but meddling with minds goes against the grain as does (in certain horror films) meddling with cross-breeding species and will, one supposes, in time, turn up in tales of cloning gone disastrously wrong. Ever since *Frankenstein*, certain writers have been suspicious of what science can do. Science, according to Bertold Brecht, "knows only one commandment—contribution to science," and thinking people may fear that there will be an abdication of moral accountability, that science will operate, in the worlds of Barbara Ehrenreich, "without any social relevance or human responsibility at all."

More recent science fiction is a huge field with many true experts. I hesitate to venture into their preserves. Sci-fi fans know their field backwards and forwards. Today political correctness is as daunting among the exponents of popular culture as it used to be in the academic establishment which haughtily pushed all such popular matters aside as trivial.

IN DREAMS BEGIN RESPONSIBILITIES

Primitive people did not understand what death was, how someone vital could suddenly die and rot. When the living began to be visited in dreams by the dead, they were terrified, and out of fear of what the dead might come back and do to the living arose burial customs and other attempts to palliate the deceased. The corpse came to be treated with awe and dread. Then various rituals were enacted so that the dead could in some sense live happily in another world and not return to this world.

Even today, in societies all over the world, there is some fear of the dead, some way to make sure the departed spirit does not return to molest the living, some hope that the spirit lives on, on some other plane of existence.

Out of dread and superstition, we are told, religion and its rituals arose. I prefer to believe that care for the dead had some element of sentiment in it and religion some trace in it of a sense that there must be some place from which we come, some place to which we go, some reason for our existence. "The grave is not the goal." Mankind began to see in nature (the obvious revelation of the divine) some hint of its eternal creator, the force which Philo was to call the *logos,* and to believe that in altered states of consciousness, dreams especially, the divine sometimes made itself manifest.

In various religions consecrated priests and learned rabbis and Muslim *imams* ("exemplars," leaders of service in the mosques), witch-doctors and shamans, miracle workers and preachers, and others, undertook to instruct us on the origins, destinations, and duties of mankind and to bring to us or interpret for us messages from the spirit world, heavenly visions, and prophetic dreams.

ALBERT BÉGUIN AND THE SOUL OF ROMANTICISM

There are libraries full of books on the nature of romanticism, either glorifying its achievements or denouncing it for the bohemian or eccentric lives of its followers. Books also criticize the substitution of sensibility for sense, intuition for reason, and emotion and sensation for morality.

Romanticism injected passion into literature. In the nineteenth-century Alexis de Toqueville observed: "In times when the passions are beginning to take charge of the conduct of human affairs, one should pay less attention to what men of experience and common sense are thinking than to what is preoccupying the imagination of dreamers." As usual, Toqueville was right.

One important modern book is Albert Béguin's *L'Âme romantique et le rêve*. Béguin's romanticism is based squarely on mythological symbolism from the unconscious, chiefly accessed in dreams. Dreams gave romantic literature ambiguous symbols and ancient archetypes, irrational order and fragmentary incompletion. They were materials from life metamorphosed by imagination; they expressed a love of the fantastic, a phantasmagoric ambiance, and the solitary dreamer.

Béguin discusses dream symbolism in Ludwig [Jo]Achim von Arnim (1781–1831), Clemens Brentano (1778–1832), Ernst Theodor Amadeus Hoffmann (1776–1832), Novalis (1772–1801), and other German romantic writers. Béguin argues that dreams as these Germans saw them were also evident in the works of French writers such as Charles-Pierre Baudelaire (1821–1867), Stéphane Mallarmé (1842–1898), Gérard de Nerval (1808–1855), Marcel Proust (1871–1922), and Arthur Rimbaud (1854–1891).

It is convenient for literary critics to speak of the Romantic Movement and to give it specific dates but there always is a romantic as well as a classical movement in art and literature. The ambiguous and fantastic symbols of dreams are still evident in painting and modern poetry, as well as experimental and commercial film.

Literature notoriously borrows from life and from earlier literature; styles and even content go in and out of favor. I think it was Stanislaw Lec who suggested in the sixties when we were out to destroy monuments that we ought to save pedestals because they come in handy later. Some of the elaborate monuments of romanticism stand and in some other cases the pedestals, as you might say, have had other constructions erected on them. Romanticism and dreams have never ceased to be important in all the arts. They never will.

"Dreams," wrote Mallarmé, "have as much influence as actions." They are a way of looking at the actual historical record. Hegel wrote: "If all the dreams which men had dreamed during a particular period were written down, they would yield an accurate idea of the spirit which prevailed at the time." There's some Hegel anyone can grasp.

Artists and writers make dreams visible and explain them, for poets, as one said, are "the dreamers of dreams."

KRISHNAMURTI

M. Krishnamurti's *The Cloth of Gold* is a dance drama, in verse, that has a "dream-epilogue." Dance dramas and ballets, naturally, have incorporate dream material from time to time. There is something essentially dreamlike about dance that seems effortlessly to lend us grace and even let us defy gravity.

HENRI GAUDIER-BRZESKA

"I dreamed last night that I visited Paris," wrote this artist, "and I came to a room where my name was written in letters of gold over the door. I went in and found all my works there, so you see, Sisik [Brzeska], I shall one day be a great sculptor."

Many years later, in 1965, in Paris' Musée de l'Art Moderne, a Salle Gaudier-Brzeska opened as part of the permanent collection. It could not contain all his works, but marked him as a great artist. The artist's name is over the door.

SOME RECENT AMERICAN AND BRITISH OCCULT REFERENCE BOOKS

Complete Book of Fortune (1988)
Dark Dimensions: A Celebration of the Occult (1977)
Dictionary of Mysticism and the Esoteric Traditions (revised, 1992)
[James Randi's] Encyclopedia of Claims, Frauds and Hoaxes of the Occult and Supernatural (1997)

Encyclopedia of Occultism and Parapsychology (1978)
Encyclopedia of Occult Sciences (1990)
Encyclopedia of the Occult Sciences (1960)
The Mammoth Book of the Supernatural (Colin Wilson, ed. Damon Wilson, 1991)
The Occult (Gareth Knight, 1975)
Occult Bibliography...1971-1975 (1978)
Occult Connection (1988)
Occult Dictionary for the Millions (1966)
Occult Illustrated Dictionary (1975)
Oxford Book of Dreams (ed. S. Brook, 1987)
Oxford Book of the Supernatural (ed. D. J. Enright, 1994)
Steinerbooks Dictionary of the Psychic, Mystic, Occult (1977)

SOME RECENT PERIODICAL LITERATURE ON DREAMS AND LITERATURE

Brewer, William Dean. "Mary Shelley on Dreams," *Southern Humanities Review* 29 (Spring 1995), 105–123.

Brown, Murray L. "Conflicting Dreams: [Richard] Lovelace and the Oneirocritical Reader," *Eighteenth Century Life* 19 (November 1995), 1–21.

Bryson, Cynthia B. "The Imperative Daily Nap; or, Aschenbach's Dream in [Thomas Mann's] *Death in Venice*," *Studies om Short Fiction* 29 (Spring 1992), 181–193.

Gandelman, Claude. "The Artist as *Traumarbeiter* [Dream Worker]: On Sketches of Dreams by Marcel Proust," *Yale French Studies* 84 (1994), 118–135.

LeBlanc, Diane C. "Pilgrimage, Duality, and Quest in Denise Levertov's *Pig Dreams*," *Essays in Literature* 18 (Spring 1991), 106–121.

Monsman, Gerald. "'Definite History and Dogmatic Interpretation': The 'White Nights' of [Walter] Pater's *Marius the Epicurian*," *Criticism* 26 (Spring 1984), 171–191.

Purdy, Strother B. "*Beowulf* and Hrothgar's Dream," *Chaucer Review* 21: 2 (1986), 257–273.

Stern, Michael Lynn. "'It Has Been Itself a Dream': The Oneiric Plot of [E. M. Forster's] *Howards End*," *Literature and Psychology* 41: 1–2 (1995), 19–36.

Elizabeth Bosse, Strindberg's much younger wife, played the lead in the first production (Svenska Teatern, April 1907) of the Swedish master of expressionism's *Ett Drömspell* (The Dream Play, written in 1902). Strindberg hoped it would have the persuasive illogicality of a dream in which a mysterious castle—the play was given a working title of *Castle Rising*—springs up. Strindberg said he wanted "to capture the inconsistent yet ostensibly logical structure of a dream" in which "anything can happen" because "Time and Place do not exist."

DREAMS AND CREATIVITY

In scientific journals and popular magazines—such as George Howe Colt's cover story, "The Power of Dreams" in *Life*, September 1995—dreams are presented as tools for the detection and even the palliation of illnesses from cancer to schizophrenia, for insights and conflict resolution, and for artistic creativity.

Recurrent dreams—these are often treated by psychology and investigated by researchers such as Ronald J. Brown and Donald C. Donderi—are particularly fruitful in providing clues to conflict, the intellectual lumber for the construction of imaginative works of art.

Today dreams are studied not only in connection with science and high culture but in terms of popular culture. In "Psychoanalysis of Dreams..." in the *Journal of Popular Culture* 32:1 (Summer 1998), 113 –120, Daniel Walden and Helena Poch take on not only Sigmund Freud, but Billy Joel.

DION McGREGOR

Dreams and dreamers in popular music particularly, could fill a whole book, so permit me to mention just one, highly unusual, recording artist, Dion McGregor.

Here's DJ David Garland on radio station WNYC in April, 2000:

Dion McGregor was a dreamer. And you can listen to him dream, because Dion McGregor talked in his sleep and his dreams were recorded! Stream of consciousness was never so natural, real or bizarre as on these tapes made while McGregor slept, and talked his way through his dreams. In addition to McGregor's virtuoso dreams, you can hear interviews with Michael Barr, who recorded them, and Phil Milstein, who produced a new CD of Dion's dreams.

On a second CD, *Dion McGregor Sings Again*, you will encounter tracks with titles such as "Dumb Fart," "The Food and What to Do with It," "Vulvina," and "Wha Deboah Yo Ya?" A lot of modern recordings are weird but you must admit that this is extraordinary.

HYPNOSIS AND EXTENDED SLEEP

In 1888 Edward Bellamy published a utopian book that has remained in print. In fact, there are several editions of *Looking Backward 2000–1887* in print now. In its century the book sold more copies than any other American novel the one President Lincoln claimed "started the great war:" *Uncle Tom's Cabin.*

In *Looking Backward* a Bostonian named Julian West is hypnotized and forgotten. The subject wakes up in the year 2000, when tremendous social and technological change has occurred. Dr. Leete brings West out of his sleep and explains to this Rip van Winkle sort of man what has occurred.

At the end of the descriptions of socialist triumph West has a nightmare in which he thinks himself to be back in the awful nineteenth century, before universal cooperation, vegetarianism, and other astounding milestones in the march toward grace.

On a lighter note, there is the Chuck Jones animated film *Froggy Evening* in which a frog, put into a cornerstone in the nineteenth-century, comes out of a long sleep in the mid-twentieth-century, dancing and singing some old vaudeville songs. The man who finds the frog cannot get it to perform for a theatrical agent and the frog is placed in the cornerstone of another building. As the cartoon ends the frog emerges again, this time in 2056.

5

Dreams and the Movies

A strange thing has happened—while all the other arts were born naked, this the youngest, has been born fully clothed. It can say everything before it has anything to say. It is as if the savage tribe, instead of finding two bars of iron to play with, had found scattering the seashore fiddles, flutes, saxophones, trumpets, grand pianos by Erhard and Bechstein, and had begun with incredible energy, but without knowing a note of music, to hammer and thump upon them all at the same time.
—Virginia Woolf, *The Captain's Death Bed*

THE MOVIES ARE NOT JUST AN
ENTERTAINMENT INDUSTRY

Thoroughly Modern Millie (1967) was a cute musical starring Julie Andrews. More significantly, with Carol Channing's camp and Mary Tyler Moore's charm, it acted out the American dream (become a secretary, marry the boss), hinted at the postwar sexual revolution (be a flapper, be "modern"). It dramatized American sociodynamics. Some of its concerns, (like white slavery), merely reflect the period but some are still central. One hit song says Americans and those influenced by America have learned how to behave from the movies.

From the movies we learned how to woo and how to win, how to dress, and talk, and conduct ourselves. We learned that smoking cigarettes was sophisticated and we indeed saw our society's values not only reflected but also reshaped.

Study the movies. They are as powerful visually as any dream. They are for anyone who can see. Images are powerful, with or without words, music, color or explanation. This chapter contains a great variety of motion pictures with powerful images of dreaming. There is nothing like it anywhere else.

SLEEPING BEAUTY

I spoke in the previous chapter of *Sleeping Beauty*. You probably saw the animated feature when you were a child. It was Disney's most expensive animation to that date (1959), with an artistic look derived from old manuscripts that were less mechanically crafted than most.

Did it affect your dreams? Movies often do, in ways that are subtle, because when we are in the dark, dreaming or at the cinema, we are especially open to ideas. We become impressionable children gambling in the Now.

The Madison Ave. boys have used dream images to great effect. There was a Schenley TV ad back in 1967 in which a psychiatrist named Dr. Strangeluv dealt with the nightmares of a liquor distributor whose products were always outsold by the Schenley corporation. The nurse brought doctor and patient—a shot of Schenley's. The ad was called *The Dream Life of Fred Ferment*.

Lately, movies have been playing with "dream linkage," the nutty notion that people can get into your dreams or you can get into theirs. One film along those lines was *Total Recall*. With a title like that you may think it had to be about US automobile manufacturers but it was about violent dreams.

Ingmar Bergman's *Persona* (1966), has his usual team of actors driven by dreams. Bergman spoke of all film as dreams: "No art passes our conscience in the way film does, and goes directly to our feelings, deep down into the dark rooms of our souls."

He has Victor Sjöstrom recall an old friend's sentiment: "Dreams are a kind of living and lunacy a kind of dream," in *Wild Strawberries* (1956), and the character adds, " but life is also supposed to be a dream, isn't it?"

How movies live in our dreams is worthy of very careful study and may in fact receive some as we progress. Mrs. Woolf told us that the movies started with technology and no idea how to make use of it. Wrong! From the first, movies learned from dreams, which are narrative and mostly pictorial. Moving pictures are what films are in essence, not words but images, occasionally not even logical but psychological—sound familiar?

In The Vulgate of St. Jerome, The Bible usually has *somnium videre*, "to see a dream," not in the sense of seeing but interpreting what you see.

What is dreaming all about? Briefly, the tiny nodes in your brain that put out adrenergic chemicals shut down as you drift off to sleep, and cholinergic chemicals decouple the networks that produce "waking cognition and behavior" (says neurobiologist Allan Hobson of Harvard). We get "pentine-geniculate-occipital waves" and we dream.

What are the movies all about? Edison filmed *The Kiss* and *The Great Train Robbery* and the movies sprang instantly into life as waking visualizations of the two major concerns of our dreams: sex and escape from normal constraints. (These are the two commonest hits on the internet today.)

Television, then video, then cable television did not kill the movies as one might have expected; they forced the movies to be bigger if not better. Like dreams, spectacle is what the movies do best; big images, unforgettable images. Today the FX experts often contribute more to a movie than do actors. It's not that Leonardo DiCaprio scores but that the ship stinks.

I think the sets of my dreams are getting more spectacular and the casts larger. I credit that to the movies, along with any new ideas I may have picked up from *The Matrix, Eyes Wide Shut, Casablanca* or *Debbie Does Dallas*.

I dream about people that look old-fashioned elegant or pseudo-elegant, rather than modern or grunge, which makes me think that older people might cast our dreams in old-fashioned style. I have never once dreamed of being on a train with Madonna and entering a tunnel.

A DREAM FOR MOVIE TREATMENT

Arthur Schnitzler (1862–1931) knew a lot about the dream fulfillments of sexual desires and wrote plays and novels about such themes. In the last year of his life he wrote in his diary—he had kept one since 1879—of the following dream. I invite you to consider how it could be put on the screen, with music, montage, close-up, and other cinematographic effects:

> Dreaming, again with particular clarity. In a concert hall Richard Strauss and Richard Wagner are playing at two pianos (the latter imprecisely)—improvising actually (somewhat like

Heini and I have often played improvisations on Mahler symphonies),—I accompany them, on one of the pianos, with one finger, not always correctly;—Heini is there and says to me something like: You're musical, but you're playing it wrong;—I stop; then Heini begins to play suddenly—at the same piano as Strauss, turned around, so that Str[auss] actually has to play on the cover (which I hardly notice). Then (without my hearing the clapping) Strauss thanks for the applause, which is actually for Heini, and applauds for himself.

The text is from Peter Michael Braunwarth's edition of Schnitzler's *Tagebuch 1931* (2000) and it appears in the review of that book in *Times Literary Supplement* for 13 October 2000 (p. 5). There Leo A. Lensing accompanies it with an elaborate interpretation of the dream.

I want to stress that it is not the meaning of the dream but the similarity of the dream to a piece of filming. I want to emphasize that you may not know science but you do know screenwriting, at least by osmosis. Today our lives are scenarios, jump cuts and all. Some of them go through drastic rewrites.

Let me offer one other dream for you to work on. You will find it surprisingly easy, however far it may be from your own sexuality, because movies have taught you so much. It is from Wayne Kostenbaum's *The Queen's Throat* (1993):

Recently I dreamt I stood in an arena, beside an upright piano, its lid piled with scores to every opera I've tapped in this pocket guide. I was finally a singer! And although I was performing *Werther* and *Lucia* next week, I decided to devote the weekend to muscle building. I walked from the arena to the gym, and lifted weights. And though at this point the dream was fading, I entered the steam room for a last few instants, and saw a gay guy with his towel protectively wrapped around his middle: to hide incipient arousal, or to hide plumpness? I knew he was gay because of his eyes, his haircut, his intensity. He opened his mouth. He was about to sing "Pourquoi me réviller." Then the dream shut down.

MOVIES IN YOUR DREAMS

If in your dreams you are watching movies you may be aware that you are too escapist or too willing to sit on the sidelines. Or you may just be entertaining yourself.

John Collick wrote an article called "Wolves through the Window: Writing Dreams/Dreaming Films/Filming Dreams," *Critical Survey* 3:3 (1991), 283–289. See also Cynthia A. Hanson, "The Hollywood Musical Biopic and the Regressive Performer," *Wide Angle* 10:2 (1988), 15–23.

Literary and film bibliographies will offer you many critical voices. This book has some lists of useful material for further reading. Even if you never look at any of it you will see the main point: there is a lot of interest in the subject.

TELEVISION DOCUMENTARIES ABOUT DREAMS

Dreams are not only vital parts of commercial movies but also the subject of documentaries, instruction films, and such. There are a great many of these, but here are a couple:

Dr. Carl Gustav Jung (1968). Hugh Burnett of the BBC interviews Jung about his life, his theories of the collective unconscious, etc. There are other such interviews on record, though I have never seen one of Freud.

Dreams (1980). A Canadian documentary on American television about how to interpret the symbols of your dreams and how people discuss these in group sessions.

DREAM IN THE MOVIES

From Ric Robertson's "The Whole World Was Watching," an advertisement in *New York Times Magazine* in 1999:

> For just about 100 years, the world has sat in the dark as hundreds of millions of frames of films flickered from screen to eye to brain and then traveled the neuron highway to settle someplace deeper. The pervasive ability of movies to affect cultural and personal behaviors and psychology extends from surface stereotypes into the deeper reaches of our cultural experience. The cinema simultaneously defines, reflects and romanticizes life as we know it, and it has done so almost from its creation, demonstrating a consistent and unique ability to instruct, amaze and influence.

I would add that the movies have changed way we structure our dreams over the last century. I think we dream differently, running movies in our heads. People didn't do that before.

For a long time Hollywood has been called America's dream factory, and today one of the leading production companies in the motion picture industry is DreamWorks.

Consider *The Wizard of Oz* or *The Sixth Sense*, a film of 1999 combining childhood dreams and adult terror. In *Something Wicked This Way Comes* the story, taken from Ray Bradbury, concerns a carnival creep who travels around changing dreams into reality or reality into dreams, or so he promises. The film starred Jason Robards as a con man of dangerous talents, Jonathan Pryce, Diane Ladd, and Pam Grier.

In *Labyrinth* (1986), a lonely daydreamer, a teenager played by Jennifer Connelly, enters a dream world to save her brother from the Goblin King (David Bowie). Terry Jones wrote the script and George Lucas produced this fantasy.

One could fill a book with films involving dreams (in all senses of the word) but my candidate for the most unforgettable dreamer is the somnambulist Cesare (played by Conrad Veidt) in the silent-screen epic, *Das Kabinett der Dr. Caligari* (Germany, 1919).

An evil small-time showman, played by Werner Krauss, has hypnotized Cesare and wanders around with him in a series of terrifically effective expressionist sets. The sets tilt this way and that in a surrealistic nightmare.

Fellini's *8 1/2*—he had presumably made 7 1/2 movies before this one—appeared in 1963. Piero Gherardi costumes and sets created the dreamworld in black and white.

Fellini is famous for turning his dreams into feature films but he is by no means the only cinema giant to have done so. One should also note certain atmospheric films that create something of the world of dreams. There is Paul Wegener's *Der Golem* (The Golem, 1920), a much more neglected silent-film creepy *Schauerroman* (horror story) than *Caligari* or *Nosferatu* (the classic vampire film).

Michael Bliss in *Dreams within a Dream* (2000) says that Australian filmmaker Peter Weir "has managed to establish for himself a distinctive place in international cinema by insisting that dreams and the unconscious...are still undervalued and overlooked in contemporary culture." Bliss relates Weir's films to Jungian theories, though the likes of *Dead Poets Society* do not fit his Procrustean format very well.

The most interesting new film involving dreams is by director Neil Jordan (of *The Crying Game*). It is *In Dreams* (1999), and pits mundane rationality against the irrational world of dreams.

The unconscious is symbolized by an underwater world. There is a beautifully photographed submerged town that holds the killer's secrets, a touch Freud would have loved.

In the story, psychic Claire Cooper (Annette Bening), who has long suffered from nightmares, begins to worry that she is actually communicating with a serial killer of children who has invaded her dreams. Robert Downey, Jr. and Stephen Rea are also in the cast. Critic Norman Green describes director Neil Jordan as "our Dr. Freud and our Hieronymus Bosch."

AWAKE IN THE STATELY PLEASURE DOME OF DREAMS

The motion picture has affected our dreams in all senses of the word, from the very first magical flickers on a screen. Here is my personal list of the most remarkable creations. I avoid a number of films I have heard of but cannot find. A single example of those will suffice: Charlie Ruggles' comedy *Early to Bed* (1936, with Mary Boland) involves the comedian who suffers from sleepwalking but catches a criminal thereby. Norman McLeod directed the comedy for Paramount.

It seems that most of the films of the last century have perished, and the scripts with them, shockingly. You need to know most about films that you can get on video and may even be able to see screened in the few remaining art houses and the museums of the moving image.

I regret the demise of the old-movie art houses like The Thalia in New York City. That was back when art movie meant "classic," not "artsy-fartsy" as seen in places like The Angelika now.

SILENTS, PLEASE

The silent screen loved trick photography. Dream sequences were easy and popular. Here is a generous sampling of early dream movies, by no means all that are known, although many are lost now:

The Absent-Minded Professor (Gaumont, 1907). A mathematician has an odd dream. Directed by Percy Stow.

The Cabby's Dream (Warwick Trading Co., 1906). A cab driver has a dream about a wild ride with a magician. Charles Raymond directed seven short scenes.

Le Cauchemar (The Nightmare, Star 1897). Just 65 feet of film by George Méliès.

Diabolo Nightmare (Urban Trading Co., 1907). A clerk devoted to diabolo dreams of playing under the sea. Walter R. Booth directed 22 short scenes.

Dick Whittington (G.A.S. Films, 1899). The lad with the cat who gets to be Lord Mayor of London in the old stories here dreams three things about his future. Directed by G. A. Smith.

Don Quixote's Dream (Hepworth, 1908). The Don dreams of some toughs kidnapping a girl. Directed by Lewin Fitzhamon.

Dream Bad, Luck Ditto (Martin, 1915). A nightmare. Directed by Edwin J. Collins.

Dream Dance (Lubin, 1915). By this time the entertainment could last half an hour, like this film, and even get beyond slapstick: in this one a man dies in a nightmare. A painting comes to life.

The Dream Fairy (Edison, 1913). A girl dreams that a fairy (Gertrude McCoy) gives her some wishes. Some are the real McCoy and come true when the girl awakes.

Dreaming of Robinson Crusoe (Fay Films, 1915). A comic film on the Crusoe story so popular on the melodrama stage of the nineteenth century, even in France.

Dreamland Adventures (Urban Trading Co., 1907). A golliwog (black doll) and another doll take children to the Arctic on an airship. The Arctic was popular: *Bobby Wideawake* dreams of going there in another early film. Directed by Walter R. Booth.

A Dreamland Frolic (Globe, 1919). Music hall star Lupino Lane is Nipper. He dreams he is a schoolboy who puts on dad's clothes for a night on the town. Donning the clothes of older persons, or men dressing as women, is a common comic device of the period. Stars from other media are entering the film business seriously.

The Dream of an Opium Fiend (from France's Star Films, date uncertain) presents a dream sequence in which a young woman turns into an old hag.

A Dream of Glory (Pathé, 1913). An actress dreams of fame but marries a poor artist. Directed by R. E. Coleby.

Dream Paintings (Ivy Close Films [Butcher], 1912). Ivy Close is the model that Austin Melford as the artist dreams of in poses from various paintings.

Dream of a Rarebit Fiend (1906, only four minutes) is based on the old belief that cheese or anything at all hard to digest at bedtime causes nightmares. This is a classic bit.

The Dream of Old Scrooge (Cinés, 1910) gives us three dreams of Dickens' old miser from *A Christmas Carol:* the ghosts of Christmas Past, of Christmas Present, and of Christmas of the Future.

A Dream of Paradise (Wrench, 1910). A tramp dreams he is invited to drink champagne.

The Dream Pill (Lubin, 1910) involves Professor Swank giving a pill to some poor tramp who then has an uncomfortable dream.

Dreams of Toyland (Alpha Trading Co., 1908). A boy dreams of toys coming alive. Directed by Arthur Cooper.

The Enchanted Toymaker (Alpha Trading Co., 1904). An old man dreams that a toy Noah's Ark, a common Victorian toy, grows larger and animals enter it. Directed by Arthur Cooper.

From Servant Girl to Duchess (Gaumont, 1909). A maid dreams of glory as in another old flick a "slavey" played by May Clark dreams of advancement. This one is directed by Alf Collins.

The Glutton's Nightmare (Hepworth, 1901). The gourmand finds cats in the rabbit pie, dogs in the sausages. Directed by Percy Stow.

His Prehistoric Past (Keystone, 1914). Charlie Chaplin dreams of earlier times. With Mark Swain, Gene Marsh, and Fritz Schade. A Mack Sennett film.

The Newsboy's Christmas Dream (1913) from C&M was an ambitious 30-minute epic with a prehistoric monster chasing the principal.

The Nursemaid's Dream starred Gertie Potter (for Hepworth in the UK) as a baby chased (very briefly) by giants in a dream.

A Policeman's Dream (Gaumont, 1902). Three scenes as a policeman dreams before a snowfall wakes him up. Policemen are featured in many early films as they chase people who steal things, people who take off their clothes to bathe, etc. Think of Keystone Kops.

Prehistoric Peeps (Hepworth, 1905). An expert on old bones dreams of prehistoric times. A dinosaur was to be among the very first animated cartoon characters.

Santa Claus and the Children (R. W. Paul, 1898). The same story as in *The Vision of Santa Claus* (see below) that was made earlier that year.

Skeleton Dance (Walt Disney animation, 1930).

The Sleepwalker (Hepworth, 1909). A female sleepwalker runs into trouble but is saved by a willing waif. Directed by Theo Bouwmeester.

Tommy Lad (Walturdaw, 1909). A tommy (Tommy Atkins=soldier) dreams his mother is dead and he deserts. She is alive and successfully pleads for him at his court-martial, a common image.

Too Much Lobster (Hepworth, 1909). Usually oysters are the aphrodisiac, but here lobster gets the man dreaming of girls. Directed by Lewin Fitzhamon.

The Nightmare of the Glad-Eye Twins (Kineto, UK, 1913). A little girl's dolls come to life, but they are not as horrible as some other toys in later horror films.

The Tramp's Dream (Hepworth, 1906). Tramps were popular comic characters, as you know from the huge success of Charlie Chaplin. They helped him rank with Garbo and a few others in the Picture Pantheon. Here a tramp dreams that a fairy takes him to be the guest of a marquis. One of a number of dream sequences directed by Lewin Fitzhamon for Hepworth.

The Tramp's Dream (Selsior Films, 1913). A tramp dreams of elves dancing (synchronized to cinema orchestras, as some early films were to organ or piano music).

A Tramp's Dream of Wealth (Hepworth, 1907). Thurston Harris as the tramp and Gertie Potter as a mermaid at Bognor (Regis) who leads him to a shipload of money. Directed by Lewin Fitzhamon.

Vision of a Crime (Lubin, 1907). Dream of a corpse found the next day.

The Vision of Santa Claus (G.A.S. Films, 1898). Children dream that Santa comes down the chimney. Directed by G. A. Smith.

Visions of an Opium Smoker (R.W. Paul, 1905). Opium and derivatives such as laudanum were in rather common use in the nineteenth-century and early twentieth-century. Even babies and the old ladies sipping cordials were into drugs.

MAIN FEATURES

The Cabinet of Dr. Caligari (1919) will crop up in this book more than once. It is a surreal masterpiece of the silent era. A creepy showman (Werner Krauss) has made Cesare (Conrad Veidt) into a somnambulist by placing him under hypnosis. He looks like a Goth punk; if the club kids think they have invented a style they should be shown that Cesare, with black lipstick and too much eye shadow, created The Look before their grandparents were born.

Cesare's expressionistic landscape of streets out of a nightmare are like nothing you have seen in Batman or TV imitations

Any movie, like a dream, approaches what Karl Jaspers described as "the infinitely interpretable" and is a sort of nightmare we can run over and over while maintaining some distance. If a movie is to be viewed more than once it has to have even more going for it than a book.

Film has been one of the most experimental arts despite its commercialism. As early as the mid-forties, Hans Richter was involved with an experimental film called *Dreams that Money Can Buy*. That had dream sequences by Marcel Duchamp, Max Ernst (whose paintings are often of weird dreamscapes), Fernand Léger, Alexander Calder (he of the toy circus and the mobiles), and the photographer who called himself Man Ray. The general goofiness of this period in art was reflected in the Man Ray Dada *duh* episode of this pretentious piece of work in which the audience is invited to watch an onscreen audience, supposedly hypnotized,

Pursuit or sex are common in dreams. Here is an image from *The Cabinet of Dr. Caligari.*

putting up with a lot of stupidity.

James Agee punctured this hot air balloon when he called *Dreams that Money Can Buy* "arch, snobbish, and sycophantic, about as experimental as a Chemcraft set."

Dead of Night (1945) is probably the best omnibus of stories about the occult ever assembled. No one who has seen it will forget Cavalcanti's direction of Sir Michael Redgrave as the schizophrenic ventriloquist with the frightening dummy. The American Film Institute omitting it from its list of the 100 best thriller movies was dumb, but the AFI's lists are often very debatable and far too anxious to hype living actors and directors.

In the story that links the dream sequence opening and the

tricky ending, an architect is called to a country house. He wakes from a dream that he is murdering someone, drives to the country house—important shot of it as he turns the last corner of the road—and in the house is told weird stories commented upon by a psychiatrist. They are tales about a haunted mirror, a hearse driver, etc. At the point of the murder the architect awakes from a dream again and as the film ends he is driving back around that corner, the country house in the distance.

Dream a Little Dream (1989). You may have seen far too many films in which the mind of an adult is transferred to a child, or *vice versa*. A bad movie with a worse sequel has an old couple on bikes run into teenagers and, lo and behold! The old couple "with the young minds" are transported to a permanent dream-like state. *VideoHound's Golden Movie Retriever* gives it two bones and claims it's the "same old switcheroo made bearable by cast:" son of Jason Robards, some relative of Rocco, Piper Laurie, etc. But I say it's a dog.

Dream Girl (1947). This was a play Elmer Rice wrote for his wife, Betty Field. It had some success on the boards on Broadway but really lost it when Betty Hutton was miscast in a movie version.

MOSTLY SECOND FEATURES OR SECOND RATE—
BUT THERE ARE ALSO SOME TERRIFIC MOVIES HERE

Maybe we had better put the plentiful losers among the occasional winners for comparison and contrast and even go alphabetical so you can keep track of things. I admit that not all these movies are great movies.

If you know little about dreams and dreamers in movies you are going to be surprised to see what evidence there is of an obsession with such material and how easily dream-related materials transfer to the screen. Bring it on!

Let's get a few duds out of the way first: *Seizure; Bad Dreams; Dream Demon; I, Madman.* These few are enough to illustrate some of the most frequent ways in which dream movies fail artistically and commercially.

Here, for instance, is a Cinerama B-movie directed by none other than Oliver Stone. In *Seizure* (1973) Jonathan Frid—remember *Dark Shadows* on the boob tube?—is joined by Martine Beswick as a Queen of Evil, a repulsive dwarf (Hérve Villechaize), a black executioner, and I don't know what all. Oh, Troy Donahue.

The baddies are materialized out of Frid's dreams. The fame of Frid, I suppose, convinced the young Oliver Stone he could cheaply rent a supposedly haunted house up in Canada and knock off a passable picture. He was wrong.

Bad Dreams (1988), Jennifer Rubin, Bruce Abbott, Susan Barnes—need I go on? It seems there's this woman who wakes up from a 13-year coma and now has to face nightmares. (Wouldn't it be awful if people in comas had recurrent nightmares?) Her former guru, a Jim Jones kind of guy, is trying to get her to kill herself. It would be a good career move. Psychiatrists often appear in dream movies; they are generally incompetent or worse. The doctors of the mad and the mad doctors of horror movies get all mixed up and patients suffer.

Dream Demon (1988). After a thrilling dream sequence at the start this one goes downhill all the way as Jemma Redgrave turns over in her mind whether she should turn over her body to Mark Greenstreet. It is set in your standard creepy British mansion with the not infrequently included American (this one played adequately by Kathleen Wilhoite). One or even more than one dream sequence does not a good movie make.

Dream Flight (1982) is a Canadian computer-animated film. P. Bergeron, N. Magnenat-Thalmann, D. Thalmann.

I, Madman (1989) has a character out of a pulp fiction of the same

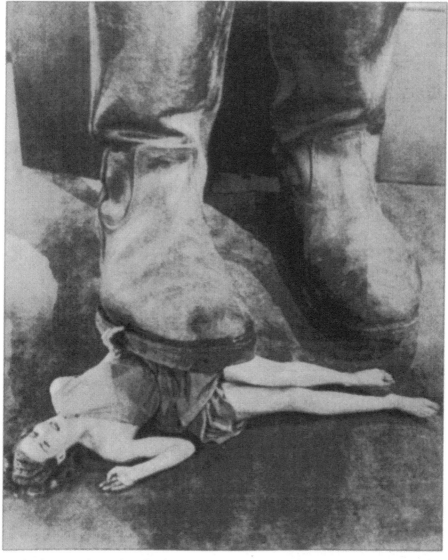

Trick photography makes the fantastic perils we may encounter in dreams visible to moviegoers when awake in the dark. Here we have the unconcious right before our eyes. "Thinking in pictures," wrote Freud in *The Ego and the Id*, "approximates more closely to the unconcious processes than thinking in words, and it is unquestionably older than the latter both ontogenetically and phylogenetically."

title that gets into a woman's dreams. The special effects are the main reason for this thing and the fellow who provided them (Randall William Cook) was rewarded with the lead in the movie. You have to see it to believe it. But this kind of movie really doesn't require acting talent.

As I write, there is a Jennifer Lopez movie where somebody gets into somebody else's dream and causes some havoc. Fads such as "dream linkage" are not solid enough basis for plots of dream movies.

Now we shall go alphabetical and a little less horrific as we consider more film features in which there are dreams and dreamers.

L'Age d'or (The Golden Age, 1930). This is essentially an anti-Catholic diatribe by Luis Buñuel. He was a bizarre maverick who attended orgies with Chaplin, smoked opium with Cocteau, and had his horoscope cast by André Breton. Though his pictures could be as enigmatic as some dreams, Buñuel was a cinema force for half a century after

Un Chien andalou (1928). The eyeball sliced in one of his shocking films or the dreamy beauty of some of his other startling films are unforgettable trademarks. The dreamlike quality in this particular film comes chiefly from the surrealism that remains from the collaboration of Salvador Dalí. Dalí wanted his name taken off the final product, but this film represents the surrealist-dream approach that was widely imitated thereafter.

Alice in den Stadten (Alice in the Cities, 1974) is a semi-amateur (Filmverlag der Authoren, which could be translated as something like Filmmakers' Collective) low-budget Wim Wenders film with Yella Rottländer as the nine-year-old Alice.

Bienvenido, Mr. Marshall (Welcome, Mr. Marshall, 1952). General Marshall of the Marshall Plan (American money to rebuild Europe after World War II) is going to help an "ordinary little village" in this comedy directed by Luis G. Berlanga with José Isbert, Manuel Morán and Lolita Seville. Each person expects a handout from the Americans, and we see the dreams of the mayor, the nobleman, and the village priest.

The Blood of Dr. Jekyll (1981, also known as *Dr. Jekyll and Miss*

Osbourne and *Dr. Jeklyll et les femmes*). Walerian Borowczyk had already shown his fetish interests in his *Une Collection particulière* of 1974 by the time he got to this retelling of the famous RLS story with an emphasis on the eroticism in clothes and other objects. What in dreams might be important symbols appear in the film as fetish objects imbued with great eroticism. It's memorable for certain images rather than the many acts of violence, an air rather than an anarchy.

A Caddy's Dream (1911 silent, only 385 feet, from Majestic). A caddy who should be searching for a golf ball dreams he has slept for 20 years.

The nuttiest rip-off of the long-

Martha Mansfield is not unruffled as John Barrymore attacks as Mr. Hyde in *Dr. Jekyll and Mr. Hyde* (1920).

sleep story may be *Iceman* (1984). John Lone is a thawed-out prehistoric man who has trouble adjusting to a changed world. Figures.

Le Cake-Walk infernal (The Hellish Cakewalk, 1903). This George Méliès silent film represents all the photographic tricks in early popular entertainments derived from dream experience in which parts of the body—in this case the bodies of skeletons in a *danse macabre*—separate and act on their own. Méliès was an imaginative pioneer of special effects.

Deadly Blessing (1981). Here we have horror-movie honcho Wes Craven among rural religious cultists with nightmares—a spider falls into a girl's mouth and an *incubus* is painted on a barn door. The barn owner is killed by a tractor, which may or may not have some relation to Stephen King's nasty car in *Christine*. One critic pointed out that in Britain the supernatural aspects of *Deadly Blessing* were played down, which, in his view, would have been much better to the fore. Ernest Borgnine, Sharon Stone, Lois Nettleton, and others do surprisingly well with this material.

Dream No Evil (1975). A crazed nightmare victim has to commit murders to protect her dream fantasies. Oh, come on! Edmond O'Brien, Brook Mills, Marc Lawrence. John Hayes directing. I am even ready to feel sorry for Susan Hayward when she gets the electric chair for overacting with malice aforethought but I cannot abide this woman in *Dream No Evil.*

Deserto Rosso (Red Desert, 1964). The films of Michelangelo Antonioni are all relevant to our subject. This example—he co-wrote the screenplay with Tonino Guerra—is pure Antonioni, with Monica Vitti, Richard Harris, and Carlo Chionetti. It is a mixture of dream and reality in high style.

A DREAM SERIES OF SHOCKERS

Slumber Party Massacre (1982) was followed by *Slumber Party Massacre 2* (1987) and *Slumber Party Massacre 3* (1990). Crystal Bernard (from *Wings*) was the star that made the series a hit.

The history is interesting. Rita Mae Brown (eventually known as the feminist author of *Rubyfruit Jungle*) wrote a screenplay entitled *Don't Open the Door.* Apparently, Roger Corman didn't open the script. It was found years later by Amy Jones, fresh out of film school at MIT, and made into a most unfeminist 1982 slasher movie.

It energized this gory genre and after the likes of *Sorority House Massacre* and other damsel-in-distress (and dismemberment) films, came the *Friday the 13th* string of frights.

MORE DREAMS

Don Chichote (*Don Quixote,* 1933) was an attempt to present the great world masterpiece on the screen. G. W. Pabst went all out with Feodor Chaliapin, George Robey, Renée Valliers and more, but (as Otto Bond says in *Fifty Foreign Films,* 1959) "*Don Quixote* is inaccessible to translation on the screen," or has proved so thus far except for the Nureyev ballet movie. Maybe emphasizing a dream structure would do it. There is a dream of the Don in a cave in the original, and the scenario could begin with the Don falling asleep over his books on chivalry and end with his waking up to reality, even the tilting at windmills being a phantasmagoric dream.

Ta Chromata tis Iridias (The Color of Iris, 1974). This gift from the Greeks, directed by Nikos Panayotopoulos (who also wrote it), has some convincing performances (Nikitas Tsakoroglu, George Dialegmenos, Vangelis Kazan) and at one point a leading character who is trying to write a musical gets his finale from a dream.

Dreamchild (1985) has a finely crafted performance by Coral

Browne and an excellent screenplay by Dennis Potter. Ian Holm is also good. The director was Gavin Miller. The story is of Alice Liddell, the little girl for whom Lewis Carroll wrote *Alice*. As the movie opens she is Mrs. Alice Hargreaves. It is some 70 years later than when she sat for the pederastic clergyman's revealing photos and was rewarded with a starring role in an immortal story. In 2001 Mrs. Hargreaves' personal effects were auctioned. She still attracts interest.

Coral Browne makes Alice into a complex if not entirely likeable old biddy. The fantasy sequences are first rate. Jim Henson and friends help a lot. Undoubtedly you have read the *Alice* stories. They are classic, so if you have not, deny it and take the earliest opportunity to rectify the problem.

Alice abounds in dream qualities.

Dreamaniac (1987). Directed by David DeCoteau (a name close enough to the French for knife) has a succubus in it. The succubus makes short work of heavy-metal rocker Adam (Thomas Bern). His psychiatrist (Brent Black) is no help and Adam should never have eaten those hash brownies in the first place.

Dreamer (1979) is worth noting to alert you to misleading titles. This movie is about bowling.

Dreaming (1944). In case you skipped over an earlier mention of this British comedy here it is again. Hazel Court, Dick Francis are on hand for the fun. It's about the level of Benny Hill and his Hill's Angels, but without as much nudity or lewdity.

The Dreaming (1989) is a video (no cinema record I could find) about a young doctor wandering between fact and fantasy in supernatural fog.

Dream Lover (1986). Kristy McNichol, Ben Masters, Paul Shenar, directed with a heavy hand by Alan Pakula. Kathy (McNichol)'s recurrent nightmares drive her into the clutches of the psychiatrist Dr. Michael Hansen (Masters) of the Yale University Sleep Laboratory. Gail Hunnicutt and some others do yeoman work to save this picture. The plot, however, works against them a good deal of the time.

Kathy feels guilty at having stabbed a guy who wanted to rape her and winds up stabbing her own father. Fathers, by the way, honestly reflected or distorted, are frequently seen in dreams as the movies report them, and are often up to no good.

A Dream of Love (1938). "A dream of love is just a dream of you, dear…" Franz Schubert's *Liebestraum* (Dream of Love) was portrayed by a pop song and a pop movie. Franz was gay, but Hollywood didn't know that in the thirties. Therefore Franz (played by Ian Colin), thwarted in heterosexual passion, dashes off a beautiful memory at the pianoforte. Not a dream in the usual sense but a dream in the biopic sense.

Dreams Come True (1984). This is just your cup of weak tea if what you are dreaming about is out-of-body body contact. It's a comedy directed by Max Kalmanowicz. There was an earlier movie (reissued in 1943) of this title, directed by Reginald Denham, in the "Dream Lover" operetta mode.

Dreamscape (1984). It's the cold war. There's a plot against POTUS (President of the United States). Bring on Dennis Quaid, Max von Sydow, Eddie Albert (as the president), Kate Capshaw, Christopher Plummer as the principal villain, and other fantasy workers.

This is essentially an action movie. The premise rests on the supposition that your therapist should go beyond listening to you rattling on about your dreams and get right *into* them to see what is rattling you. "Don't just raise the hood, Doc, get under the car." That would be nice.

Dream Street (1921). Obviously an old silent, but it can stand for all the more modern dreamers, whether they are constructing baseball diamonds (*Field of Dreams*) or just yearning for money and fame, like Katharine Hepburn in *The Rainmaker*. Have a look at the beginning of *Risky Business* or the end of *Pretty Woman* for the oft-repeated Hollywood and Dreams mantra.

This movie is set in Limehouse, an East End milieu in London, attractive to cinematographers because of its fog-shrouded dockland alleys, rough sailors, inscrutable Chinese, etc. The three who have dreams are Carol Dempster, Ralph Graves, and Charles Emmett Mack. Tyrone Powers' father is in this one, too.

Dream Trap (1990). The girl of your dreams can interfere with establishing a successful relationship in the real world. People mooning about are often dismissed as "dreamers," and so, of course, are those whose imaginations and inventions go unappreciated by ordinary folks. This film was written and directed by Tom Logan. It starred Kristy Swanson, Sasha Jensen, *et al.* Audiences expecting to enjoy someone trapped in dreams were only trapped in the movie theater.

The Electronic Monster (also called *The Dream Machine*) and based on Eric Maine's novel *Escapement*) was directed by Montgomery Tully and starred Rod Cameron, Mary Murphy, Meredith Edwards, Peter Illing, and Kay Callard in a story of a machine supposed to cure psychosis which really only produced hallucinations allowing the baddy to gain power over the patients. Cinema historians debate but are not vocal enough in complaint about the film being released, whenever it was made.

Farewell, My Lovely (1975) is based on Raymond Chandler's Philip Marlowe detective story *Murder, My Sweet*. Detective stories permit us to get involved in sticky situations without danger or guilt. We have all of the fun of identifying with the Bad Guy while feeling sure, most of the time, that the Good Guys will get him.

In this outing, Robert Mitchum plays the dick. The way he portrays Marlowe looks half-awake or half-stoned; it is impossible to tell which. The plot, the soul of all stories says Aristotle, is honest enough. Looking into the past always involves some night dreaming and day-dreaming.

Fear in the Night (1946). Did you ever dream you had murdered someone? The protagonist of this thriller is worried that he has committed the crimes that crop up in his nightmares. He hires a private detective and they wind up in a creepy mansion. (Where else?) This one has a room of mirrors as well as a lot of smoke and mirrors in a tricky plot. Paul Kelly, DeForest Kelley, Ann Doran, Robert Emmet Keane, screenplay and direction by Maxwell Shane.

Paul Kelly may have been assisted in this film by the fact that in real life he spent a couple of years in jail in the twenties for manslaughter. He killed the ex-husband of the woman he later married.

Fröken Julie (Countess Julie, usually translated as Miss Julie, 1951). Alf Sjöberg's masterful handling of August Strindberg's classic play of the aristocrat with a recurrent dream and a dangerous liaison. This is one of the great Swedish films.

Glen or Glenda (1953). Ed Wood has been singled out as the klutziest of Hollywood directors. I happen to think that is like trying to identify the ugliest horse in a glue factory. People mock his sci-fi movies, in which paper plates are used for UFOs, and his employment of Béla Lugosi on his last legs, and of course this "documentary" about transvestism, starring Wood himself. The dream sequences are especially bad, but the whole thing is ridiculous. You will swear at it or by it, depending upon your cult condition.

L'Histoire d'Adèle H. (The Story of Adele H., 1975). The initial stands for *Hugo;* she is the daughter of the famous French writer of the nineteenth-century, and this film is by one of the most famous film *auteurs* of the twentieth-century, François Truffault. Every one of his movies relates much more than superficially to dreams and dreamers. Isabelle Adjani makes this film a must-see.

Horror Dream (1947)—not seen—was Sidney Peterson's underground dance film. Dance was the excuse for many dream sequences (or vice versa) in old musicals, you know.

In Between (1992). For those who regard death as an awakening to an afterlife, there is this thinking-man's drama about three people (Amy, Jack, and Margo) who wake up to discover they are "in between" this life and the next. They have to review their lives and decide whether they want to "wake up" and continue living or accept death and enter the next world.

Jujiro (Crossroads, Japanese, 1928). Directed by Teinosuke Kinugasa, this film has a hero who dreams that arrows are being shot at him, cats are attracted to his wounds, and more.

Juliet of the Spirits (1965). In this dreamy wonder Federico Fellini features his wife, Guillietta Massina, and offers what well might be regarded as the feminine answer to *Otto e mezze* (1963), the famous *81/2*. Not everyone approved of the way Fellini made his dreams into movies. John Simon called *Guilietta degli spiriti* "brilliant, precise, and tasteless."

Juliette ou la clef des songes (Juliet or the Key to Dreams, French, 1950). Marcel Carné directed this screenplay by Jacques Viot with Gérard Phillipe and Suzanne Cloutier. It is about escape into a world of dreams.

Kavalier Zolotoy Zvezdy (1950), they tell me, has something to do with dreams but I suspect Semion Babayevsky was perpetuating socialist realism.

Lady in the Dark (1944). The stage play was pop psychology, by Moss Hart, an unthinking man's thinking man. The movie version, I think, was improved by the substitution of dream sequences for some of the banal banter. Once in a while we are tempted to say with Shirlee the radio advice-maven in *Straight Talk* (1992): "Get off the cross. Somebody needs the wood."

The Last House on the Left (1972). The famous chisel nightmare, forever recalled by anyone who has seen this Wes Craven movie more or less stolen from Ingmar Bergman's *The Virgin Spring* (1959), but while in Bergman (who borrowed from a medieval ballad) the parent mourns over the daughter raped and killed and exacts a very messy revenge, the action is a bit different here.

In this period of American life, certain movies pretended to be down on sexual degradation and violence but really were exploiting it, all the while tut-tutting that such things were all around us.

The Lathe of Heaven (1980). This is based on popular science-fiction writer Ursula LeGuin's superior novel. A young fellow has dreams of a better and less polluted world but the dreams can have bad fallout. Directed by David Loxton, it stars Bruce Davidson, Margaret Avery, and Kevin Conway.

Marius (1931). To "dream of" can mean simply "yearn for" rather than to actually dream about, but we need to note at least one of these. So here is the first of Marcel Pagnol's trilogy. *Fanny*, a film of 1932, and *César*, a film of 1936, complete the set. You have probably heard more about *Fanny* the film of 1961. Marius dreams of going to sea and leaves Fanny behind, no pun intended.

Mirt sost shi amit (Harvest 3000, 1975). Hold onto your hats, because I have reached very far for some example of the fact that dreams and dreamers occur in even the most obscure and unlikely movies. This one is not a clumsy Philippine horror movie or anything like that. It is Ethiopian! Directed by Haile Gerima (an Ethiopian trained at UCLA's film school), this tale is about how Kebebe (played by Gebru Kassa), is thought to be off his rocker but is merely demonstrating the craziness of his society. It touches on dreams.

Moemoea (The Dream, 1980) was shot in Tahiti, the paradise of many people's dreams. An escaped convict winds up in the hay (or palm fronds) with not one but two beautiful maidens—but it may all be a dream.

Monkey Bone (2001). An accident produces a coma and animated nightmares. Not funny.

Mondo di notte 3 (World of Night 3, 1963). This is one of the trashy *mondo* movies the Italians churned out. This one was also called *Ecco* (Look). It has a piece on hypnosis used to try to stop Japanese tots from bedwetting. The *Mondo cane* (World of Dogs) approach was to present the sleazy as sociology. Don't look.

Murder in the Old Red Barn (1931) was a filming of the nineteenth-century melodramatic but true story of Maria Marten that was mentioned in the chapter on dreams in literature. This awkward version starred Tod Slaughter and Sophie Stewart.

Nightmare (1963) is a Jimmy Sangster UK thriller in which a young woman, who, witnessed her crazy mother killing her father as a child. Now she has nightmares that she, too, might be insane. The fear you might go insane can drive you entirely around the bend. That's what happened to Guy de Maupassant. Here it's the nightmare in which an insane mother invites a girl to join her in the looney bin, a plot of a

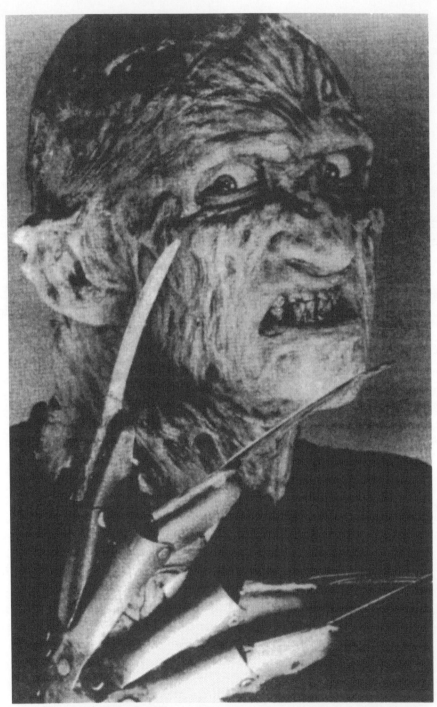

The scariest thing about Freddy from *Nightmare on Elm Street* was that the picture was not laughed off the screen by the American cinemagoers.

wicked guardian to drive the girl to murder. There's a better *Nightmare* film, starring Edward G. Robinson.

In the world of literature and narrative, all sorts of nightmares can be used to punish the guilty, but on occasion they punish the innocent.

Nightmares can be much more dangerous than Vincent Philip d'Onofrio tells Michael Lewis they are: "Dreams are just stories people tell themselves when they are asleep." (*Signs of Life*, 1989.)

Nightmare Castle (1966). Mario Caians directed this Italian production—his real name is Alan Grunewald—with horror Queen Barbara Steele. Murder and disfigurement, ghosts and vampires, and hearts in an urn, causing nightmares. They would, wouldn't they?

Nightmare on Elm Street (1984) brought horror to quiet suburban neighborhoods and vast riches to Wes Craven. Kids started to worry about highschool staff. Teens rule.

Nightmares (1983) is a clutch of horror tales resembling *Tales from the Crypt*, *Twilight Zone*, *Creepshow*, and others of a type little Daisy Ashford would describe as "piffle in the wind." Moviemakers would describe such shows as blockbusters. They make money hand over fist. They introduce into terrene life the terrors of the supernatural and are (to some) scarier than real-life maniacs with chainsaws or serial killers with human heads in the fridge. Everyday occurrences take on the ingredients of a nightmare when one of these unexplained horrors breaks through into suburban life. One episode of *Nightmares* has my favorite appearance of Moon Unit Zappa, not easy to find on film. There are few other rewards for your patience.

The Night My Number Came Up (1955). Leslie Norman directed this film when Ealing Studios were making an international name. Victor Goddard wrote the true story of a dream of a plane falling out of the sky that came true. R. C. Sheriff (playwright of *Journey's End*) wrote the screenplay. The cast boasted Sir Michael Redgrave, Denholm Eliot, Michael Horden, Mary Campbell, and Alfie Bass. We have here an unusual example of a veridical dream in a movie.

Night Scare (1993). Since Mary Shelley's *Frankenstein* the general public has been afraid of scientific progress, or afraid it will go wrong and create a huge Love Canal, a worldwide Three Mile Island, another *Island of Dr. Moreau*. In the loser now before the court, Dr. Stephanie Lyell (played by attractive Elizabeth Hurley) tries still another of those attempts to rehabilitate a serial killer that always seem to go astray, so Marc Gilmour (Keith Allen) is able to get at new victims through their dreams. The story is by Harry Adam Wright; the decision to make this one is wrong.

The Night Walker (1964) finds Barbara Stanwyck chewing up the scenery over a faceless lover who keeps popping up in nightmares. Could it be her dead husband? Or is her husband, in fact, not really dead? William Castle's film of a Robert Block screenplay. Cast includes Robert Taylor, Llyod Bochner, Judith Meredith, Rochelle Hudson, and Jess Barker.

Nightwish (1989). A group of students conducting dream research gets caught up in this nightmarish plot and there are strange goings-on in a haunted house with threats both apparently real and imagined. In the end it all turns out to be a bad dream—or maybe not. Who cares? Bruce R. Cook and a crowd of unknowns (Clayton Rohner, Alysha Das, Elizabeth Kaitan, and more) are to be held responsible.

An Occurrence at Owl Creek Bridge (1962). If you have seen the movie, now read the Ambrose Bierce story. Bierce's puzzling disappearance in Mexico, by the way, became a novel by Carlos Fuentes and then a movie with Gregory Peck and Jane Fonda, *Old Gringo* (1989).

Oklahoma! (1955). Made in Arizona, the film of what may be Broadway's most hyped hit certainly did not actually need the standard musical dream ballet to flesh it out—it runs over two hours—but it can be mentioned to point out still again that the dream ballet was once as standard Broadway practice as bringing big musicals to the screen. Shirley Jones was first seen on screen in this big Rogers & Hammerstein film directed by Fred Zimmerman.

Orphée (1950). Jean Cocteau did the play, the screenplay, and the "realization" as the French say. Jean Marais and Maria Casarès move in a dream world of symbolism. This is a justly famous work of art.

Paperhouse (1988). In this British horror story a young girl draws a house on a piece of paper and visits it in her dreams. The screenplay by Matthew Jacobs is from Catherine Storr's novel *Marianne Dreams*. The British do this kind of thing pretty well.

En Passion (Passion, usually translated as The Passion of Anna, 1969). Ingmar Bergman's characters (Max von Sydow, Liv Ullman, Bibi Andersson) seem to behave as they do because of some underlying mechanisms, similar to the not unmotivated though puzzling violence often found in dreams.

Paul Delveaux (1987) is a Belgian film released under the English title *The Sleepwalker of Saint Iclesbald, Paul Delveaux*. It's an art film (Adrian Mabken), not much noticed.

Quai des brumes (Foggy Quay, 1938). French film idol Jean Gabin is Jean, gorgeous Michèle Morgan is Nelly. The Mediterranean port atmosphere is made palpable and Eugene C. McCreary writes in a reference book, "Almost every character in the film has a dream which is either unreal or unrealizable."

Reaching for the Moon (1917). Daydreams fulfilled were a staple of the silent movies. In this example Douglas Fairbanks, athletic and handsome if vertically challenged, is a moony department store worker who winds up as ruler of a kingdom. Directed by John Emerson.

A Romance of Wastdale (1921). This silent film, based on A. E. W. Mason's novel about life in Lancashire a long time ago, maybe one of the first important films to use the now intolerable "It was all a dream" excuse for closure. Anyone know any one earlier?

Sai ehaien bolan de bad (Tall Shadows of the Wind, Iranian, 1978). Directed by Bahman Farmanara with Faramarz Gharibian, Saïd Nikpour, and Nadia Khalipur. There is a terrible one-legged scarecrow in the field and Abdollah (Abdullah, Slave of God) has a nightmare of 16 scarecrows, etc.

Secrets of a Soul (1925, *Geheimnisse einer Seele*) may not be the first but it is certainly the first significant film with a really good dream sequence. A professor's incipient madness, brought on by sexual problems, among others, is cured by Freudian dream analysis.

Simon del Desierto (Simon of the Desert, Mexican, 1965). St. Simon Stylites sat on top of a pillar for years. He was one of the Christian equivalents of those Hindu holy men who do what we think of as totally nutty things. Luis Buñuel satirizes such sanctity (or silliness) in this typically Spanish *olla podrida* (sin, salvation, leatherboys on bikes, the inevitable Spanish-speaking dwarfs), with some dream or nightmare aspects.

Spellbound (1945), and I do not mean another movie of the same title (though that is also called *The Spell of Amy Nugent*, 1941) but the Ingrid Bergman and Gregory Peck film, directed by Alfred Hitchcock. The dream sequence was designed by Salvador Dalí.

Stairway to Heaven (1946, *A Matter of Life and Death* in its native UK) was the first motion picture to bring out the Royals for a Command Performance. To some Britons this was regarded as tantamount to Queen Victoria knighting an actor and making the profession respectable. I believe the Royals were not needed to make film important. In this positive and postwar film an engaging Royal Air Force pilot undergoing brain surgery dreams he is being put on trial in heaven.

The RAF pilot, foreground, watches himself on the operating table and, on the stairway, a heavenly host watches too.

Sleeping Beauty (1983). You can get this story in Disney animation (1959) or live-action (1989) but I prefer Bernadette Peters live with animation added, as in this "Faerie Tale Theater" version. I tend to think of fairytales as part reality and part art anyway.

Sleepstalker (1994). You can't keep a bad man down. Even though he's dead, The Sandman returns to strip the flesh from the bones of his victims. One reporter escapes from one of The Sandman's attacks and teams up with Kathryn Morris to defeat this monster cropping up in the reporter's nightmares. Also starring Jay Underwood and Michael Harris, this one is directed by Turi Meyer.

Steven King's Sleepwalkers (1992) drew what audience it did on the basis of the name of this modern master of the gory gothic. It is far from the best of King's works on the screen. Stephen King, Clive Barker, and others make brief appearances. The actors include Brian Krause, Madchen Amick, and others you never heard of. The mother and son in this movie go about at night as human sleepwalkers. You may doze off yourself despite cheap shocks that vainly hope to keep you riveted.

The Strange Ones (*Les Enfants terribles*, 1950) really came out of Jean Cocteau's opium dreams of decades before. Cocteau proves to be an interesting narrator of this film with Jean-Pierre Melville. The children are rather frightening orphans.

A Tale of Tails (1933). Horace Shepherd directs and comic Tony Handley narrates as Bert Coote, a drunk, dreams of foreign models. Bits of foreign film are shown.

Three Cases of Murder (1955) consists of short stories tied together by theme. There is some dream stuff in these stories of a haunted politician, a crazy taxidermist, and more. Directed by Wendy Toye, with David Eady, and George More O'Ferrall.

Topio stin omichli (Misty Landscape, Greek, 1988). This movie has a symbolic, mist-shrouded, stark setting rather like those in dreams and is equally imaginary: in the film Greece is supposed to border on Germany. This is an international production co-written and directed by Theo Angelopoulos. If "Greek movie" means *Never on Sunday* to you, see this.

If you can get over the fact that both of the lovers are played by females (males played by females is a Chinese tradition), you will love the sumptuousness of Li Han-hsiang's production from Hong Kong of *Chin-yu liang-yuan hung-lou meng* (rendered in English as *The Dream of the Red Chamber* [1977]).

Los Traidores (Traitors, Argentinian, 1973). Politically dangerous, this film has an unacknowledged director (he was really Raymundo Gleyzer) and an anonymous cast. In the film, Robert Barrera, a labor leader, dreams of his own assassination, and then it happens.

Un tranquillo posto di campagna (A Quiet Country Place, Italian, 1970). Directed by Elio Petri from a story by Petri and Tonino Guerra and a screenplay by Petri and Luciano Vincenzoni. The story is not bad: it is about an artist, beset by terrible nightmares, who retires to the peace of a country house but—wouldn't you know?—the house may be haunted. Or maybe someone or ones is/are determined to drive the artist 'round the bend.

Tristana (1970). One of those international productions, but this one has Catherine Deneuve in the title role. Don Lope (Fernando Rey) is her aging aristocrat lover. But she falls big time for the younger Franco Nero. There is a deaf and dumb son (Saturno), a campanile, dreams, more. Most of all, there is Catherine Deneuve.

Tuzoltó utca 25 (25 Fireman Street, 1973). A Hungarian goulash of fact and fancy, reality and dream. For a foreign-language oddity, try this one. It *does* relate to our subject.

Maybe this is the place to mention that dreams are prominent in both Chinese movies and in the products of Bollywood (Asian subcontinent) but I don't know much about them, and probably we cannot get to see them anyway or appreciate them if we do.

Tystnaden (The Silence, 1964). It would look less pompous to list films under their English titles but I want to put emphasis on dream material in foreign films, which can be (though never in the case of a Bergman movie) hard to come by. Still they make the point that it is not just Hollywood that has been a dream factory or an exporter of culture through the cinema. Here we have a film very unlike a Hollywood production in that the architecture of the screenplay is from dreams and the characters can be thought of as parts of the mind. Johan represents the ego, Ingrid Thulin as Ester is the superego, and Gunnel Lindblom as Anna is the id. Read Freud—or see Montgomery Clift in the movie bio. ("Could it be that dreams are ideas escaping from repressions in disguise?" You betcha, Doc.)

Ukigusa (Floating Weeds, made in Japan in 1959, released in the U.S. in 1970) can stand for a huge number of foreign films that are dreamlike in one way or another, from fuzzy photography to fuzzy thinking. The Japanese director Yasujiro Ozu made this one from a story of his own which had been knocking around for a long time: he had done a short and silent version much earlier in his long career. The story involves those colossal bores—as we in our culture see them unless we are precious and arty—Kabuki actors. It is tedious and melodramatic both, in the way that long dreams can sometimes be. But it does have the immediacy of dreams. What little occurs here does seem to be happening.

Valerie a týden divu (Valerie and the Wonder Week, Czech, 1970). Lots of dreamy people inhabit Czech movies, where yearning is a fulltime occupation. Vítézslav based this movie directed by Jaromil Jirés on a book. This is a classic. Jaroslava Schallerovna plays the little girl who has a wonderful week of dreams, fantasies, and nightmares, accompanied by some very strange actual occurrences. Helena Ányzova and Petr Kopriva are also excellent.

La Vie rêvée (1971) is a Canadian feminist film (Mireille Dansereau) also known as *The Dreamed Life* or *Dreamed Life*.

Wet Dreams (1977) is also known as *Dreams of Thirteen* but actually consists of the "dreams" of eight different directors. That of Nicholas Ray, says James L. Limbacher in his very useful book on *Sexuality in World Cinema*, shows himself "trying to exorcise his fear of incest."

When Knights were Bold (1936, reissued 1942, 1947). This comedy is in *The Connecticut Yankee at King Arthur's Court* mode. Jack Raymond directed it with bravura. Singers and comedian Jack Buchanan romp through medieval times in a dream and Martita Hunt turns up. She may have wound up on horror movies, true, but so did Maria Ouspenskaya and Bette Davis. Here Martita Hunt is a howl.

The Wiz (1978). Miss Ross is too old to be Supreme in this African-American version of *The Wizard of Oz*. This is Motown in Notown. Nonetheless, Lena Horne as the good witch is better than good—she is delightful. Michael Jackson plays a perky scarecrow. The movie was much hyped but lost millions of dollars despite lavish sets, Sidney Lumet direction, and Quincy Jones musical score.

The Wizard of Oz (1939). WOZ may or may not be about the gold standard but it does teach children to question authority. Oz is said to come from L. Frank Baum's filing cabinet (O-Z). (Possible. I once found a filing cabinet in the street with drawers marked M, N, O. I dragged it home and I use it for Miscellaneous, Non-Miscellaneous, and Other.)

But back to Kansas. Dorothy is hit on the head and in a dream is transported from Kansas. The whole famous children's story works "behind the curtain" of dream symbolism. Many have been the political, sexual, and other readings of this dream of a movie, a favorite with generations of movie lovers.

Your author may be one of the very few living proponents of the theory that the whole thing would have been a better flick had Shirley Temple not turned down the lead and someone who could act rather than just mug had been given the lion's share. Bert Lahr's insufferable simpering and clumsy overacting mar a good show. If you are very intellectual, subject this object to Walter Benjamin in terms of fantasy and fashion, allegory and reality. If you are interested in background, see Mark Evan Swartz, *Oz before the Rainbow* (2000); he describes what preceded the 1939 filming of the story.

I do not state my opinions to offend you but I do want to point out that *opinions differ*. People can get quite upset when someone states a opinion contrary to the one they cherish. That is a tried and true fact and technique, therefore we have to be considerate and cautious when we approach the reading of symbols in art or in life. These are open to reaction and to different readings; just like scripts, just like dreams.

The way to fight the most tenaciously held beliefs that people have is with your hat. Grab it and run. If you do stand and fight, expect bitter resistance: nobody loves a fact man.

The Wonderful Ice Cream Suit (1998). Ray Bradbury's "The Magic White Suit" is the basis of this comedy in which several people get to don the suit that can make their dreams (daydreams or actual dreams) come true.

I'LL SEE YOU IN MY DREAMS

This is the title of a memorable song by Gus Kahn and of the genial biopic starring Danny Thomas and Doris Day (1951). It is a remarkable movie in many ways besides the fact that a Christian plays a Jew. The title underlines one of the most important aspects of dreams: the ful-

fillment of wishes. In dreams if only in dreams we get what we want and need, which just goes to show you that the pop gurus are telling the truth; that you *are* OK and that in your unconscious you may even be your *own best friend*. If you have no friends you can watch TV, cable, and movies or at a stretch read for escape. When you go to sleep you can have friends, fun and frolic.

IT WAS ALL A DREAM

The producers requested silence about the ending of *The Strange Affair of Uncle Harry* (1945), starring George Sanders and Geraldine Fitzgerald, directed by Robert Siodmak, but at this junction I suppose we can let the cat out of the bag. The same kind of ending was put on the Jack Benny feature *The Horn Blows at Midnight* (also 1945). However, there we are alerted from the start: Benny falls asleep and dreams that he is an angel who has to sound the trumpet to announce the end of the world. Later he wakes up. "I just had the craziest dream. You know, if you saw it in the movies, you'd never believe it." Damn right.

HYPNOSIS

The person under hypnosis is (as the Greek word suggests) asleep, to some extent, but I would not say it involves dreaming. In any case, it will not hurt to notice that in *Svengali* (1931, etc.) a girl is hypnotized to make her sing, in *The Climax* (1944) another is hypnotized to prevent her from singing, and Dracula in innumerable films transfixes victims with his stare. In *The Double Life* (1912) a man hypnotizes his wife and, because he has lost money gambling, makes her rob her father. Her guilt is overwhelming and a psychiatrist figures out what has occurred. The doctor hypnotizes the wife and before witnesses she tells what her husband made her do under his hypnotic spell. The wily Dr. Mabuse (more later) and Dr. Fu Manchu are also criminally hypnotic.

In the two reels of *Double Trouble* (1915) Douglas Fairbanks plays wimpy Florian Amidon who, accidentally hit on the head, turns into blustering and pushy Eugene Brassford. Mde. Leclaire (played by Olga Grey) can call up either personality through hypnosis and, taking the best from both, creates a character that his lovely fiancée (played by Elizabeth Waldron) can safely marry. In *The Mask of Dijon* (1944) a madman who cannot cut the mustard hypnotizes an unfaithful wife to get her to shoot the paramour (but she loads up with blanks). The husband may have been shooting blanks as well, which would go far to explain her infidelity. In *Black Magic* (1948) Orson Welles played the mesmerizing charlatan.

Cagliostro was featured in a number of early films. There are always fads like this. The historical count was featured in *The Mirror of Cagliostro*.

Franz Anton Mesmer himself occurs in some films. Hypnotism is everywhere. In *Whirlpool* (1949), says Leslie Halliwell, Jose Ferrer "immediately after major surgery...hypnotized himself into leaving his bed and committing a murder." That was an Otto Preminger film.

See also *Fear in the Night* (1947, remade as *Nightmare* 1956) for murder under hypnosis. Hypnosis is not only a good way to get good information out of troubled or unwilling people; it is also a good plot device to get bad actions out of good people. Or someone can slip drugs into the punch.

Naturally, hypnosis is distinguishable from sleepwalking and drugged zombies (a fun feature of numerous films) as well as supernatural nightstalkers.

Here are some other selected films dealing with hypnosis:

The Criminal Hypnotist (1909). Directed by D. W. Griffith. I have not seen it and perhaps it has perished with other early celluloid.

Dr. Mabuse, der Spieler (Dr. Mabuse, the Gambler, German, 1921). Fritz Lang not only had his wife (Thea von Harbou) helping with the script but convinced her ex-husband (Rudolf Klein-Rogge) to play the bad doctor. He followed up next year with a sequel and the two films were put together for release as *The Fatal Passions* (1927). But that was not all. Then Lang did what we call *The Testament of Dr. Mabuse* (1932), but Dr. M. still would not die. There was more in a series, taken over by Wolfgang Preiss when Lang dropped it and more recently *Dr. M.* (1990) by Claude Chabrol. It was also released as *Club Extinction*, but for all we know Dr. M. is not extinct yet. He uses hypnotism well when he is up to no good.

The Evil of Frankenstein (1964). Freddie Francis (who turned from cameraman to director with great success for Hammer Films) directs Peter Cushing as Dr. F., who finds that he can thaw out his frozen monster for still another outing. The monster gets hypnotized this time.

Hypnotic Suggestion (Cricks & Martin, 1901). A hypnotist makes a man think he is a horse. Directed by Dave Aylott.

Invasion U.S.A. (1952). Regrettable fallout from nuclear-scare days. Story by Robert Smith (coauthor of screenplay) is alleged to have some hypnotism in it. I didn't bother to check when I saw it got only one bone from Videohound's critic. But we do need to note that hypnotism occurs even in some of the worst films.

The Mesmerist (G.A.S. Films, 1898). A hypnotist draws the "spirit" out of a person and then puts it back. Directed by G. A. Smith.

On a Clear Day You Can See Forever (1970). From the musical, with Barbra Streisand, Bob Newhart, Yves Montand. Director Vincente Minnelli. "Go To Sleep" is one of the lesser songs, not a direction to the audience. Previous incarnation revealed through hypnosis. Past-lives garbage is still popular with the mentally feeble. (Please do not write to me about that remark.)

Rasputin the Mad Monk (1965). A Hammer production with Christopher Lee as the randy Russian, Renée Asherton as the Czarina in his thrall, Barbara Shelley. Directed by Don Sharp. The movies love Rasputin, who was extremely difficult to kill.

The Rival Mesmerist (Hepworth, 1909). A brief comedy directed by Lewin Fitzhamon.

The Search for Bridey Murphy (1956). For quite a while a Colorado woman had some people convinced that under hypnosis she could describe a previous life as an Irish woman. Written and directed by Noel Langley, based on the book by her hypnotist, Morey Bernstein. Bridey Murphy was too often wrong about the Old Days. Today even past-lifers find the Bridey Murphy phase rather embarrassing.

Spell of the Hypnotist (1956). Seems to have sunk without a trace. Not available on video.

Svengali (1931). This film with John Barrymore is the best, despite his acting manner or mannered acting. Weaker remakes came in 1955 (Sir Donald Wolfitt) and, for TV, in 1983 (Peter O'Toole). The part encourages excess.

Zerakalo (The Mirror, 1975). Directed by Andrei Tarkovsky, a Russian filmmaker of whom I am especially fond, not solely because of his interest in dreams. Here hypnosis enters the picture. For dreams, see the dream-obsessed Andrei Gortchakov (played well by Oleg Yankovsky) in Tarkovsky's film known in English as *Nostalgia* (1983).

THE MAVENS AND THE MOVIES

Babington, Bruce & Peter William Evans, "The Life of the Interior—Dreams in the Films of Luis Buñuel, *Critical Quarterly* 27, (1985), 5–20.

Gledhill, Christine & Linda Williams, *Reinventing Film Studies* (2001).

Jean Marais as the beast and Josette Day as the beauty in Jean
Cocteau's film, *La Belle et le Bête* (1946).

Hollows, Joanne, *et al.*, *The Film Studies Reader* (2000).

Kaufmann, Stanley, *Regarding Film* (2001).

Kinder, Marsha, "The Adaptation of [Fellini] Cinematic Dreams,"
Dreamworks 1 (1980), 54–68.

Lederman, Marie Jean, "Dreams and Vision in Fellini's *City of Women*,"
Journal of Popular Fiction and Television 9:3 (1981), 114–122.

Mitry, Jean, *Semiotics and the Analysis of Film* (trans. C. King, 2000).

Petric, Vlada, "[Ingmar] Bergman and Dreams," *Film Comment* 17
(1981), 57–59.

Prince, Stephen, ed., *Screening Violence* (2000).

Stamp, Shelley, *Movie-Struck Girls* (2000).

Stempel, Tom, *American Audiences on Movies and Moviegoing* (2000).

THE SLEEPER'S SOUL IN FOLKLORE

Folklore in many cultures says you know that in sleep, as well as in
death, the soul can leave the body.

The movies, with their special effects and unusual hold over audiences, are extremely well-equipped to show you souls voyaging. The
movies consider death as oblivion trite, so they sometimes undertake to
show us other worlds. It is amazing that with all the drive to get new
story material the movies have not made more of relevant old folklore.

When they do snatch at its archetypes they can get *Star Wars* and other great hits.

SORGE

There has been a much closer connection between the other arts and that of the cinema than historians of the movies recognize. Literary critics focus on words, not movies. Films are seen chiefly by film people from the technical or the sociological angles. Let us turn to an example of literary work that demands more attention as influence on the twentieth-century cinema.

Der Bettler (1912), was directed by Reinhard Johannes Sorge, born in 1892 and killed at The Battle of the Somme (1916). His brief but important career in German literature initiated Expressionism, a "natural" for the movies. Sorge the poet's patricidal struggle against the oppressive father is the very essence of Freudianism, and so is the symbolism introduced into scenery and characters in this play.

THE MOVIEGOER

Lewis A. Lawson in "The Dream Screen in *The Moviegoer*," *Papers on Language and Literature* 30 (Winter 1994), 25–56, writes of how the central character, Binx, in Walker Percy's celebrated novel realizes his desire to return to the womb by his compulsive moviegoing and how the author finds a clever way of mediating Binx's feelings in the cinema. Walker Percy is one of those writers whose every line could inspire a filmmaker. Southern writers seem to have something special going for them in terms of movie raw material.

LATE-NIGHT NEWS

Martine Beswick was cast to appear in that Oliver Stone low-budget horror movie called *Seizure* (1973) and she later told the fanzine *Fangoria* 55: "Before I read the script, I had a nightmare about a giant threatening me with a knife. The next day I discovered it was a scene from the picture."

SOME RECENT PERIODICAL LITERATURE

Lindroth, James. "Down the Yellow Brick Road: Two Dorothys and the Journey of Initiation in Dream and Nightmare," *Literature/Film Quarterly* 18: 3 (1990), 160–163.

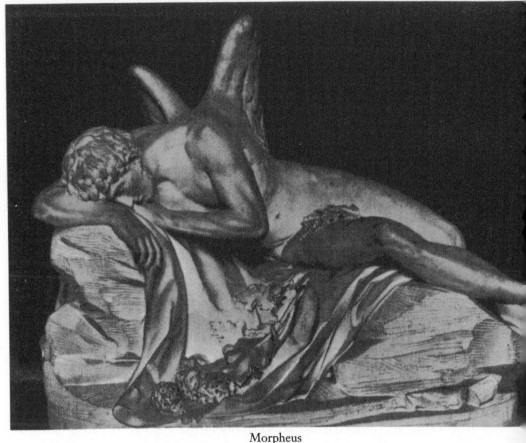

Morpheus

Petric, Vlada. "[Andrei] Tarkovsky's Dream Imagery," *Film Quarterly* 43 (Winter 1989- 1990), 28–34.
Thompson, Frank T. "Video Classics; Dream Logic," *American Film* 15 (March 1990), 68–70.
Wood, Michael. "Double Lives," *Sight & Sound* [NS] 1 (1992), 20–23.

DREAMS IN PORNOGRAPHY

"It was all a dream" is some help to porn merchants desperate for some scintilla of plot. This gimmick is sometimes used in such gay porn that bothers to have a story line. It likewise occurs in such heterosexual porn as *Dreams of Misty* (1985) with Long John Holmes and Misty Dawn, and *Dreams of Pleasure* (1988) with Ms. Dawn again, Ron Jeremy and Shana Grant.

Dream sequences are a natural for sexploitation films. These films must compete with the "dirty movies" we sometimes run in our sleeping heads and in which we make, out of the day's detritus and disappointments, stimuli and satisfactions.

TEN FAMOUS DREAMS OF THE MOVIES

Nina Foch, showing her psychiatrist sand in her shoes in *Shadows in the Night* (1944):

> I dream a woman comes to my window dripping wet. She looks as if she just walked out of the sea. She looks like a woman from another time. She seems to be part of the fog that drifts through the window. She crosses to the door. And, as she leaves she beckons to me to follow.... When the dream kept coming back night after night, I began to get the feeling that I was going to follow her into the ocean. Tonight, in my sleep, I must have gone down on the beach. Look."

Dorothy McGuire was not plain but she played a plain woman in *The Enchanted Cottage* (1945), "Women like me find refuge in our dreams, in which we are lovely and desirable as the most beautiful woman."

In *The Secret beyond the Door* (1948) Joan Bennett is an heiress and says on her wedding day to mentally disturbed millionaire Michael Redgrave, "I remember long ago I read a book that told the meaning of dreams. If a girl dreams of a boat or a ship she will reach a safe harbor. But if she dreams of daffodils she will be in great danger."

Eventually everyone has to give up the old childish act and do something important (marry, go to Hollywood), so Ann Jillian leaves Rosalind Russell—Rosalind Russell! whatever happened to Ethel Merman?—a farewell note in *Gypsy* (1962), the movie of the musical:

> I had a dream: me. My dream is like a nightmare, Mama. I dreamed I was a very old lady, but I was still doing the same old act. I was so ashamed of myself. I ran away, Mama—from the act, from your dreams, because they only made you happy and I want a dream of my own, my very own. I have to be like you, Mama. I have to fight for it. I started toward my dream three weeks ago, between shows. I-I married—Jerry.

Oskar Werner is not the name of a hot dog. It's the name of the ship's doctor in Katherine Anne Porter's *Ship of Fools* (1965). He moans:

When I had my heart attack, there was a dream I had. You can talk about death. I've seen it many times as a doctor, but you never know what it's like until it almost happens to you. I dreamed I had already died. I dreamed I was in a box. The sweat broke out all over my body. I wanted to cry out, "I can't be dead—I haven't lived!"

The grammar is not as good as the sentiment as Martin Sheen says to Jack Albertson (Academy Award for best supporting actor) in *The Subject was Roses* (1968):

There was a dream I used to have about you and I. It was always the same. I'd be told that you were dead, and I would run crying into the street. Someone would stop and ask, "Why are you crying?" And I would say, "Because my father is dead and he never said he loved me."

The cynical old novelist played by Sir John Gielgud in *Providence* (1977), "Oh, well, if one has led a fatuous life, one might as well have fatuous nightmares."

The Shakespearian actor on his last legs (and in *Lear*)—he's supposed to be Sir Donald Wolfitt—played by Albert Finney confides to his long-time dresser (Tom Courtenay) in *The Dresser* (1983), "I've had my dream again. Unseen hands driving wooden stakes into my feet, and I can't move."

Even cowgirls get the dreams. Consider Shari Shattuck as the woman confronting loneliness and lesbianism in prison in Paul Nicholas' *The Naked Cage* (1986), "Sometimes I have dreams about home. Like right now, I'm riding on Misty. That's my horse."

The German visitor's Polish dream-boy in *Death in Venice*.

VIDEOS

There are a number of videotapes on the subject of dreaming, few of them any good, from the physicist Fred Wolf on the dream state (*The Dreaming Universe*) to the Reverend Jim Wolfe's eight 55-minute sermons (*Dreams, the Divine Spark Within*). Dr. Stephan LaBerge discusses *Lucid Dreaming* techniques, Marcel Marceau has a mime called *The Dream*, and there is a two-part discussion of *Dream Appreciation* in Western culture. You can learn about Native American *Dream Catchers* or the *Dream Time* diary of a five-year-old. Wishing Well Distributors is one of the sources for videotapes on dreams. Also on videotape, of course, are many films dealing with dreams and dreamers. See your local Blockbuster or an equivalent.

DREAMS IN THE VISUAL ARTS

The film is the best medium so far for the translation of dreams into art that reaches the general public. In the cinema, or in films on television and video, the twentieth-century made the most influential use of the unconscious and the imaginative. Movies deal in powerful ways with the most crucial of human experiences. "Dreams and Fantasy," wrote Novalis [Friedrich von Hardenberg, 1772–1801] in his *Hymns to the Night* (1800), "are our most unique possessions."

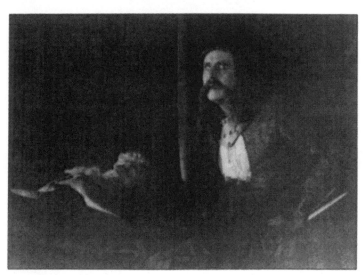

The first U.S. film (John Emerson, 1916) of Shakespeare's Scottish Play. King Duncan sleeps, and Macbeth (Sir Herbert Beerboh Tree, mugging) is going to go sleepless over this murder.

Detail of a Victorian painting imaginatively depicting Charles Dickens dreaming up his immortal characters.

6

A Little Treasury of Short Stories

Those who write clearly have readers; those who write obscurely have commentators.

—Albert Camus

HERE'S THE STORY

We all have dreams, but some people make them into prophecies— Euripides said that the best seers are those who guess the best—and some people make them into fictions. In this section, I offer you a small collection of short stories, as much as space allows, and I have chosen unusual popular tales. From exotic sources rather than more familiar or accessible ones.

We cannot begin to include all the works of fiction whose dénouements admit "it was all a dream." One interesting fictional dream is the Dionysian revel in the famous *Der Tod in Venedig* (Death in Venice, 1913) by Thomas Mann (1875-1955). Enraptured by a young Polish lad, Gustave von Aschenbach, an elderly German from Munich, finds his moral sense collapsing and in a dream his desires break out:

> That night he experienced a fearful dream—if dream is the right word for a mental and physical experience which did indeed come upon him in deep sleep as something apart from but real to his sense....its theater seemed to be his own soul, and the events burst in from outside it, violently overwhelming the

strong resistance of his spirit; it passed through him and left him, left the whole cultural construction of a lifetime trampled on, ravaged, and destroyed.

In fact Aschenbach does more than just observe, as in a theater, the orgy swirling around the strange god as the abandoned celebrants scream their wild cries (which end, Aschenbach notes, in a prolonged *u* sound as do the nicknames of the golden boy, Tadziu or Adziu) he finds himself shockingly and joyfully fully engaged in it. That is what he would like.

100 SHORT STORIES ABOUT DREAMS

Agnon, S. Y. *Metamorphosis.*
Aikens, C. P. *Mr. Arcularis.*
Alcott, Louisa May. *A Christmas Dream, and How It Came True.*
Asimov, Issac. *Dreaming is a Private Thing.*
Asquith, Lady. *In a Nutshell.*
Bartheleme, David. *A Few Moments of Sleeping and Waking.*
Bashford, H. H. *Crossing the Bridge.*
Bates, H. E. *Ring of Truth.*
Benét, Stephen Vincent. *The Danger of Shadows.*
Bennett, Arnold. *Dream.*
Blackwood, Algernon. *World-Dream of McCallister.*
Bloch, Robert. *All on a Golden Afternoon.*
Borges, José Luis. *The Circular Ruins.*
Bradbury, Ray. *The Last Night of the World.*
Brontë, Charlotte. *Adventure in Ireland.*
Buchan, John (Lord Tweedsmuir). *Basilissa.*
Burke, T. *The Dream of Ah Lum.*
Caldwell, Erskine. *The Dream.*
Carroll, Gladys H. *Three Times Dreamed.*
Cheever, John. *A Vision of the World.*
Clarke, Arthur C. *Inheritance.*
Cobb, Irvin S. *The Finger that Kills.*
Collins, Wilkie. *Dream-Woman.*
Coppard, A. E. *Big Game.*
Cost, M. *The Lady of Great Occasions.*
Deeping, Warwick. *Sand Dunes.*
de la Mare, Walter. *What Dreams May Come.*
Dickens, Charles. *A Christmas Carol.*

Dinesen, Isaak. *Echoes from the Hills.*

Dostoievsky, Feodor. *The Dream of a Ridiculous Man.*

Dumas, Alexandre. *Jean Ollier.*

Dunsany, Lord. *Jorkens' Ride.*

Ekberg, I. D. *Astral Plain—Land of Dreams.*

Farrell, James T. *When Boyhood Dreams Come True.*

Fiedler, Leslie A. *The Stain.*

Field, Eugene. *Sweet-One-Darling and the Dream-Fairies.*

Fitzgerald, F. Scott. *Winter Dreams.*

France, Anatole. *Jean Marteau.*

Freeman, Mary E. Wilkins. *Pot of Gold.*

Gale, Zona. *Herself.*

Gautier, Théophile. *The Mummy's Foot.*

Gogol, Nikolai. *Nevsky Prospekt.*

Harte, Bret. *Romance of the Line.*

Hawthorne, Nathaniel. *The Old Woman's Tale.*

Hearn, Lafcadio. *The Dream of Akinosuké.*

Henry, O. (W. S. Porter). *The Dream.*

Hughes, L. *Rude Awakening.*

Jacobs, W. W. *The Dreamer.*

James, Henry. *Great Good Place.*

James, Montague Rhodes. *Rose Garden.*

Kipling, Rudyard. *The Brushwood Boy.*

Korolenko, Vladimir. *Makar's Dream.*

Lägerlof, Selma. *Story from Jerusalem.*

LeFanu, James Sheridan. *Dream.*

Lessing, Doris. *Two Potters.*

Li Kung-tso. *A Lifetime in a Dream.*

Lovecraft, H. P. *Beyond the Wall of Sleep.*

Mansfield, Katherine. *Taking the Veil.*

Márquez, Gabriel García. *Monologue of Isabelle Watching it Rain in Macondo.*

Maugham, W. Somerset. *The Dream.*

Maupassant, Guy de. *The Horla.*

Maurois, André. *The House.*

Mérimée, Propser. *Djoumane.*

McCloy, H. *The Other Side of the Curtain.*

Moore, C.L. *Scarlet Dream.*

Morang, A. *Dream.*

Moravia, Alberto. *Words and the Night.*

Morris, William. *A Dream.*
Nemerov, Howard. *A Commodity of Dreams.*
Nin, Anaïs. *The Voice.*
Noailles, Countess of. *Fear of Being Useless.*
O'Byrne, C. *The Dream of Pilate's Wife.*
Onions, Oliver. *Phantasm.*
Pemberton, Sir M. *The Devil to Pay.*

Peretz, I. L. *The Days of the Messiah.*
Petrov, Alexander. *Dream of a Ridiculous Man.*
Phillpots, Eden. *The Dream.*
Pirandello, Luigi. *A Dream of Christmas.*
Poe, Edgar Allen. *The Angel of the Odd.*
Robin, R. *Pleasant Dreams.*
Russell, Bertrand (Earl Russell). *Dr. Southport Vulpes' Nightmare.*
Saki (H. H. Munro). *Bread and Butter Miss.*
Saroyan, William. *The Dream.*
Schreiner, Olive. *Three Dreams in a Desert.*
Schwartz, Delmore. *In Dreams Begin Responsibilities.*
Seawell, M. E. *Maid Marian.*
Shaw, Irving. *Age of Reason.*
Steele, Wilbur Daniel. *Due North.*
Tabori, Paul. *Fear.*
Thurber, James. *The Secret Life of Walter Mitty.*
Tolstoi, Leo (Count Tolstoi). *The Dream.*
Turgenev, Ivan. *Dream.*
Twain, Mark (Samuel L. Clemens). *My Platonic Sweetheart.*
Van Doren, Mark. *The Dream.*
Van Dyke, H. *Remembered Dream.*
Voltaire (Jean-Marie Arouet). *Plato's Dream.*
Wells, H. G. *The Dream.*
Wilde, Oscar. *The Young King.*
Wilhelm, K. *Perchance to Dream.*
Wilson, Leon. *Not Quite Martin.*
Wren, P. C. *As in a Glass Darkly.*
Young, R. F. *Wish upon a Star.*

And now a story in which it is up to you to say how much of it is a dream.

MAKAR'S DREAM

By Vladimir Galaktionovich Korolenko
(1852-1921)

This dream was dreamed by poor Makar, who herded his calves in a stern and distant land, by that same Makar upon whose head all troubles are said to fall.

Makar's birthplace was the lonely village of Chalgan, lost in the far forests of Yakutsk. His parents and grandparents had wrested a strip of land from the forest, and their courage had not failed even when the dark thickets still stood about them like a hostile wall. Rail fences began to stretch across the clearing; small, smoky huts began to crowd thickly upon it; hay and straw stacks sprang up; and at last, from a knoll in the center of the encampment, a church spire had shot toward heaven like a banner of victory.

Chalgan had become a village.

But while Makar's forebears had been striving with the forest, burning it with fire and hewing it with steel, they themselves had slowly become savage in their turn. They married Yakut women, spoke the language of the Yakuts, adopted their customs, and gradually the characteristics of the Great Russian race had been obliterated and lost.

Nevertheless, my Makar firmly believed that he was a Russian peasant of Chalgan, and not a nomad Yakut. In Chalgan he had been born, there he lived and there he meant to die. He was very proud of his birth and station, and when he wished to vilify his fellow-townsmen would call them his "heathen Yakuts," though if the truth must be told, he differed from them neither in habits nor manner of living. He seldom spoke Russian and, when he did, spoke it badly. He dressed in skins, wore "torbas" on his feet, ate doughcakes and drank brick-tea, supplemented on holidays and special occasions with as much cooked butter as happened to be on the table before him. He could ride very skillfully on an ox, and when he fell ill he always summoned a wizard, who would go mad and spring at him, gnashing his teeth, hoping to frighten the malady out of the patient and so drive it away.

Makar worked so desperately hard, lived in poverty, and suffered from hunger and cold. Had he thought beyond his unceasing anxiety to obtain his doughcakes and brick-tea? Yes, he had.

When he was drunk he would weep and cry, "Oh, Lord my God, what a life!" sometimes adding that he would like to give it all up and go on the "mountain." There he need neither sow nor reap, nor cut and haul wood, nor even grind grain on a hand millstone. He would be "be saved," that was all. He did not know exactly where the mountain was, nor what it was like, he only knew there was such a place, and that it was somewhere far away, so far that not even the District Policeman could find him. Of course there he would pay no taxes.

When sober he abandoned these thoughts, realizing perchance the impossibility of finding that beautiful mountain, but when drunk he grew bolder. Admitting he might not find that particular mountain, but some other, he would say: "In that case I should die." But he was prepared to start, nevertheless. If he did not carry out his intention, it was because Tartars in the village always sold him vile vodka with an infusion of mahorka [cheap tobacco] for strength, and this quickly made him ill and laid him by his heels.

It was Christmas Eve, and Makar knew that tomorrow would be a great holiday. This being the case, he was overpowered for a longing for a drink, but to drink there was nothing. His resources were at an end. His flour was all gone, he was already in debt to the village merchants and the Tartars, yet tomorrow was a great holiday, he would not be able to work, what could he do if he did not get drunk? This reflection made him unhappy. What a life it was! He had not even one bottle of vodka to drink on the great winter holiday.

Then a happy thought came to him. He got up and put on his ragged fur coat. His wife, a sturdy, sinewy woman, remarkably strong and equally remarkably ugly, who saw through all his simple wiles, guessing his intentions as usual.

"Where are you going you wretch? To drink vodka alone?"

"Be quiet I'm going to buy one bottle. We'll drink it together tomorrow."

He gave her a sly wink and clapped her on the shoulder with such force that she staggered. A woman's heart is like that; though she knew that Makar was deceiving her, she surrendered to the charms of that conjugal caress.

He went out of the house, caught his old piebald pony in the courtyard, led him by the mane to the sleigh, and put him in harness. The piebald soon carried Makar through the gates and then stopped and looked enquiringly at his Master, who was sitting plunging in thought. At this Makar pulled the left rein, and drove to the outskirts of the village.

On the edge of the village stood a little hut out of which, as out of the other huts, the smoke of a little fire rose high, high into the air, veiling the bright moon and the white, glittering hosts of stars. The flames crackled merrily and sparkled through the dim icicles that hung above the doorway. All was quiet inside the courtyard gates.

Strangers from a foreign land lived here. How had they come, what tempest had cast them up in that lonely clearing, Makar knew not, neither cared to know, but he liked to trade with them, for they neither pressed him too hard nor insisted upon payment.

On entering the hut, Makar went straight to the fireplace and stretched out his frozen hands over the blaze crying "Tcha" to explain just how the frost had nipped him.

The foreigners were at home; a candle was burning at the table although no work was being done. One man was lying on the bed blowing rings of smoke, pensively following their winding curves with his eyes, and intertwining with them the long threads of his thoughts.

The other was sitting over the fire thoughtfully watching the sparks that crept across the burning wood.

"Hello!" said Makar, to break the oppressive silence.

He did not know—how should he—that sadness filled the hearts of the two strangers, the memories that crowded their brains that evening, the visions they saw in the fantastic play of fire and smoke. Besides, he had troubles of his own.

The young man who sat by the chimney raised his head and looked at Makar with puzzled eyes, as if not recognizing him. Then, with a shake of his head, he quickly got up from his chair.

"Ah, good evening, good evening, Makar. Good. Will you have tea with us?"

"Tea?" Makar repeated after him. "That's good. That's good, brother; that's fine."

He began quickly to take off his things. Once free of his fur coat and cap he felt much more at ease, and, seeing the red coals already glowing in the samovar, he turned to the young man with exaggerated enthusiasm.

"I like you, that is the truth. I like you so, so very much; at night I don't sleep—"

The stranger turned, and Iabitter smile crept over his face.

"You like me do you?" he asked. "What do you want?"

"Business," Makar answered. "But how did you know?"

"All right. When I've had tea I'll tell you."

As his hosts themselves had offered him tea, Makar thought the moment opportune to press the point farther.

"Have you any roast meat?" he asked. "I like it."

"No, we haven't."

"Well, never mind," replied Makar soothingly. "We'll have that some other time, won't we?" And he repeated his question: "We'll have that some other time?"

"Very well."

Makar now considered that the strangers owed him a piece of roast meat, and he never failed to collect a debt of this kind.

Another hour found him seated once more in his sled, having made one whole ruble by selling five loads of wood in advance on fairly good terms. Now, although he had vowed and sworn not to drink up the money until tomorrow, he nevertheless made up his mind to do so today. What odds? The pleasure ahead silenced the voice of his conscience; he didn't forget the cruel dubbing in store for his self from his wife, the faithful and the deceived.

"Where are you going, Makar?" called the stranger laughing, as Makar's horse, instead of going straight ahead, turned off to the left in the direction of the Tartar settlement.

"Whoa! Whoa! Will you look where the brute is going?" cried Makar to exculpate himself, tugging hard at the left rein nevertheless and slyly slapping the pony's side with the right.

The clever little horse stumbled patiently away in the direction required by his master, and the scraping of the runners soon stopped in front of a Tartar house.

At the gate stood several horses with high peaked Yakut saddles on their backs.

The air in the crowded hut was stifling and hot; a dense cloud of acrid mahorka smoke hung in the air and wound slowly up the chimney. Yakut visitors were sitting on benches about the room or had clustered around tables set with mugs full of vodka. Here and there little groups were gathered over a game of cards. The faces of all were flushed and shining with sweat. The eyes of the gamblers were fiercely intent on their play, and the money came and went in a flash from pocket to pocket. On a pile of straw in a corner sat a drunken Yakut, rocking his body to and fro and droning an endless song. He drew the wild rasping sounds from his throat in every possible key, repeating always that tomorrow was a great holiday and that to-day he was drunk.

Makar paid his ruble and received in return a bottle of vodka. He slipped it into the breast of his coat and retired unnoticed into a corner. There he filled mug after mug in rapid succession and gulped them down one after another. The liquor was vile, diluted for the holiday with more than three-quarters of water, but if the dole of vodka was scant, the mahorka had not been stinted. Makar caught his breath after each draught, and purple spots circled before his eyes.

The liquor soon overpowered him; he also sank down on the straw, folded his arms around his knees, and laid his heavy head upon them. The same dreary, rasping sounds burst on their own accord from his throat; he sang that tomorrow was a holiday and that he had drunk up five loads of wood.

Meanwhile the hut was filling with other Yakuts who had come to town to go to church and to drink Tartar vodka, and the host saw that soon there would be no room for more. He rose from the table and looked at the company, and, as he did so, his eye fell upon Makar and the Yakut, sitting in their dark corner. He made his way to the Yakut, seized his by the coat collar, and flung him out of the hut. Then he approached Makar.

As citizens of Chalgan, the Tartar showed his greater respect; he threw the door open wide and gave the poor fellow such a kick from behind that Makar shot out of the hut and buried his nose in a snow-drift.

It would be difficult to say whether Makar was offended by this treatment or not. He felt snow up his sleeves and on his face, picked himself up somehow out of the drift, and staggered to where his piebald was standing.

The moon had by now risen high in the heavens and the tail of the Great Bear was dipping toward the horizon. The cold was tightening its grasp. The first fiery shafts of the Aurora were flaring up fitfully out of a dark, semicircular cloud in the north and playing softly across the sky.

The piebald, realizing, it seemed, his master's condition, trudged carefully and soberly homeward. Makar sat in his sled, swaying from side to side, and continued his song. He sang that he had drunk away five loads of wood, and that his old woman would kill him when he got home.

The sounds that burst from his throat rasped and groaned so dismally through the evening air that his friend the foreigner, who had climbed up onto his roof to close the mouth of the chimney, felt more than ever unhappy to hear Makar's song.

Meanwhile the piebald had drawn the sled to the top of a little hill from where the surrounding country could be distinctly seen. The snowy expanse lay shining brightly, bathed in the rays of the moon, but from time to time the moonlight faded and the white fields grew dark until with a sudden flash, the radiance of the Northern Lights streamed across them. Then it seemed as if the snowy hills and the forest that clothed them were coming very close, to withdraw one again into the distant shadow. Makar spied plainly through the trees the silvery bald crown of the little knoll behind which his traps were waiting for all the wild dwellers of the forest. The sight of this hill changed the tenor of his thoughts. He sang that a fox had been caught in one of his snares; he would sell the pelt in the morning, and so his wife would not kill him.

The first chimes of the church bells were ringing through the frosty air as Makar re-entered his hut. His first words were to tell his wife that a fox was caught in one of his traps, and as he had forgotten entirely that the old woman had not shared his vodka, he was violently surprised when she gave him a cruel kick, without paying any attention to his good news.

Later, as he lay prostrate on his bed, she managed to give him another blow to the back with her fist.

Meanwhile, the solemn, festal chiming of the bells broke over the Chalgan and floated far, far away into the distance.

He lay on the bed with his head burning and his vitals on fire. The strong mixture of vodka and mahorka was coursing through his veins and trickles of melting snow were running down his face and back.

His wife thought him asleep, but he was not sleeping. He could not get the idea of that fox out of his head. He had succeeded in convincing himself absolutely that a fox had been caught in one of the traps, and he even knew what trap it was. He saw the fox pinned under the heavy log, saw it tearing at the snow with its claws and struggling to be free, while the moonbeam stole into the thicket and played over its red-gold fur. The eyes of the wild creature were glowing at his approach.

He could stand it no longer. He rose from his bed, and started to find his faithful pony who was to carry him to the forest.

But what was this? Had the strong arms of his wife really seized him by the collar of his fur coat and thrown him back onto the bed?

No, here he was, already beyond the village. The runners of his sleigh were creaking smoothly over the hard snow. Chalgan had been left behind. The solemn tones of the church bells came floating along his trail, and on the black line of the horizon bands of dark horsemen in tall, pointed hats were silhouetted against the bright sky. The Yakuts were hurrying to church.

The moon went down, and a small, whitish cloud appeared in the zenith, shining and suffused, phosphorescent luster. It gathered size, it broke, it flickered, and rays of iridescent light spread swiftly from it in all directions, while the dark, semicircular cloud in the north grew blacker and blacker, more somber than the forest which Makar was approaching.

The road wound through a dense, low thicket with hills rising on either hand; the farther it advanced, the higher grew the trees, until at last the forest closed about it, mute and pregnant with mystery. The naked branches of the larches drooped under their loads of silvery rime. The soft radiance of the Aurora filtered through the treetops, and strayed across the frosty earth, unveiling now an icy glade, now the fallen trunk of some giant of the forest half-buried in the grass.

Another moment, and again all was sunk in murky darkness, full fraught with secrecy and silence. Makar stopped. Here, almost at the side of the road, were the first set of an elaborate system of traps. He could see clearly in the phosphorescent light the low stockade of fallen timber and the first trap—three long, heavy logs resting upon an upright post, and held in place by a complicated arrangement of levers and horse-hair ropes.

To be sure, these traps were not his, but might not a fox have been caught in them too? Makar quickly got out of his sled, left the clever piebald standing in the road, and listened attentively.

Not a sound in the forest! Only the solemn ringing of the church bells came floating as before from the distant, invisible village.

There was nothing to fear. Aliosha, the owner of the traps and Makar's neighbor and bitter enemy, was no doubt in church. Not a track could be seen on the smooth breast of the new-fallen snow.

Makar struck into the thicket—no one was there.

The snow creaked under foot. The log traps lay side by side like a row of cannon with gaping jaws, in silent expectation.

Makar walked up and down the line without finding anything, and turned back up the road.

But what was that? A faint rustle! The gleam of red fur near at hand in a spot of light! Makar clearly saw the pointed ears of a fox; it waved its bushy tail from side to side as if to beckon him into the forest, and it vanished among the tree trunks in the direction of his traps. Next moment a dull, heavy thud resounded through the forest, ringing out clearly at first, and the echoing more faintly under the canopy of trees, until it died softly away in the dark abysses of the forest.

Makar's heart leapt—a trap had fallen!

He sprang toward the sound, pushing his way through the undergrowth. The icy twigs whipped his eyes and showered snow in his face; he stumbled and lost his breath.

At last he ran into a clearing that he himself had made. Hoary white trees surrounded the little glade, and a shrinking path crept across it, with the mouth of a large trap guarding its farther end. A few more steps and—

Suddenly a figure of a man appeared on the path near the trap—appeared and vanished. Makar recognized Aliosha. He saw distinctly his short, massive, stooping form, and his walk like a bear's. His dark face look blacker than he had ever seen it, Makar thought, and his large teeth showed a wider grin than ever.

Makar was seized with genuine anger. "The scoundrel! He has been at my traps!" It was true that Makar had just made the rounds at Aliosha's traps, but that was a different matter. The difference was that when he visited other men's traps he felt afraid of being discovered, but when other men came to his traps, he felt indignation and a longing to lay hands on the man who had violated his rights.

He darted toward the fallen trap. There was the fox! Aliosha, too, was approaching with his shuffling bear walk; Makar must reach the trap first!

There lay the fallen log and under it glistened the ruddy coat of the captive creature. The fox was scratching at the snow with its paws exactly as Makar had seen it scratching in his dream, and was watching his approaching with bright, burning eyes, just as he dreamt it would.

"Titima! (Don't touch it!) It is mine!" cried Makar to Aliosha.

"Titima!" came Aliosha's voice like an echo. "It is mine!"

Both men ran up at the same moment, and both began quickly to raise the log, freeing the animal beneath it. As the log was lifted the fox rose too. It gave a little jump, stopped, looked at the two men with mocking eyes, and then, lowering its nose, licked the place that had been caught under the log. This done it hopped gaily away with a farewell flirt of its tail.

Aliosha would have thrown himself after it, but Makar caught him by the coat tails.

"Titima!" he cried. "It is mine!" And he started after the fox.

"Titima!" echoed Aliosha's voice again, and Makar felt himself seized, in turn, by the tails of his coat, and saw Aliosha dart forward.

Makar was furious. He forgot the fox and rushed after Aliosha, who now turned to flee.

They ran faster and faster. The twigs of the larches knocked the cap from Aliosha's head, but he could not stop to regain it,

Makar was already upon him with a fierce cry. But Aliosha had always been more crafty than poor Makar. He suddenly stopped, turned around, and lowered his head; Makar ran straight into it with his stomach and turned head over heels in the snow. As he fell that infernal Aliosha snatched the cap from his head and vanished into the forest.

Makar rose slowly to his feet. He felt thoroughly beaten and miserable. The state of his mind was pitiful. The fox had been in his hands and now—he thought he saw it again in the darkening forest wave its tail gaily once more and vanish forever.

Darkness was falling. The little white cloud in the zenith could barely be seen, and beams of fading light were flowing wearily and languidly from it as it gently melted away.

Sharp rivulets of icy water were running in streams over Makar's heated body; the snow had gone up his sleeves and was trickling down his back into his boots. That infernal Aliosha had taken his cap and Makar knew that pitiless cold does not jest with men who go into the forest without gloves and a hat.

He had already walked far. According to his calculations he should long since have been in sight of the church steeple, but here he was still in the forest. The forest held him in its embrace like a witch. The same solemn ringing came to his ears from afar; he thought he was walking toward it, but the sound kept growing more and more distant, and a dull despair crept into Makar's heart as its echoes came ever more faintly to his ears.

He was tired; he was choking; his legs were shaking under him. His bruised body ached miserably, his breathing strangled him, his feet and hands were growing numb, and red-hot bands seemed tightening around his bare head.

"I shall die!" came more and more frequently into his mind, but he still walked on.

The forest held its peace. It closed about him with obdurate hostility and gave him no light and no hope.

"I shall die!" Makar kept thinking.

His strength left him altogether. The saplings now beat him squarely in the face without the least of shame, in derision at his helpless plight. As he crossed one little glade a white hare ran out, sat up on its hind legs, waved its long, black-tipped ears, and began to wash its face, making the rudest grimaces at Makar. It gave him to understand that it knew him well, knew him to be the same Makar who had devised cunning means of destruction of it in the forest; but now it was its turn to jeer.

Makar felt bitterly sad. The forest grew more animated, but with a malign activity. Even the distant trees now threw their long branches across his way, snatched at his hair, and beat his face and eyes. The ptarmigans came out of their secret coverts and fixed their round, curious eyes upon him, and the wood-grouse ran in and out among them with dropping tails and angry, spreading wings, loudly telling their mates of him, Makar, and of his snares. Finally a thousand fox faces glanced from the distant thickets; they sniffed the air and looked derisively at him, pricking their sharp ears. Then the hares came and stood on their hind legs before him and shouted with laughter as they told of Makar's misfortune.

That was too much.

"I shall die!" thought Makar, and he decided to do so as quickly as possible.

He lay down on the snow.

The cold increased. The last rays of the Aurora flickered faintly and stretched across the sky to peep at Makar through the treetops. The last echoes of the church bells came floating to him from far away Chalgan.

The Northern Lights flared up and went out. The bells ceased ringing.

Makar died.

He did not notice how this came to pass. He knew that something should come out of him, and waited, thinking every moment that it would come, but nothing ever appeared.

Nevertheless, he realized that he was now dead, and therefore lay very still; he lay so long that he grew tired.

The night was very dark when Makar felt someone push him with his foot. He turned his head and opened his eyes,

The larches were now standing meekly and quietly over him, as if ashamed of their former pranks. The shaggy spruces stretched out their long snow-covered arms and rocked themselves gently, gently, and the starry snowflakes settled softly through the air.

The kind, bright stars looked down through the branches from the dark blue sky, and seemed to be saying: "See, a poor man has died!"

Over Makar's prostrate form and prodding him with his foot stood the old priest Ivan. His long dark cassock was white with snow; snow lay upon his fur hat, his shoulders, his beard. Most surprising of all was the fact that this was the same Father Ivan who had died five years ago.

He had been a good priest. He had never pressed Makar for his tithes and had not even asked to be paid for the services of the church; Makar had always fixed the price of his own christenings and requiems, and he now remembered with confusion that it had sometimes been extremely low and that sometimes he had not even been paid at all. Father Ivan never resented this, he had only required one thing; a bottle of vodka on every occasion. If Makar had no money, Father Ivan would send him for the bottle himself, and they would drink it together. The good priest always grew as drunk as a lord, but he fought neither fiercely or often. Makar would see him home, and hand him over, helpless and defenseless, to the care of the Mother Priestess, his wife.

He had been a good priest, but his end had been bad.

One day, when there was no one else at home, the fuddled Father, who was lying alone in bed, had taken into his head to smoke. He got up and staggered toward the great, fiercely heated fireplace to light his pipe at the blaze. But he was too drunk, he swayed and fell into the fire. When his family returned, all that remained of the little Father were his feet.

Everyone regretted good Father Ivan, but no doctor on earth could have saved him, as only his feet remained. So they buried the feet, and a new priest was appointed to replace Father Ivan.

And now Ivan himself, sound and whole, was standing over Makar, prodding him with his foot.

"Get up, Makar, old man!" he was saying, "and let us be going."

"Where must I go?" asked Makar with displeasure. He supposed that once dead he ought to be able to lie still, and there was no need now for him to be wandering through the forest, losing his way. If he had to do that why had he died.

"Let us go to the great Chief."

"Why should I go to him?" Makar asked.

"He is going to judge you," answered the priest in a sorrowful, compassionate voice.

Makar recollected that, in fact, one did have to appear at some judgment after one died. He had heard that in church. The priest was right after all, he would have to get up.

So Makar rose, muttering under his breath that they couldn't even let a man alone after he was dead.

The priest walked before and Makar followed. They went always straight ahead, and the larches stood meekly aside and allowed them to pass; they were going eastward.

Makar noted with surprise that Father Ivan left no tracks in the snow behind him; he looked under his own feet and saw no tracks either; the snow lay fresh and smooth as a tablecloth.

How easy it would be now he reflected, to rob other men's traps, as no one could find him out! But the priest must have read his secret thought, for he turned and said: "Kabis! (stop that!) You don't know what you will get for thoughts like that."

"Well, I declare!" exclaimed the disgusted Makar. "Can't I even think what I please? What makes you so strict these days? Hold your tongue!"

The priest shook his head and walked on.

"Have we far to go?" asked Makar.

"Yes, a long way," answered the priest sadly.

"And what shall we have to eat?" Makar inquired with anxiety.

"You have forgotten that you are dead," the priest answered turning toward him. "You won't have to eat or drink now."

Makar didn't like the idea in the least. Of course it would be all right in case there were nothing to eat, but then one ought to lie still as he did at first after his death. But to walk, and to walk a long way, and to eat nothing, that seemed to him to be absolutely outrageous. He began muttering again.

"Don't grumble!"

"All right!" he answered in an injured voice and went on complaining and growling to himself about such a stupid arrangement.

"They make a man walk and yet he shouldn't eat! Who ever heard of such a thing?"

He was extremely discontented as he followed the priest. And they walked a long way. Though Makar could not see the dawn, they seemed, by the distance they had covered, to have been walking a week. They had left so many ravines and hills behind them, so many rivers and lakes, so many forests and plains! Whenever Makar looked back the dark forest seemed to be running away behind them and the high snowclad mountains seemed to be melting into the murky night and hiding swiftly behind the horizon.

They appeared to be climbing higher and higher. The stars grew larger and brighter; from the crest of the height to which they had risen they could see the rim of the setting moon. It seemed to have been in haste to escape, but Makar and the priest had overtaken it. Then it rose again over the horizon, and the travelers found themselves on a level, very high plain. It was light now, much lighter than early in the night, and this was due, of course, to the fact that they were much nearer the stars than they had been before. Each one of these, in size like an apple, glittered with ineffable brightness; the moon, as large as a huge barrelhead, blazed with the brilliance of the sun, lighting up the vast expanse from one edge to another.

Every snowflake on the path was sharply discernable, and countless paths stretched across it, all converging toward the same point in the east. Men of various aspects and in many different garbs were walking and riding along these roads.

"Stop! Stop!" cried the priest, but Makar didn't even hear him. He had recognized a Tartar, an old acquaintance of his, who had stolen a piebald horse from him once, and who had died five years ago. That was the very same Tartar now, riding along on the very same horse! The animal was skimming over the ground, clouds of snowy dust were rising under its hoofs, glittering with the rainbow colors of twinkling stars. Makar was surprised that he should be able, on foot, to overtake the Tartar so easily on his mad gallop. Besides, when he perceived Makar a few steps behind him, he stopped with readiness. Makar fell upon him with passion.

"Come to the sheriff with me!" he cried. "That is my horse; he has a split right ear. Look at the man, how smart he is, riding along on a stolen horse while the owner follows along like a beggar!"

"Gently," said the Tartar. "No need to go for the sheriff!

You say this is your horse, take him and be damned to the brute! This is the fifth year I have been riding him up and down on one and the same spot! Every foot-passenger overtakes me. It is humiliating for a good Tartar, it is indeed."

He threw his leg over the saddle in an act to alight, but at that moment the panting priest came running and seized Makar by the arm.

"Unfortunate man!" he cried. "What are you about? Can't you see that the Tartar is fooling you?"

"Of course he is fooling me!" shouted Makar waving his arms. "That was a lovely horse, a real gentleman's horse; I was offered forty rubles for him before his third spring. Never you mind, brother! If you have spoilt that horse for me I shall cut him up for meat, and you shall pay me his full value in money! Do you think, because you are a Tartar, there are no laws for you?"

Makar was flying into a passion and shouting in order to about him, for he was afraid of Tartars from habit, but the priest broke in on his outburst.

"Gently, gently, Makar you keep forgetting that you are dead! What do you want with a horse? Can't you see that you travel much faster on foot than the Tartar does on horseback? Would you like to be forced to ride for a whole thousand years?"

Makar now understood why the Tartar had been so willing to give up his horse.

"They're a crooked lot!" he thought, and he turned to the Tartar.

"Very well then," he said. "Take the horse, brother; I forgive you!"

The Tartar angrily pulled his fur cap over his ears and lashed his horse. The pony galloped madly, and clouds of snow flew under its hoofs, but as long as Makar and the priest stood still, the Tartar did not budge an inch from their side.

He angrily spit and turned to Makar.

"Listen friend, haven't you got a bit of mahorka with you? I do want to smoke so badly, and I finished all mine five years ago."

"You are a friend of dogs but no friend of mine," retorted Makar in a rage. "You have stolen my horse and now you ask for mahorka! Confound you altogether, I'm not sorry for you one bit!"

With these words Makar moved on.

"You made a mistake not to give him a little mahoraka," said Father Ivan. "The Chief would have forgiven you for at least one hundred sins for that at the judgement."

"Then why didn't you tell me that before?" snapped Makar.

"Ah, it is too late to teach you anything now. You should have learnt it from your priest while you were alive."

Makar was furious. He saw no sense in priests who took their tithes and did not even teach a man when to give a leaf of mahorka to a Tartar in order to gain forgiveness for his sins. One hundred sins were no joke! And all for a leaf of tobacco! The mistake had cost him dear.

"Wait a moment!" he exclaimed. "One leaf will do very well for us two. Let me give the other four to the Tartar this minute and that will mean four hundred sins!"

"Look behind you." Answered the priest.

Makar looked round. The white, empty plain lay stretched out far behind them; the Tartar appeared for a second upon it, a tiny, distant dot. Makar thought he could distinguish the white cloud rising from under the hoofs of his piebald, but the next moment the dot, too, had vanished.

"Well, well, the Tartar will manage alright without his mahoraka. You see how he ruined my horse, the scoundral!"

"No, he has not ruined your horse," answered the priest. "That horse was stolen. Have you not heard old men say that a stolen horse will never go far?"

Makar had certainly heard this from old men, but as he had often seen Tartars ride all the way to the city on horses that they had stolen, he had never put much belief in the saying. He now concluded that old men were sometimes right.

They now began to pass many other horsemen on the plain. All were hurrying along as fast as the first; the horses were flying like birds, the riders dripping with sweat, yet Makar and the priest kept over-taking them and leaving them behind.

Most of these horsemen were Tartars, and muttering every time he passed one of that the fellow had deserved much worse than this, but when he met a peasant from Chalgan he would stop and chat amicably with them, as they were friends, after all, even if they were thieves! Sometimes he would even show his fellow-feeling by picking up a lump of ice and diligently beating the ox or horse from behind, but let him take so much as one step forward himself, and horse and rider would be left far in the rear, a scarcely visible dot.

The plain seemed boundless. Though Makar and his companion occasionally overtook these riders and pedestrians, the country around was deserted, and the travelers seemed to be separated by hundreds of thousands of miles.

Among others, Makar fell in with an old man unknown to him, who plainly hailed from Chalgan; this could be discerned from his face, his clothes, and even from his walk, but Makar could not remember ever seeing him before. The old man wore a ragged fur coat, a great shaggy hat, tattered and worn leather breeches, and still older calf-skin boots. Worst of all, he was carrying on his shoulders, in spite of his old age, a crone still more ancient than himself, whose feet trailed on the ground. The old man was wheezing and staggering along, leaning heavily on his stick. Makar felt sorry for him. He stopped and the old man stopped too.

"Kansi! (speak!)" said Makar pleasantly.

"No" answered the greybeard.

"What have you seen?"

"Nothing."

"What have you heard?"

"Nothing."

Makar was silent for awhile, and then thought that he might ask the old man who he was and whence he had crawled.

The old man told his name. Long since, he said—he did not know himself how many years ago—he left Chalgan and gone up to the "mountain" to save himself. There he had done no work, had lived on roots and berries, and had neither ploughed nor sowed nor ground wheat nor paid taxes. When he died he went to Judgment of the Toyon. The Toyon asked him who he was, and what he had done. He answered that he had gone up the mountain and had saved himself. "Very well," the Toyon answered, "but where is your wife? Go and fetch her here." So he went back for his old woman. But she had been forced to beg before she died, as there had been no one to support her, and she had neither house, nor cow, nor bread. Her strength had failed, and now finally she was not able to move her legs. So he was obliged to carry her to the Toyon on his back.

As he said this, the old man burst into tears, but the old woman kicked him with her heels as if he had been an ox, and cried in a weak, cross voice:

"Go on!"

Makar felt more sorry than ever for the old man, and heartily thanked his stars that he had not succeeded in going to the "mountain" himself. His wife was large and lusty, and his burden would have been heavier than that of the old man; if, in addition to this, she had begun to kick him as if he were an ox, he would certainly die a second death.

He tried to hold the old woman's feet out of pity for his friend, but he scarcely had taken three steps before he was forced to drop them hastily, or they would have certainly been left in his hands; another minute, and the old man and his burden were left far out of sight.

For the remainder of his journey Makar met no more travelers whom he honored with marked attention. Here were thieves crawling along step-by-step, laden like beasts of burden with stolen goods; here rode fat Yakut chieftains towering in their high saddles, their peaked hats brushing the clouds; here, skipping beside them, ran poor workmen, and lean and light as hares; here strode a gloomy murderer, blood-drenched, with haggard, furtive eyes. He kept casting himself in vain into the pure snow, hoping to wash out the crimson stains; the snow around him was instantly dyed red, but the blood upon the murderer started out more vividly than ever, and in his eyes gleamed wild horror and despair. So he ran on, shunning the frightened gaze of all men.

From time to time little souls of children came flying through the air like birds, winging their way in great flocks, and this was no surprise to Makar. Bad, coarse food, dirt, heat from the fireplaces, and the old draughts in the huts drove them from Chalgan in bunches. As they overtook the murderer, the startled flocks wheeled swiftly aside, and long after their passage the air was filled with the quick, anxious whirl of their little pinions.

Makar could not help remarking that, in comparison with the other travelers, he was moving at a fairly swift pace, and he hastened to ascribe this to his own virtue.

"Listen, Asabit! (Father!)" he said, "What do you think, even if I was fond of drinking I was a good man, wasn't I? God loves me, doesn't he?"

He looked inquiringly at Father Ivan. He had a secret motive for asking this question, he wanted to find out something from the old priest, but the latter answered curtly:

"Don't be conceited! We are near the end now. You will soon find that out for yourself."

Makar had not noticed until then that a light seemed to be breaking over the plain. First a few lambent rays flashed up over breaking over the horizon, spreading swiftly across the stars. They went out, the moon set, and the plain lay in darkness.

Then mists arose on the plain and stood round about it like a guard of honor.

And at a certain point in the east the mists grew bright like a legion of warriors in golden armor.

And the mists stirred, and the warriors prostrated themselves upon the ground.

And the sun rose from their midst, and rested upon the golden ranks, and looked across the plain.

And the whole plain shone with wonderful, dazzling radience.

And the mists rose triumphantly in a mighty host, parted in the south, swayed, and swept upwards.

And Makar seemed to hear the most enchanting melody, the immemorial paean with which the earth daily greets the rising sun. He had never before given it due attention, and only now felt for the first time the beauty of the song.

He stood and hearkened and would not go any farther; he wanted to stand there forever and listen.

But Father Ivan touched him on the arm.

"We have arrived," he said. "Let us go in."

Thereupon Makar noticed that they were standing before a large door which had previously been hidden by the mist.

He was very loath to proceed, but he could not fail to comply.

They entered a large and spacious hut, and not until then did Makar reflect that it had been very cold outside. In the middle of the hut was a chimney of pure silver marvelously engraved, and in it blazed logs of gold, radiating such an even heat that one's whole body was penetrated by it in an instant. The flames in this beautiful fireplace neither scorched nor dazzled the eyes, they only warmed, and once more Makar wanted to stand there and toast himself before the fire, stretching out his frozen hands to the blaze.

Four doors opened out of the room, and of these only one led into the open air; through the other three young men in long white gowns were coming and going. Makar imagined that they must be the servants of this Toyon. He seemed to remember having seen them somewhere before, but could not recollect exactly where. He was not a little surprised to note that each servant wore a pair of large white wings upon his back, and decided that Toyon must have other workmen besides these, for surely they, encumbered with their wings, could never make it through the forest thickets when they went to cut wood or poles.

One of the servants approached the fire, and turning his back to the blaze, addressed Father Ivan:

"Speak!"

"There is nothing to say."

"What did you hear in the world?"

"Nothing."

"What did you see?"

Both were silent and then the priest said:

"I have brought this one."

"Is he from Chalgan?" asked the servant.

"Yes, from Chalgan."

"Then we must get ready for the big scales."

He left the room to make his preparations, and Makar asked the priest why the scales were needed and why they must be large.

"You see," answered the priest a trifle embarrassed, "the scales are needed to weigh the good and evil you did when you were alive. With all other people the good and evil almost balance one another, but the inhabitants of Chalgan bring so many sins with them that the Toyon had to have special scales made with one of the bowls extra large to contain them all."

At these words Makar quailed, and felt his heartstrings tighten.

The servant brought in and set up the big scales. One bowl was small and gold, the other was wooden and of huge proportions. A deep black pit suddenly opened up beneath the wooden bowl.

Makar approached the scales and carefully inspected them to make sure they were not false. They proved to be correct; the bowls hung motionless, without movement up or down.

To tell the truth, he did not exactly understand their mechanism, and would have preferred to have done business with the simple balances by whose aid he had learned to buy and sell with great profit to himself during the course of his long life.

"The Toyon is coming!" cried Father Ivan suddenly, and hastily began to pull his cassock straight.

The central door opened and in came an ancient, venerable Toyon, his silvery long beard hanging below his waist. He was dressed in rich furs and tissues unknown to Makar, and on his feet he wore warm velvet-lined boots, such as Makar had seen depicted on antique icons.

Makar recognized him at a glance the same old greybeard whose picture he had seen in church, only here he was unattended by his son. Makar decided that the latter must have gone out on business. The dove flew into the room, however, and after circling about the old man's head, settled upon his knee. The old Toyon stroked the dove with his hand as he sat on the seat that had been especially prepared for him.

The Toyon's face was kind, and when Makar became too downcast, he looked at it and felt better.

His heart was heavy because he was suddenly remembering all his past life down to the smallest detail; he remembered every step he had taken, every blow of his axe, every tree he had felled, every deceit he had practiced, every glass of vodka he had drunk.

He grew frightened and ashamed, but he took heart as he looked at the face of the old Toyon.

And as he took heart it occurred to him that there might be some things that he could manage to conceal.

The old Toyon looked searchingly at him and asked him who he was and whence he had come, what his name was and what his age might be.

When Makar had replied to his questions, the old Toyon asked:

"What have you done in your life?"

"You know that yourself," answered Makar. "Surely it is written in your book!"

Makar wanted to test Toyon and find out whether everything was really inscribed in there or not.

"Tell me yourself," answered the old Toyon.

Makar took courage.

He began enumerating all his works, and although he remembered every blow he had struck with his axe, every pole he had cut, and every furrow he plowed, he added to his reckoning thousands of poles and hundreds of loads of wood and hundreds of logs and hundreds of pounds of sown seed.

When all had been told, the old Toyon turned to Father Ivan and said:

"Bring hither the book."

Makar saw from this that Father Ivan was secretary to the Toyon, and was annoyed that the other had given him no friendly hint of the fact.

Father Ivan brought the great book, opened it, and began to read.

"Just look and see how many poles are inscribed there," said the Toyon.

Father Ivan looked and answered sorrowfully:

"He added around three thousand to his reckoning."

"It's a lie!" shouted Makar vehemently. "He must be wrong because he was a drunkard and died a wicked death!"

"Be quiet!" commanded the Toyon. "Did he charge you more than was fair for christenings and weddings? Did he ever press you for tithes?"

"Why waste words?" asked Makar.

"You see," the Toyon said, "I know without assistance from you that he was fond of the drink—"

And the old Toyon lost his temper. "Read his sins from the book now; he is a cheat and I can't believe his words!" he cried to Father Ivan.

Meanwhile the servants were heaping into the golden bowl all Makar's poles, and his wood, and his ploughing, and all his work. And there proved to be so much that the golden bowl sank, and the wooden bowl rose out of reach, high, high, into the air. So the young servants of God flew up to it on the pinions and hundreds of them pulled it to the floor with ropes.

Heavy is the labor of a native of Chalgan!

Then Father Ivan began adding up the number of frauds

that Makar had committed, and there proved to be twenty-one thousand, three hundred and three. Then he added up the number of bottles of vodka he had drunk, and there proved to be four hundred. And the priest read on and Makar saw that the wooden bowl was pulling on the gold one; it sank into the hole, and, as the priest read, it descended deeper and deeper.

Makar realized that things were going badly for him; he stepped up to the scales and furtively tried to block them with his foot.

But one on the servants saw him, and a clamor arose.

"What is the matter there?" asked the old Toyon.

"Why, he is trying to block the scales with his foot!" cried the servant.

At that the Toyon wrathfully turned to Makar exclaiming:

"I see you are a cheat, a sluggard, and a drunkard. You have left your arrears unpaid behind you, you owe tithes to the priest, and the policeman is steadily sinning on your account by swearing everytime he speaks your name."

Then, turning to Father Ivan, the old Toyon asked:

"Who in Chalgan gives the heaviest loads to his horses to pull and how works them the hardiest?"

Father Ivan answered:

"The church warden. He carries all the mail and drives the district policeman."

To that Toyon answered:

"Hand over this sluggard to the church warden for a horse and let him pull the policeman until he drops—we shall see what will happen next."

Just as the Toyon was saying these words, the door opened; his son entered the hut and sat at his right hand.

And the son said:

"I have heard the sentence pronounced by you. I have lived long on earth, and I know the ways of the world. It will be hard for the poor man to take the place of the district policeman's horse. However, so be it, only mayhap he still has something to say: speak, baraksan! (poor fellow!)"

Then there happened a strange thing Makar, the Makar who had never before in his life uttered more than ten words at a time, suddenly found himself possessed of the gift of eloquence. He began speaking, and wondered at himself. There seemed to be two Makars, the one talking, the other listening and marveling. He could scarcely believe his ears. The discourse flowed from his lips with fluency and passion; the words pursued one another swiftly, and ranged themselves in long and graceful rows. He did not hesitate. If by any chance he became confused, he corrected himself and shouted twice louder than before. But above all he felt his words were carrying conviction.

The ancient Toyon, who had at first been a little annoyed by his boldness, began listening with rapt attention, as if he were being persuaded that Makar was not the fool that he seemed to be. Father Ivan had been frightened for an instant and had plucked Makar by the coattails, but Makar had pushed him aside and continued with his speech. The fears of the old priest were quickly allayed; he even beamed at Makar as he heard his old parishioner boldly declaring the truth, and saw that the truth was pleasing to the heart of the ancient Toyon. Even the young servants of the Toyon with the long gowns and their white wings came out of their quarters and stood in the doorways listening with wonder to Makar's words, nudging one another with their elbows.

Makar commenced his plea by saying that he did not want to take the place of the church warden's horse. Not because he was afraid of hard work, but because the sentence was unjust. And because the sentence was unjust, he would not submit to it; he would not do a stroke of work nor move one single foot. Let them do what they will with him! Let them hand him over to the devils forever, he would not haul a policeman, because to condemn him to do so was an injustice. And let them not imagine that he was afraid of being a horse. Although the church warden drove his horse hard, he fed him with oats, but he, Makar, had been goaded all his life, and no one had ever fed him.

"Who has goaded you?" asked the Toyon.

Yes, all his life he had been goaded. The baliff had goaded him; the tax assessor and the policeman had goaded him, demanding taxes and tallage; hunger and want had goaded him; cold and heat, rain and drought had goaded him; the frozen earth and the ruthless forest had goaded him. The horse had trudged on with its eyes on the ground, ignorant of its journey's end; so he had trudged through life. Had he known the meaning of what the priest read in church or for what his tithes were demanded? Had he known why his eldest son had been taken away as a soldier and where had he gone? Had he known he had died and where his poor bones had been laid?

He was a drunk it was charged, too much vodka; so he had, for his heart had craved it.

"How many bottles did you say that he drank?" the Toyon asked.

"Four hundred," answered Father Ivan, with a glance at the book.

That might be so, pleaded Makar, but was it all really vodka? Three quarters of it was water; only one quarter was vodka and that was stiffened with vile mahorka. Three hundred bottles may well be deducted from his account.

"Is what he says true?" asked the ancient Toyon of Father Ivan, and it was plain that his anger was not yet appeased.

"Absolutely true," the priest answered quickly, and Makar continued his tale.

It was true that he added three thousand poles to his account, but what if he had? What if he had only cut sixteen thousand? Was that so small a number? Besides, while he had cut two thousand his first wife had been ill. His heart had been aching, he longed to sit by her bedside, but want had driven him into the forest, and in the forest he wept, and the tears had frozen on his eyelashes, and because of his grief, the cold had struck into his very heart, and still he had chopped.

And then his old woman had died. He had to bury her, but he had no money to pay for her burial. So he hired himself out to chop wood to pay for his wife's abode in the world beyond. The merchant had seen how great was his need, and had only paid him ten kopecks—and his old woman had laid alone in that icy hut while he once more chopped wood and wept. Surely each one of those loads should be counted for four or more!

Tears rose in the eyes of old Toyon, and Makar saw the scales trembling and the wooden bowl rising as the golden one sank.

And still he talked on.

Everything was written down in their book, he said, let them look and see if anyone had ever done him a kindness or brought him happiness and joy! Where were his children? If they had died his heart had been heavy and sad; if they lived to grow up they had left him, to carry on their fight alone with their own grinding needs. So he remained to grow old with his second wife, and had felt his strength failing and had seen that a pitiless, homeless old age was creeping upon him. They two had solitary as two lorn fir trees on the steppe, buffeted every hand by the merciless winds.

"Is it true?" asked the Toyon again, and the priest hastened an answer:

"Absolutely true."

And the scales trembled once more—but the old Toyon pondered.

"How is this?" he asked. "Have I not many on earth who are truly righteous? Their eyes are clear, their faces are bright, and their garments are without a stain. Their hearts are mellow as well-tilled soil in which flourishes good seed, sending up strong and fragrant shoots whose odor is pleasant to my nostrils. But you—look at yourself!"

All eyes were now turned on Makar, and he felt ashamed. He knew that his eyes were dim, that his face was dull, that his hair and beard were unkempt, that his raiment was torn. And though for some time before his death he had intended to buy a new pair of boots in which to appear at the Judgment, he had somehow always managed to drink up the money, and now stood before the Toyon in wretched fur shoes like a Yakut.

"Your face is dull," the Toyon went on. "Your eyes are bleared and your clothes are torn. Your heart is choked with weeds and thistles and bitter wormwood. That is why I love my righteous and turn my face from the ungodly such as you."

Makar's heart contracted and he blushed for his own existence. He hung his head for a moment and then suddenly raised it and took up his tale once more.

Which righteous men did the Toyon mean? he asked. If he meant those that lived on earth in rich houses at the same time that Makar was there, then he knew all about them! Their eyes, were clear because they had not shed the tears he had shed; their faces were bright because they bathed in perfume, and their spotless garments were sewn by other hands than their own.

Again Makar hung his head and raised it.

And did not the Toyon know that he too had come into the world with clear, candid eyes in which heaven and earth lay reflected? That he had been born with a pure heart, ready to expand to all the beauty of the world? Whose fault was it if he now longed to hide his besmirched and dishonored head under the ground? He could not say. But this he did know, that the patience of his soul was exhausted!

Of course Makar could have been calmer could he have seen the effect that his speech was having on the Toyon, or how each of his wrathful words fell into the golden bowl like a plummet of lead. But he saw nothing of this because his heart was overwhelmed with blind despair.

He had gone over again the whole of his bitter existence. How had he managed to bear the terrible burden until now? He had borne it because the star of hope had still beckoned him onward, shining through the watch-fire through mists of toil and doubt. He was alive, therefore he might, he would, know a happier fate. But now he stood at the end, and the star had gone out. Darkness fell on his soul, and rage broke over it as a tempest breaks over the steppe at night. He forgot who he was and before whose face he stood; he forgot all about his wrath.

But the old Toyon said to him: "What a moment, baraksan! You are not on earth. There is justice for you here, also."

At that Makar trembled. The idea that someone pitied him dawned up on his mind and filled and softened his heart, but because his whole miserable existence now lay exposed before him from his first day to his last, unbearable self-pity overwhelmed him and he burst into tears.

And the ancient Toyon wept with him. And the old Father Ivan wept, and the young servants of God shed tears and wiped them away with their wide sleeves.

And the scales wavered, and the wooden bowl rose ever higher and higher!

AN OCCURRENCE AT OWL CREEK BRIDGE

by

Ambrose Bierce (1842-1914)

A man stood upon a railroad bridge in northern Alabama, looking down into the swift water twenty feet below. The man's hands were behind his back, the wrists bound with a cord. A rope closely encircled his neck. It was attached to a stout cross-timber above his head and the slack fell to the level of his knees. Some loose boards laid upon the ties supporting the rails of the railway supplied a footing for him and his executioners—two private soldiers of the Federal army, directed by a sergeant who in civil life may have been a deputy sheriff. At a short remove upon the same temporary platform was an officer in the uniform of his rank, armed. He was a captain. A sentinel at each end of the bridge stood with his rifle in the position known as "support," that is to say, vertical in front of the left shoulder, the hammer resting on the forearm thrown straight across the chest—a formal and unnatural position, enforcing an erect carriage of the body. It did not appear to be the duty of these two men to know what was occurring at the center of the bridge; they merely blockaded the two ends of the foot planking that traversed it.

Beyond one of the sentinels nobody was in sight; the railroad ran straight away into a forest for a hundred yards, then, curving, was lost to view. Doubtless there was an outpost farther along. The other bank of the stream was open ground—a gentle slope topped with a stockade of vertical tree trunks, loopholed for rifles, with a single embrasure through which protruded the muzzle of a brass cannon commanding the bridge. Midway up the slope between the bridge and fort were the spectators—a single company of infantry in line, at "parade rest," the butts of their rifles on the ground, the barrels inclining slightly backward against the right shoulder, the hands crossed upon the stock.

A lieutenant stood at the right of the line, the point of his sword upon the ground, his left hand resting upon his right. Excepting the group of four at the center of the bridge, not a man moved. The company faced the bridge, staring stonily, motionless. The sentinels, facing the banks of the stream, might have been statues to adorn the bridge. The captain stood with folded arms, silent, observing the work of his subordinates, but making no sign. Death is a dignitary who when he comes announced is to be received with formal manifestations of respect, even by those most familiar with him. In the code of military etiquette silence and fixity are forms of deference.

The man who was engaged in being hanged was apparently about thirty-five years of age. He was a civilian, if one might judge from his habit, which was that of a planter. His features were good—a straight nose, firm mouth, broad forehead, from which his long, dark hair was combed straight back, falling behind his ears to the collar of his well fitting frock coat. He wore a moustache and pointed beard, but no whiskers; his eyes were large and dark gray, and had a kindly expression which one would hardly have expected in one whose neck was in the hemp. Evidently this was no vulgar assassin. The liberal military code makes provision for hanging many kinds of persons, and gentlemen are not excluded.

The preparations being complete, the two private soldiers stepped aside and each drew away the plank upon which he had been standing. The sergeant turned to the captain, saluted and placed himself immediately behind that officer, who in turn moved apart one pace. These movements left the condemned man and the sergeant standing on the two ends of the same plank, which spanned three of the cross-ties of the bridge. The end upon which the civilian stood almost, but not quite, reached a fourth. This plank had been held in place by the weight of the captain; it was now held by that of the sergeant. At a signal from the former the latter would step aside, the plank would tilt and the condemned man go down between two ties. The arrangement commended itself to his judgement as simple and effective. His face had not been covered nor his eyes bandaged. He looked a moment at his "unsteadfast footing," then let his gaze wander to the swirling water of the stream racing madly beneath his feet. A piece of dancing driftwood caught his attention and his eyes followed it down the current. How slowly it appeared to move! What a sluggish stream!

He closed his eyes in order to fix his last thoughts upon his wife and children. The water, touched to gold by the early sun, the brooding mists under the banks at some distance down the

stream, the fort, the soldiers, the piece of drift—all had distract-
ed him. And now he became conscious of a new disturbance.
Striking through the thought of his dear ones was sound which
he could neither ignore nor understand, a sharp, distinct, metal-
lic percussion like the stroke of a blacksmith's hammer upon the
anvil; it had the same ringing quality. He wondered what it was,
and whether immeasurably distant or near by—it seemed both.
Its recurrence was regular, but as slow as the tolling of a death
knell. He awaited each new stroke with impatience and—he
knew not why—apprehension. The intervals of silence grew
progressively longer; the delays became maddening. With their
greater infrequency the sounds increased in strength and sharp-
ness. They hurt his ear like the trust of a knife; he feared he
would shriek. What he heard was the ticking of his watch.

He unclosed his eyes and saw again the water below him. "If
I could free my hands," he thought, "I might throw off the
noose and spring into the stream. By diving I could evade the
bullets and, swimming vigorously, reach the bank, take to the
woods and get away home. My home, thank God, is as yet outside their lines; my wife and little ones are still beyond the
invader's farthest advance."

As these thoughts, which have here to be set down in words,
were flashed into the doomed man's brain rather than evolved
from it the captain nodded to the sergeant. The sergeant
stepped aside.

II

Peyton Fahrquhar was a well to do planter, of an old and
highly respected Alabama family. Being a slave owner and like
other slave owners a politician, he was naturally an original
secessionist and ardently devoted to the Southern cause.
Circumstances of an imperious nature, which it is unnecessary
to relate here, had prevented him from taking service with that
gallant army which had fought the disastrous campaigns ending
with the fall of Corinth, and he chafed under the inglorious
restraint, longing for the release of his energies, the larger life of
the soldier, the opportunity for distinction. That opportunity,
he felt, would come, as it comes to all in wartime. Meanwhile he
did what he could. No service was too humble for him to perform in the aid of the South, no adventure too perilous for him

to undertake if consistent with the character of a civilian who was at heart a soldier, and who in good faith and without too much qualification assented to at least a part of the frankly villainous dictum that all is fair in love and war.

One evening while Fahrquhar and his wife were sitting on a rustic bench near the entrance to his grounds, a gray-clad soldier rode up to the gate and asked for a drink of water. Mrs. Fahrquhar was only too happy to serve him with her own white hands. While she was fetching the water her husband approached the dusty horseman and inquired eagerly for news from the front.

"The Yanks are repairing the railroads," said the man, "and are getting ready for another advance. They have reached the Owl Creek bridge, put it in order and built a stockade on the north bank. The commandant has issued an order, which is posted everywhere, declaring that any civilian caught interfering with the railroad, its bridges, tunnels, or trains will be summarily hanged. I saw the order."

"How far is it to the Owl Creek bridge?" Fahrquhar asked.

"About thirty miles."

"Is there no force on this side of the creek?"

"Only a picket post half a mile out, on the railroad, and a single sentinel at this end of the bridge."

"Suppose a man—a civilian and student of hanging—should elude the picket post and perhaps get the better of the sentinel," said Fahrquhar, smiling, "what could he accomplish?"

The soldier reflected. "I was there a month ago," he replied. "I observed that the flood of last winter had lodged a great quantity of driftwood against the wooden pier at this end of the bridge. It is now dry and would burn like tinder."

The lady had now brought the water, which the soldier drank. He thanked her ceremoniously, bowed to her husband and rode away. An hour later, after nightfall, he repassed the plantation, going northward in the direction from which he had come. He was a Federal scout.

III

As Peyton Fahrquhar fell straight downward through the bridge he lost consciousness and was as one already dead. From this state he was awakened—ages later, it seemed to him—by the pain of a sharp pressure upon his throat, followed by a sense of suffocation. Keen, poignant agonies seemed to shoot from his neck downward through every fiber of his body and limbs. These pains appeared to flash along well defined lines of ramification and to beat with an inconceivably rapid periodicity. They seemed like streams of pulsating fire heating him to an intolerable temperature. As to his head, he was conscious of nothing but a feeling of fullness—of congestion. These sensations were unaccompanied by thought. The intellectual part of his nature was already effaced; he had power only to feel, and feeling was torment. He was conscious of motion. Encompassed in a luminous cloud, of which he was now merely the fiery heart, without material substance, he swung through unthinkable arcs of oscillation, like a vast pendulum. Then all at once, with terrible suddenness, the light about him shot upward with the noise of a loud splash; a frightful roaring was in his ears, and all was cold and dark. The power of thought was restored; he knew that the rope had broken and he had fallen into the stream. There was no additional strangulation; the noose about his neck was already suffocating him and kept the water from his lungs. To die of hanging at the bottom of a river!—the idea seemed to him ludicrous. He opened his eyes in the darkness and saw above him a gleam of light, but how distant, how inaccessible! He was still sinking, for the light became fainter and fainter until it was a mere glimmer. Then it began to grow and brighten, and he knew that he was rising toward the surface—knew it with reluctance, for he was now very comfortable. "To be hanged and drowned," he thought, "that is not so bad; but I do not wish to be shot. No; I will not be shot; that is not fair."

He was not conscious of an effort, but a sharp pain in his wrist apprised him that he was trying to free his hands. He gave the struggle his attention, as an idler might observe the feat of a juggler, without interest in the outcome. What splendid effort!—what magnificent, what superhuman strength! Ah, that was a fine endeavor! Bravo! The cord fell away; his arms parted and floated upward, the hands dimly seen on each side in the growing light. He watched them with a new interest as first one and then the other pounced upon the noose at his neck. They tore it away and thrust it fiercely aside, its undulations resembling those of a water snake. "Put it back, put it back!" He thought he shouted these words to his hands, for the undoing of the noose had been succeeded by the direst pang that he had yet experienced. His neck ached horribly; his brain was on fire, his heart, which had been fluttering faintly, gave a great leap, trying to force itself out at his mouth. His whole body was racked and wrenched with an insupportable anguish! But his disobedient hands gave no heed to the command. They beat the water vigorously with quick, downward strokes, forcing him to the surface. He felt his head emerge; his eyes were blinded by the sunlight; his chest expanded convulsively, and with a supreme and crowning agony his lungs engulfed a great draught of air, which instantly he expelled in a shriek!

He was now in full possession of his physical senses. They were, indeed, preternaturally keen and alert. Something in the awful disturbance of his organic system had so exalted and refined them that they made record of things never before perceived. He felt the ripples upon his face and heard their separate sounds as they struck. He looked at the forest on the bank of the stream, saw the individual trees, the leaves and the veining of each leaf—he saw the very insects upon them: the locusts, the brilliant bodied flies, the gray spiders stretching their webs from twig to twig. He noted the prismatic colors in all the dewdrops upon a million blades of grass. The humming of the gnats that danced above the eddies of the stream, the beating of the dragon flies' wings, the strokes of the water spiders' legs, like oars which had lifted their boat—all these made audible music. A fish slid along beneath his eyes and he heard the rush of its body parting the water.

He had come to the surface facing down the stream; in a moment the visible world seemed to wheel slowly round, himself the pivotal point, and he saw the bridge, the fort, the soldiers upon the bridge, the captain, the sergeant, the two privates, his executioners. They were in silhouette against the blue sky. They shouted and gesticulated, pointing at him. The captain had drawn his pistol, but did not fire; the others were unarmed. Their movements were grotesque and horrible, their forms gigantic.

Suddenly he heard a sharp report and something struck the water smartly within a few inches of his head, spattering his face with spray. He heard a second report, and saw one of the sentinels with his rifle at his shoulder, a light cloud of blue smoke rising from the muzzle. The man in the water saw the eye of the man on the bridge gazing into his own through the sights of the rifle. He observed that it was a gray eye and remembered having read that gray eyes were keenest, and that all famous marksmen had them. Nevertheless, this one had missed.

A counter-swirl had caught Fahrquhar and turned him half round; he was again looking at the forest on the bank opposite the fort. The sound of a clear, high voice in a monotonous singsong now rang out behind him and came across the water with a distinctness that pierced and subdued all other sounds, even the beating of the ripples in his ears. Although no soldier, he had frequented camps enough to know the dread significance of that deliberate, drawling, aspirated chant; the lieutenant on shore was taking a part in the morning's work. How coldly and pitilessly—with what an even, calm intonation, presaging, and enforcing tranquility in the men—with what accurately measured interval fell those cruel words:

"Company!...Attention!...Shoulder arms!...Ready!...Aim!... Fire!"

Fahrquhar dived—dived as deeply as he could. The water roared in his ears like the voice of Niagara, yet he heard the dull thunder of the volley and, rising again toward the surface, met shining bits of metal, singularly flattened, oscillating slowly downward. Some of them touched him on the face and hands, then fell away, continuing their descent. One lodged between his collar and neck; it was uncomfortably warm and he snatched it out.

As he rose to the surface, gasping for breath, he saw that he had been a long time under water; he was perceptibly farther downstream—nearer to safety. The soldiers had almost finished reloading; the metal ramrods flashed all at once in the sunshine as they were drawn from the barrels, turned in the air, and thrust into their sockets. The two sentinels fired again, independently and ineffectually.

The hunted man saw all this over his shoulder; he was now swimming vigorously with the current. His brain was as energetic as his arms and legs; he thought with the rapidity of lightning:

"The officer," he reasoned, "will not make that martinet's error a second time. It is as easy to dodge a volley as a single shot. He has probably already given the command to fire at will. God help me, I cannot dodge them all!"

An appalling splash within two yards of him was followed by a loud, rushing sound, DIMINUENDO, which seemed to travel back through the air to the fort and died in an explosion which stirred the very river to its deeps! A rising sheet of water curved over him, fell down upon him, blinded him, strangled him! The cannon had taken a hand in the game. As he shook his head free from the commotion of the smitten water he heard the deflected shot humming through the air ahead, and in an instant it was cracking and smashing the branches in the forest beyond.

"They will not do that again," he thought; "the next time they will use a charge of grape. I must keep my eye upon the gun; the smoke will apprise me—the report arrives too late; it lags behind the missile. That is a good gun."

Suddenly he felt himself whirled round and round—spinning like a top. The water, the banks, the forests, the now distant bridge, fort and men, all were commingled and blurred. Objects were represented by their colors only; circular horizontal streaks of color—that was all he saw. He had been caught in a vortex and was being whirled on with a velocity of advance and gyration that made him giddy and sick. In a few moments he was flung upon the gravel at the foot of the left bank of the stream— the southern bank—and behind a projecting point which concealed him from his enemies. The sudden arrest of his motion, the abrasion of one of his hands on the gravel, restored him, and he wept with delight. He dug his fingers into the sand, threw it over himself in handfuls and audibly blessed it. It looked like diamonds, rubies, emeralds; he could think of nothing beautiful which it did not resemble. The trees upon the bank were giant garden plants; he noted a definite order in their arrangement, inhaled the fragrance of their blooms. A strange roseate light shone through the spaces among their trunks and the wind made in their branches the music of Æolian harps. He had not wish to perfect his escape—he was content to remain in that enchanting spot until retaken. A whiz and a rattle of grapeshot among the branches high above his head roused him from his dream. The baffled cannoneer had fired him a random farewell. He sprang to his feet, rushed up the sloping bank, and plunged into the forest.

All that day he traveled, laying his course by the rounding

sun. The forest seemed interminable; nowhere did he discover a break in it, not even a woodman's road. He had not known that he lived in so wild a region. There was something uncanny in the revelation. By nightfall he was fatigued, footsore, famished. The thought of his wife and children urged him on. At last he found a road which led him in what he knew to be the right direction. It was as wide and straight as a city street, yet it seemed untraveled. No fields bordered it, no dwelling anywhere. Not so much as the barking of a dog suggested human habitation. The black bodies of the trees formed a straight wall on both sides, terminating on the horizon in a point, like a diagram in a lesson in perspective. Overhead, as he looked up through this rift in the wood, shone great golden stars looking unfamiliar and grouped in strange constellations. He was sure they were arranged in some order which had a secret and malign significance. The wood on either side was full of singular noises, among which—once, twice, and again—he distinctly heard whispers in an unknown tongue.

His neck was in pain and lifting his hand to it found it horribly swollen. He knew that it had a circle of black where the rope had bruised it. His eyes felt congested; he could no longer close them. His tongue was swollen with thirst; he relieved its fever by thrusting it forward from between his teeth into the cold air. How softly the turf had carpeted the untraveled avenue—he could no longer feel the roadway beneath his feet!

Doubtless, despite his suffering, he had fallen asleep while walking, for now he sees another scene—perhaps he has merely recovered from a delirium. He stands at the gate of his own home. All is as he left it, and all bright and beautiful in the morning sunshine. He must have traveled the entire night. As he pushes open the gate and passes up the wide white walk, he sees a flutter of female garments; his wife, looking fresh and cool and sweet, steps down from the veranda to meet him. At the bottom of the steps she stands waiting, with a smile of ineffable joy, an attitude of matchless grace and dignity. Ah, how beautiful she is! He springs forwards with extended arms. As he is about to clasp her he feels a stunning blow upon the back of the neck; a blinding white light blazes all about him with a sound like the shock of a cannon—then all is darkness and silence!

Peyton Fahrquhar was dead; his body, with a broken neck, swung gently from side to side beneath the timbers of the Owl Creek bridge.

DREAM OF OWEN O'MULREADY

There was a man long ago living near Ballaghadereen named Owen O'Mulready, who was a workman for the gentleman of the place, and was a prosperous, quiet, contented man. There was no one but himself and his wife Margaret, and they had a nice little house and enough potatoes in the year, in addition to their share of wages, from their master. There wasn't a want or anxiety on Owen, except one desire, and that was to have a dream—for he had never had one.

One day when he was digging potatoes, his master—James Taafe—came out to his ridge, and they began talking, as was the custom with them. The talk fell on dreams, and said Owen that he would like better than anything if he could only have one.

"You'll have one tonight," says his master, "if you do as I tell you."

"Musha, I'll do it, and welcome," says Owen.

"Now," says his master, "when you go home tonight, draw the fire from the hearth, put it out, make your bed in its place and sleep there tonight, and you'll get your enough of dreaming before the morning."

Owen promised to do this. When, however, he began to draw the fire out, Margaret thought that he had lost his senses, so he explained everything James Taafe had said to him, had his own way, and they went to lie down together on the hearth.

Not long was Owen asleep when there came a knock at the door.

"Get up, Owen O'Mulready, and go with a letter from the master to America."

Owen got up, and put his feet into his boots, saying to himself, "It's late you come, messenger."

He took the letter, and he went forward and never tarried till he came to the foot of Sliabh Charn, where he met a cowboy, and he herding cows.

"The blessing of God be with you, Owen O'Mulready," says the boy.

"The blessing of God and Mary be with you, my boy," says Owen. "Every one knows me, and I don't know any one at all."

"Where are you going this time of night?" says the boy.

"I'm going to America, with a letter from the master; is this the right road ?" says Owen.

"It is; keep straight to the west; but how are you going to get over the water?" says the boy.

"Time enough to think of that when I get to it," replied Owen.

He went on the road again, till he came to the brink of the sea; there he saw a crane standing on one foot on the shore.

"The blessing of God be with you, Owen O'Mulready," says the crane.

"The blessing of God and Mary be with you, Mrs. Crane," says Owen. "Everybody knows me, and I don't know any one."

"What are you doing here?"

Owen told her his business, and that he didn't know how he'd get over the water.

"Leave your two feet on my two wings, and sit on my back, and I'll take you to the other side," says the crane.

"What would I do if tiredness should come on you before we got over?" says Owen.

"Don't be afraid, I won't be tired or wearied till I fly over."

Then Owen went on the back of the crane, and she arose over the sea and went forward, but she hadn't flown more than half-way, when she cried out:

"Owen O'Mulready get off me; I'm tired."

"That you may be seven times worse this day twelvemonths, you rogue of a crane," says Owen; "I can't get off you now, so don't ask me."

"I don't care," replied the crane, "if you'll rise off me a while till I'll take a rest."

With that they saw threshers over their heads, and Owen shouted:

"Och ! thresher, thresher, leave down your flail at me, that I may give the crane a rest!"

The thresher left down the flail, but when Owen took a hold with his two hands, the crane went from him laughing and mocking.

"My share of misfortunes go with you!" said Owen, "It's you've left me in a fix hanging between the heavens and the water in the middle of the great sea."

It wasn't long till the thresher shouted to him to leave go the flail.

"I won't let it go," said Owen; "shan't I be drowned ?"

"If you don't let it go, I'll cut the whang."

"I don't care," says Owen; "I have the flail;" and with that he looked away from him, and what should he see but a boat a long way off.

"O sailor dear, sailor, come, come ; perhaps you'll take my lot of bones," said Owen.

"Are we under you now? " says the sailor.

"Not yet, not yet," says Owen.

"Fling down one of your shoes, till we see the way it falls," says the captain.

Owen shook one foot, and down fell the shoe.

"Uill, uill, puil, uil, liu—who is killing me?" came a scream from Margaret in the bed. "Where are you, Owen?"

"I didn't know whether 'twas you were in it, Margaret."

"Indeed, then it is," says she, "who else would it be?"

She got up and lit the candle. She found Owen halfway up the chimney, climbing by the hands on the crook, and he black with soot! He had one shoe on, but the point of the other struck Margaret, and 'twas that which awoke her.

Owen came down off the crook and washed himself and from that out there was no envy on him ever to have a dream again.

THE DREAM OF RHONABWY
(TRANSLATION BY LADY CHARLOTTE GUEST)

Madawc the son of Maredudd possessed Powys within its boundaries, from Porfoed to Gwauan in the uplands of Arwystli. And at that time he had a brother, Iorwerth the son of Maredudd, in rank not equal to himself. And Iorwerth had great sorrow and heaviness because of the honour and power that his brother enjoyed, which he shared not. And he sought his fellows and his foster-brothers, and took counsel with them what he should do in this matter. And they resolved to despatch some of their number to go and seek a maintenance for him. Then Madawc offered him to become Master of the Household and to have horses, and arms, and honour, and to fare like as himself. But Iorwerth refused this.

And Iorwerth made an inroad into Loegria, slaying the inhabitants, and burning houses, and carrying away prisoners. And Madawc took counsel with the men of Powys, and they determined to place a hundred men in each of the three Commots of Powys to seek for him. And thus did they in the plains of Powys from Aber Ceirawc, and in Allictwn Ver, and in Rhyd Wilure, on the Vyrnwy, the three best Commots of Powys. So he was none the better, he nor his household, in Powys, nor in the plains thereof. And they spread these men over the plains as far as Nillystwn Trevan.

Now one of the men who was upon this quest was called Rhonabwy. And Rhonabwy and Kynwrig Vrychgoch, a man of Mawddwy, and Cadwgan Vras, a man of Moelvre in Kynlleith, came together to the house of Heilyn Goch the son of Cadwgan the son of Iddon. And when they came near to the house, they saw an old hall, very black and having an upright gable, whence issued a great smoke; and on entering, they found the floor full of puddles and mounds; and it was difficult to stand thereon, so slippery was it with the mire of cattle. And where the puddles were, a man might go up to his ankles in water and dirt. And there were boughs of holly spread over the floor, whereof the cattle had browsed the sprigs. When they came to the hall of the house, they beheld cells full of dust, and very gloomy, and on one side an old hag making a fire. And whenever she felt cold, she cast a lapful of chaff upon the fire, and raised such a smoke, that it was scarcely to be borne, as it rose up the nostrils. And on the other side was a yellow calf-skin on the floor; a main privilege was it to any one who should get upon that hide.

And when they had sat down, they asked the hag where were the people of the house. And the hag spoke not, but muttered. Thereupon behold the people of the house entered; a ruddy, clownish, curly-headed man, with a burthen of faggots on his back, and a pale slender woman, also carrying a bundle under her arm. And they barely welcomed the men, and kindled a fire with the boughs. And the woman cooked something, and gave them to eat, barley bread, and cheese, and milk and water.

And there arose a storm of wind and rain, so that it was hardly possible to go forth with safety. And being weary with their journey, they laid themselves down and sought to sleep. And when they looked at the couch, it seemed to be made but of a little coarse straw full of dust and vermin, with the stems of boughs sticking up there through, for the cattle had eaten all the straw that was placed at the head and the foot. And upon it was stretched an old russet-coloured rug, threadbare and ragged; and a coarse sheet, full of slits, was upon the rug, and an ill-stuffed pillow, and a worn-out cover upon the sheet. And after much suffering from the vermin, and from the discomfort of their couch, a heavy sleep fell on Rhonabwy's companions. But Rhonabwy, not being able either to sleep or to rest, thought he should suffer less if he went to lie upon the yellow calf-skin that was stretched out on the floor. And there he slept.

As soon as sleep had come upon his eyes, it seemed to him that he was journeying with his companions across the plain of Argyngroeg, and he thought that he went towards Rhyd y Groes on the Severn. As he journeyed, he heard a mighty noise, the like whereof heard he never before; and looking behind him, he beheld a youth with yellow curling hair, and with his beard newly trimmed, mounted on a chestnut horse, whereof the legs were grey from the top of the forelegs, and from the bend of the hindlegs downwards. And the rider wore a coat of yellow satin sewn with green silk, and on his thigh was a gold-hilted sword, with a scabbard of new leather of Cordova, belted with the skin of the deer, and clasped with gold. And over this was a scarf of yellow satin wrought with green silk, the borders whereof were likewise green. And the green of the caparison of the horse, and of his rider, was as green as the leaves of the fir tree, and the yellow was as yellow as the blossom of the broom. So fierce was the aspect of the knight, that fear seized upon them, and they began to flee. And the knight pursued them. And when the horse breathed forth, the men became distant from him, and when he drew his breath, they were drawn near to him, even to the horse's chest. And when he had overtaken them, they besought his mercy. "You have it gladly," said he, "fear nought."

"Ha, chieftain, since thou hast mercy upon me, tell me also who thou art," said Rhonabwy. "I will not conceal my lineage from thee, I am Iddawc the son of Mynyo, yet not by my name, but by my nickname am I best known."

"And wilt thou tell us what thy nickname is?"

"I will tell you; it is Iddawc Cordd Prydain."

"Ha, chieftain," said Rhonabwy, "why art thou called thus?"

"I will tell thee. I was one of the messengers between Arthur and Medrawd his nephew, at the battle of Camlan; and I was then a reckless youth, and through my desire for battle, I kindled strife between them, and stirred up wrath, when I was sent by Arthur the Emperor to reason with Medrawd, and to show him, that he was his foster-father and his uncle, and to seek for peace, lest the sons of the Kings of the Island of Britain, and of the nobles, should be slain. And whereas Arthur charged me with the fairest sayings he could think of, I uttered unto Medrawd the harshest I could devise. And therefore am I called Iddawc Cordd Prydain, for from this did the battle of Camlan ensue. And three nights before the end of the battle of Camlan I left them, and went to the Llech Las in North Britain to do penance. And there I remained doing penance seven years, and after that I gained pardon."

Then lo! They heard a mighty sound which was much louder than that which they heard before, and when they looked round towards the sound, they beheld a ruddy youth, without beard or whiskers, noble of mien, and mounted on a stately courser. And from the shoulders and the front of the knees downwards the horse was bay. And upon the man was a dress of red satin wrought with yellow silk, and yellow were the borders of his scarf. And such parts of his apparel and of the trappings of his horse as were yellow, as yellow were they as the blossom of the broom, and such as were red, were as ruddy as the ruddiest blood in the world.

Then, behold the horseman overtook them, and he asked of Iddawc a share of the little men that were with him. "That which is fitting for me to grant I will grant, and thou shalt be a companion to them as I have been."

And the horseman went away. "Iddawc," inquired Rhonabwy, "who was that horseman?"

"Rhuvawn Pebyr the son of Prince Deorthach."

And they journeyed over the plain of Argyngroeg as far as the ford of Rhyd y Groes on the Severn. And for a mile around the ford on both sides of the road, they saw tents and encampments, and there was the clamour of a mighty host. And they came to the edge of the ford, and there they beheld Arthur sitting on a flat island below the ford, having Bedwini the Bishop on one side of him, and Gwarthegyd the son of Kaw on the other. And a tall, auburn-haired youth stood before him, with his sheathed sword in his hand, and clad in a coat and cap of jet black satin. And his face was white as ivory, and his eyebrows black as jet, and such part of his wrist as could be seen between his glove and his sleeve, was whiter than the lily, and thicker than a warrior's ankle.

Then came Iddawc and they that were with him, and stood before Arthur and saluted him. "Heaven grant thee good," said Arthur. "And where, Iddawc, didst thou find these little men?"

"I found them, lord, up yonder on the road."

Then the Emperor smiled.

"Lord," said Iddawc, "wherefore dost thou laugh?"

"Iddawc," replied Arthur, "I laugh not; but it pitieth me that men of such stature as these should have this island in their keeping, after the men that guarded it of yore."

Then said Iddawc, "Rhonabwy, dost thou see the ring with a stone set in it, that is upon the Emperor's hand?"

"I see it," he answered. "It is one of the properties of that stone to enable thee to remember that thou seest here to-night, and hadst thou not seen the stone, thou wouldest never have been able to remember aught thereof."

After this they saw a troop coming towards the ford. "Iddawc," inquired Rhonabwy, "to whom does yonder troop belong?"

"They are the fellows of Rhuvawn Pebyr the son of Prince Doerthach. And these men are honourably served with mead and bragget, and are freely beloved by the daughters of the kings of the Island of Britain. And this they merit, for they were ever in the front and the rear in every peril."

And he saw but one hue upon the men and the horses of this troop, for they were all as red as blood. And when one of the knights rode forth from the troop, he looked like a pillar of fire glancing athwart the sky. And this troop encamped above the ford.

Then they beheld another troop coming towards the ford, and these from their horses' chests upwards were whiter than the lily, and below blacker than jet. And they saw one of these knights go before the rest, and spur his horse into the ford in such a manner that the water dashed over Arthur and the Bishop, and those holding counsel with them, so that they were as wet as if they had been drenched in the river. And as he turned the head of his horse, the youth who stood before Arthur struck the horse over the nostrils with his sheathed sword, so that, had it been with the bare blade, it would have been a marvel if the bone had not been wounded as well as the flesh. And the knight drew his sword half out of the scabbard, and asked of him, "Wherefore didst thou strike my horse? Whether was it in insult or in counsel unto me?"

"Thou dost indeed lack counsel. What madness caused thee to ride so furiously as to dash the water of the ford over Arthur, and the consecrated Bishop, and their counsellors, so that they were as wet as if they had been dragged out of the river?"

"As counsel then will I take it." So he turned his horse's head round towards his army.

"Iddawc," said Rhonabwy, "who was yonder knight?"

"The most eloquent and the wisest youth that is in this island; Adaon, the son of Taliesin."

"Who was the man that struck his horse?" "A youth of froward nature; Elphin, the son of Gwyddno."

Then spake a tall and stately man, of noble and flowing speech, saying that it was a marvel that so vast a host should be assembled in so narrow a space, and that it was a still greater marvel that those should be there at that time who had promised to be by mid-day in the battle of Badon, fighting with Osla

Gyllellvawr. "Whether thou mayest choose to proceed or not, I will proceed."

"Thou sayest well," said Arthur, "and we will go altogether."

"Iddawc," said Rhonabwy, "who was the man who spoke so marvellously unto Arthur erewhile?"

"A man who may speak as boldly as he listeth, Caradawc Vreichvras, the son of Llyr Marini, his chief counsellor and his cousin."

Then Iddawc took Rhonabwy behind him on his horse, and that mighty host moved forward, each troop in its order, towards Cevndigoll. And when they came to the middle of the ford of the Severn, Iddawc turned his horse's head, and Rhonabwy looked along the valley of the Severn. And he beheld two fair troops coming towards the ford. One troop there came of brilliant white, whereof every one of the men had a scarf of white satin with jet-black borders. And the knees and the tops of the shoulders of their horses were jet-black, though they were of a pure white in every other part. And their banners were pure white, with black points to them all.

"Iddawc," said Rhonabwy, "who are yonder pure white troop?"

"They are the men of Norway, and March the son of Meirchion is their prince. And he is cousin unto Arthur." And further on he saw a troop, whereof each man wore garments of jet-black, with borders of pure white to every scarf; and the tops of the shoulders and the knees of their horses were pure white. And their banners were jet-black with pure white at the point of each.

"Iddawc," said Rhonabwy, "who are the jet-black troop yonder?"

"They are the men of Denmark, and Edeyrn the son of Nudd is their prince."

And when they had overtaken the host, Arthur and his army of mighty ones dismounted below Caer Badou, and he perceived that he and Iddawc journeyed the same road as Arthur. And after they had dismounted he heard a great tumult and confusion amongst the host, and such as were then at the flanks turned to the centre, and such as had been in the centre moved to the flanks. And then, behold, he saw a knight coming, clad, both he and his horse, in mail, of which the rings were whiter than the whitest lily, and the rivets redder than the ruddiest blood. And he rode amongst the host.

"Iddawc," said Rhonabwy, "will yonder host flee?" "King Arthur never fled, and if this discourse of thine were heard, thou wert a lost man. But as to the knight whom thou seest yonder, it is Kai. The fairest horseman is Kai in all Arthur's Court; and the men who are at the front of the army hasten to the rear to see Kai ride, and the men who are in the centre flee to the side, from the shock of his horse. And this is the cause of the confusion of the host."

Thereupon they heard a call made for Kadwr, Earl of Cornwall, and behold he arose with the sword of Arthur in his hand. And the similitude of two serpents was upon the sword in gold. And when the sword was drawn from its scabbard, it seemed as if two flames of fire burst forth from the jaws of the serpents, and then, so wonderful was the sword, that it was hard for any one to look upon it. And the host became still, and the tumult ceased, and the Earl returned to the tent.

"Iddawc, said Rhonabwy, "who is the man who bore the sword of Arthur?"

"Kadwr, the Earl of Cornwall, whose duty it is to arm the King on the days of battle and warfare."

And they heard a call made for Eirynwych Amheibyn, Arthur's servant, a red, rough, ill-favoured man, having red whiskers and bristly hairs. And behold he came upon a tall red horse with the mane parted on each side, and he brought with him a large and beautiful sumpter pack. And the huge red youth dismounted before Arthur, and he drew a golden chair out of the pack, and a carpet of diapered satin. And he spread the carpet before Arthur, and there was an apple of ruddy gold at each corner thereof, and he placed the chair upon the carpet. And so large was the chair that three armed warriors might have sat therein. Gwenn was the name of the carpet, and it was one of its properties that whoever was upon it no one could see him, and he could see every one. And it would retain no colour but its own.

And Arthur sat within the carpet, and Owain the son of Urien was standing before him. "Owain," said Arthur, "wilt thou play chess?" "I will, Lord," said Owain. And the red youth brought the chess for Arthur and Owain; golden pieces and a board of silver. And they began to play.

And while they were thus, and when they were best amused with their game, behold they saw a white tent with a red canopy, and the figure of a jet-black serpent on the top of the tent, and red glaring venomous eyes in the head of the serpent, and a red flaming tongue. And there came a young page with yellow curling hair, and blue eyes, and a newly springing beard, wearing a coat and a surcoat of yellow satin, and hose of thin greenish-yellow cloth upon his feet, and over his hose shoes of particoloured leather, fastened at the insteps with golden clasps. And he bore a heavy three-edged sword with a golden hilt, in a scabbard of black leather tipped with fine gold. And he came to the place where the Emperor and Owain were playing at chess.

And the youth saluted Owain. And Owain marvelled that the youth should salute him and should not have saluted the Emperor Arthur. And Arthur knew what was in Owain's thought. And he said to Owain, "Marvel not that the youth salutes thee now, for he saluted me erewhile; and it is unto thee that his errand is."

Then said the youth unto Owain, "Lord, is it with thy leave that the young pages and attendants of the Emperor harass and torment and worry thy Ravens? And if it be not with thy leave, cause the Emperor to forbid them."

"Lord," said Owain, "thou hearest what the youth says; if it seem good to thee, forbid them from my Ravens."

"Play thy game," said he. Then the youth returned to the tent.

That game did they finish, and another they began, and when they were in the midst of the game, behold, a ruddy young man with auburn curling hair and large eyes, well-grown, and having his beard new-shorn, came forth from a bright yellow tent, upon the summit of which was the figure of a bright red lion. And he was clad in a coat of yellow satin, falling as low as the small of his leg, and embroidered with threads of red silk. And on his feet were hose of fine white buckram, and buskins of black leather were over his hose, whereon were golden clasps. And in his hand a huge, heavy, three-edged sword, with a scabbard of red deer-hide, tipped with gold. And he came to the place where Arthur and Owain were playing at chess. And he saluted him. And Owain was troubled at his salutation, but Arthur minded it no more than before. And the youth said unto

Owain, "Is it not against thy will that the attendants of the Emperor harass thy Ravens, killing some and worrying others? If against thy will it be, beseech him to forbid them."

"Lord," said Owain, "forbid thy men, if it seem good to thee."

"Play thy game," said the Emperor. And the youth returned to the tent.

And that game was ended and another begun. And as they were beginning the first move of the game, they beheld at a small distance from them a tent speckled yellow, the largest ever seen, and the figure of an eagle of gold upon it, and a precious stone on the eagle's head. And coming out of the tent, they saw a youth with thick yellow hair upon his head, fair and comely, and a scarf of blue satin upon him, and a brooch of gold in the scarf upon his right shoulder as large as a warrior's middle finger. And upon his feet were hose of fine Totness, and shoes of parti-coloured leather, clasped with gold, and the youth was of noble bearing, fair of face, with ruddy cheeks and large hawk's eyes. In the hand of the youth was a mighty lance, speckled yellow, with a newly sharpened head; and upon the lance a banner displayed.

Fiercely angry, and with rapid pace, came the youth to the place where Arthur was playing at chess with Owain. And they perceived that he was wroth. And thereupon he saluted Owain, and told him that his Ravens had been killed, the chief part of them, and that such of them as were not slain were so wounded and bruised that not one of them could raise its wings a single fathom above the earth.

"Lord," said Owain, "forbid thy men."

"Play," said he, "if it please thee."

Then said Owain to the youth, "Go back, and wherever thou findest the strife at the thickest, there lift up the banner, and let come what pleases Heaven."

So the youth returned back to the place where the strife bore hardest upon the Ravens, and he lifted up the banner; and as he did so they all rose up in the air, wrathful and fierce and high of spirit, clapping their wings in the wind, and shaking off the weariness that was upon them. And recovering their energy and courage, furiously and with exultation did they, with one sweep, descend upon the heads of the men, who had erewhile caused them anger and pain and damage, and they seized some by the heads and others by the eyes, and some by the ears, and others by the arms, and carried them up into the air; and in the air there was a mighty tumult with the flapping of the wings of the triumphant Ravens, and with their croaking; and there was another mighty tumult with the groaning of the men, that were being torn and wounded, and some of whom were slain.

And Arthur and Owain marvelled at the tumult as they played at chess; and, looking, they perceived a knight upon a dun-coloured horse coming towards them. And marvellous was the hue of the dun horse. Bright red was his right shoulder, and from the top of his legs to the centre of his hoof was bright yellow. Both the knight and his horse were fully equipped with heavy foreign armour. The clothing of the horse from the front opening upwards was of bright red sendal, and from thence opening downwards was of bright yellow sendal. A large gold-hilted one-edged sword had the youth upon his thigh, in a scabbard of light blue, and tipped with Spanish laton. The belt of the sword was of dark green leather with golden slides and a clasp of ivory upon it, and a buckle of jet-black upon the clasp. A helmet of gold was on the head of the knight, set with precious stones of great virtue, and at the top of the helmet was the image of a flame-coloured leopard with two ruby-red stones in its head, so that it was astounding for a warrior, however stout his heart, to look at the face of the leopard, much more at the face of the knight. He had in his hand a blue-shafted lance, but from the haft to the point it was stained crimson-red with the blood of the Ravens and their plumage.

The knight came to the place where Arthur and Owain were seated at chess. And they perceived that he was harassed and vexed and weary as he came towards them. And the youth saluted Arthur, and told him that the Ravens of Owain were slaying his young men and attendants. And Arthur looked at Owain and said, "Forbid thy Ravens."

"Lord," answered Owain, "play thy game." And they played. And the knight returned back towards the strife, and the Ravens were not forbidden any more than before.

And when they had played awhile, they heard a mighty tumult, and a wailing of men, and a croaking of Ravens, as they carried the men in their strength into the air, and, tearing them betwixt them, let them fall piecemeal to the earth. And during the tumult they saw a knight coming towards them, on a light grey horse, and the left foreleg of the horse was jet-black to the centre of his hoof. And the knight and the horse were fully accoutred with huge heavy blue armour. And a robe of honour of yellow diapered satin was upon the knight, and the borders of the robe were blue. And the housings of the horse were jet-black, with borders of bright yellow. And on the thigh of the youth was a sword, long, and three-edged, and heavy. And the scabbard was of red cut leather, and the belt of new red deer-skin, having upon it many golden slides and a buckle of the bone of the sea-horse, the tongue of which was jet-black. A golden helmet was upon the head of the knight, wherein were set sapphire-stones of great virtue. And at the top of the helmet was the figure of a flame-coloured lion, with a fiery-red tongue, issuing above a foot from his mouth, and with venomous eyes, crimson-red, in his head. And the knight came, bearing in his hand a thick ashen lance, the head whereof, which had been newly steeped in blood, was overlaid with silver.

And the youth saluted the Emperor: "Lord," said he, "carest thou not for the slaying of thy pages, and thy young men, and the sons of the nobles of the Island of Britain, whereby it will be difficult to defend this island from henceforward for ever?"

"Owain," said Arthur, "forbid thy Ravens." "Play this game, Lord," said Owain.

So they finished the game and began another; and as they were finishing that game, lo, they heard a great tumult and a clamour of armed men, and a croaking of Ravens, and a flapping of wings in the air, as they flung down the armour entire to the ground, and the men and the horses piecemeal. Then they saw coming a knight on a lofty-headed piebald horse. And the left shoulder of the horse was of bright red, and its right leg from the chest to the hollow of the hoof was pure white. And the knight and horse were equipped with arms of speckled yellow, variegated with Spanish laton. And there was a robe of honour upon him, and upon his horse, divided in two parts, white and black, and the borders of the robe of honour were of golden purple. And above the robe he wore a sword three-edged and bright, with a golden hilt. And the belt of the sword was of yellow goldwork, having a clasp upon it of the eyelid of a black sea-horse, and a tongue of yellow gold to the clasp. Upon the head of the knight was a bright helmet of yellow laton, with sparkling stones of crystal in it, and at the crest of the helmet was the figure of a griffin, with a stone of many virtues in his head. And he had an ashen spear in his hand, with a round shaft, coloured with azure-blue. And the head of the spear was newly stained with blood, and was overlaid with fine silver.

Wrathfully came the knight to the place where Arthur was, and he told him that the Ravens had slain his household and the sons of the chief men of the island, and he besought him to cause Owain to forbid his Ravens. And Arthur besought Owain to forbid them. Then Arthur took the golden chessmen that were upon the board, and crushed them until they became as dust. Then Owain ordered Gwres the son of Rheged to lower his banner. So it was lowered, and all was peace.

Then Rhonabwy inquired of Iddawc who were the first three men that came to Owain, to tell him his Ravens were being slain.

Said Iddawc, "They were men who grieved that Owain should suffer loss, his fellow-chieftains and companions, Selyv the son of Kyan Garwyn of Powys, and Gwgawn Gleddyvrudd, and Gwres the son of Rheged, he who bears the banner in the day of battle and strife."

"Who," said Rhonabwy, "were the last three men who came to Arthur, and told him that the Ravens were slaughtering his men?"

"The best of men," said Iddawc, "and the bravest, and who would grieve exceedingly that Arthur should have damage in aught; Blathaon the son of Mawrheth, and Rhuvawn Pebyr the son of Prince Deorthach, and Hyveidd Unllenn."

And with that behold four-and-twenty knights came from Olsa Gyllellvawr to crave a truce of Arthur for a fortnight and a month. And Arthur arose and went to take counsel. And he came to where a tall, auburn, curly-headed man was a little way off, and there he assembled his counsellors. Bedwini, the Bishop, and Gwarthegyd the son of Kaw, and March the son of Meirchawn, and Caradawc Vreichvras, and Gwalchmai the son of Gwyar, and Edeyrn the son of Nudd, and Rhuvawn Pebyr the son of Prince Deorthach, and Rhiogan the son of the King of Ireland, and Gwenwynwyn the son of Nav, Howel the son of Emyr Llydaw, Gwilym the son of Rhwyf Freinc, and Daned the son of Ath, and Goreu Custennin, and Mabon the son of Modron, and Peredur Paladyr Hir, and Hyveidd Unllenn, and Twrch the son of Perif, and Nerth the son of Kadarn, and Gobrwy the son of Echel Vorddwyttwll, Gwair the son of Gwestyl, and Gadwy the son of Geraint, Trystan the son of Tallwch, Moryen Manawc, Granwen the son of Llyr, and Llacheu the son of Arthur, and Llawvrodedd Varvawc, and Kadwr Earl of Cornwall, Morvran the son of Tegid, and Rhyawd the son of Morgant, and Dyvyr the son of Alun Dyved, Gwrhyr Gwalstawd Ieithoedd, Adaon the son of Taliesin, Llary the son of Kasnar Wledig, and Fflewddur Fflam, and Greidawl Galldovydd, Gilbert the son of Kadgyffro, Menw the son of Teirgwaedd, Gwrthmwl Wledig, Cawrdav the son of Caradawc Vreichvras, Gildas the son of Kaw, Kadyriaith the son of Saidi, and many of the men of Norway, and Denmark, and many of the men of Greece, and a crowd of the men of the host came to that council.

"Iddawc," said Rhonabwy, "who was the auburn-haired man to whom they came just now?"

"Rhun the son of Maelgwm Gwynedd, a man whose prerogative it is, that he may join in counsel with all." "And wherefore did they admit into counsel with men of such dignity as are yonder a stripling so young as Kadyriaith the son of Saidi?"

"Because there is not throughout Britain a man better skilled in counsel than he."

Thereupon, behold, bards came and recited verses before Arthur, and no man understood those verses but Kadyriaith only, save that they were in Arthur's praise.

And lo, there came four-and-twenty asses with their burdens of gold and silver, and a tired wayworn man with each of them, bringing tribute to Arthur from the Islands of Greece. Then Kadyriaith the son of Saidi besought that a truce might be granted to Osla Gyllellvawr for the space of a fortnight and a month, and that the asses and the burdens they carried might be given to the bards, to be to them as the reward for their stay and that their verse might be recompensed during the time of the truce. And thus it was settled.

"Rhonabwy," said Iddawc, "would it not be wrong to forbid a youth who can give counsel so liberal as this from coming to the councils of his Lord?"

Then Kai arose, and he said, "Whosoever will follow Arthur, let him be with him to-night in Cornwall, and whosoever will not, let him be opposed to Arthur even during the truce." And through the greatness of the tumult that ensued, Rhonabwy awoke. And when he awoke he was upon the yellow calf-skin, having slept three nights and three days.

And this tale is called the Dream of Rhonabwy. And this is the reason that no one knows the dream without a book, neither bard nor gifted seer; because of the various colours that were upon the horses, and the many wondrous colours of the arms and of the panoply, and of the precious scarfs, and of the virtue-bearing stones.

Fifteenth-century picture of gypsies on the road.

7

The Interpretation of Dreams

> What Freud does not sufficiently recognize is that dreams do not all
> follow similar courses because dreamers have different psychologies.
> —Joseph Jastrow (1863–1944)

AN OPENING WORD FOR THIS CHAPTER

This is what this book is chiefly about, dream interpretation. Dream
interpretation is probably why you picked up this book in the first place.

This last chapter may well be the first thing you have turned to. It
will certainly assist you in deciphering what your dreams mean, though
the book differs from most dream-books because it puts the process of
interpretation into perspective, connecting it to religious, scientific, and
other traditions. Books that have only simple lists of symbols and
"meanings" are not only unoriginal but arbitrary. Sure, there are some
common symbols we can all agree on, but not enough to fill a "gypsy
dream-book." So most of that stuff is garbage.

It is important to go beyond "looking up your dreams;" you must
decode them. You have to interpret your dreams in the light of your personal language, and "come at it crabwise" as Hunter S. Thompson
would say.

Psychiatry or psychotherapy can assist but the work is essentially
yours. Some dream-books spin out what I have given you briefly into
whole books, but, as with many other aspects of my topic, I present all
you need as concisely as possible.

When this book was first proposed, I was warned that "the market is flooded with dream books." My response was that I agreed, had sampled a great many of them in my research and separated the wheat from the chaff, and would create a new book with all their virtues plus a sensible context for what dreams mean.

I won't take 100 or 250 pages to tell you that you need to keep a dream journal as accurately as you can. The quick fix dream books are not effective. You simply look up in some list that "rhinoceros=phallus" because you vaguely recall a rhino in a dream. Maybe your dream really had something to do with Reno, or Reno Sweeney, who knows? As for something that may turn up in your dream such as a dark blue computer diskette, the run of the mill dream-books are useless anyway.

The big answers in life are not in books. They are inside you from birth. Dream interpretation is one kind of self-examination. A long time ago a great philosopher told us that "the unexamined life is not worth living." The unexamined dream is wasted, too. It can be a key to self-knowledge and betterment.

Esquire for January 2001 notes that dream interpretation is one of the self-help and self-improvement standbys and that Freud's *The Interpretation of Dreams* is a classic. "There are few things more self-indulgent than keeping a dream journal," says *Esquire*. While I can think of quite a few more self-indulgences than *Esquire* seems able to dredge up, I agree with the magazine writer that "the king of shrinks makes a persuasive case that understanding yourself starts with understanding that nightmare about the octopus, the train, and Heidi Klum."

So keep a dream journal as conscientiously as you can if you want to interpret your dreams, read this last chapter with special care,

A gypsy

and do not be a slave to symbols. Face it: no book of reasonable length could list all the things that turn up in your dreams. That's first. Second: what a thing means to you is colored by your personal experience. It does not necessarily carry the same significance for you as it does for others.

You have your very own idiolect of the unconscious, or, to put it more simply, you share with others enough "words" so that communication is possible but—this is important—when I say *dog* we all know what kind of an animal is meant but you may be thinking of your little Chihuahua and I may be thinking of my big sheepdog.

Few or none of the dream-books can guarantee you what the Amerindians call the instant "great seeing," that moment of insight when (as in the cartoons) the light bulb goes on.

Therefore I have resisted the argument that a book such as mine is a waste of time in a flooded market. It reminds me of a student of mine who wrote about the problems of college admission, "Nobody can get in because everybody's going."

There also seems to me to be some need here for my book, as I said at the start and reiterate as I come near the end. What I want to do is give you a final push to make something of your dreams. This means that *you*, not some gypsy or even some psychiatrist, has to decode, translate, weigh as well as identify the things that you can recall turning up in your nighttime adventures of the unconscious.

All you really have to do is to have the courage and the persistence to solve the problem by applying brutally honest introspection.

WHEN INTERPRETATION OF DREAMS STARTED

According to a *Dictionary of Dates* published way back in 1861: "The first who attempted to give an interpretation to dreams, and to draw prognostics from omens, was Amphictyon of Athens, 1497 BC."

I question this. I believe that human beings have tried since time immemorial to figure out what their dreams mean. Even the earliest people must have had some superstitious belief that their dreams might tell the future. The Chaldeans and the Egyptians had systems of dream interpretations and later, as you are aware if you have read earlier chapters here, the Jews claimed they were the only ones who could read dreams right. The Old Testament has, as you know, many interpreted dreams. The Talmud, you may not know, has loads of material on the causes of dreams (angels, demons, indigestion among them) and dream readings.

Whether your dream interpretation book is from ancient Egypt or tenth-century Islam, modern Tibet or Britain, it probably tells you more about the society that produced it than it does about the symbols that occur in dreams. Even what is noted and what is not noted is a clue to the mindset of individuals united by little more than the universal human attraction to superstition, "blyndnesse of old misbelieve."

WHAT DO DREAMS MEAN?

Flying, falling, naked, trapped, lost, thirsty, eating, sexually aroused (or engaged), meeting dead friends or relatives, younger, richer, apprehensive, pursued—"Some dreadful thing doth close behind him tread"…. What does it mean?

This is not easy to say. We could consult the experts, but who are they? Presumably not dream-books that crib from each other and repeat the same inane stuff century after century. Should we consult experts in the sciences of the mind? If I'm OK and you're OK, are *they* OK? In my opinion, psychologists, psychiatrists, and psychotherapists are as a lot almost as derided, even despised, as lawyers. There may be something in that. There may not.

Perhaps it is just as well the experts do not usually agree. Way back in the second-century before Christ, when Artemidoris published a huge compendium on the symbols of dreams, (and assigned a meaning to each one), he got flak. This despite the fact that he tried to avoid problems and was so vague and open to interpretation himself that his book was no use at all.

If the experts could agree on symbols, they would be putting themselves out of business. You could buy the book and go in for DIY analysis. Better mental health and increased self-awareness at home in your spare time, only minutes a day.

After all, Migene González-Wippler's little paperback, *Dreams and What They Mean to You*, had 12 printings of the first edition by 2000. This is despite the fact that her appeal is chiefly in the dream-book section where she says—on what basis we do not know—what dream symbols commonly mean to other people, not to *You*.

We all have our personal associations. True, some associations are obvious: Dawn suggests a new beginning. But "Geranium—You will have considerable wealth in your life?" Where does she get that? How does she defend it. Deponent saith not.

Most importantly, if we are going to do anything useful with the symbols in our dreams we have to know what those symbols mean not to Sra. Gonzalez-Wippler but to each of us as an individual. Geranium, to me, suggests Charles Dickens. (He liked to wear one in his button-hole.) I have personal associations with a host of other symbols, from Azalea Bush to Zinc. You may have special meanings you attach to, for instance, Basketball, Crab Grass, and Fishing Fly—none of which she addresses. What she does mention is *superstés*, mere left-over ideas.

"I believe it to be true that dreams are the reliable interpretations of our inclinations," wrote Michel de Montaigne in his *Essais*, "but art is required to sort out and comprehend them." The art of free association is a personal matter. It is also ever-changing: your brain is altered con-tinually by what you experience and even by what you eat. (See Jean Carper's *Your Miracle Brain.)*

You will not get accurate, updated information from books. You develop that by recalling vivid symbols from your dreams and letting your waking mind freely react to the names.

There is even a book that offers to make you better in bed when awake: Les Peto's *Dream Lover: Transforming Relationships through Dreams* (1991). Yes, you can change yourself and your relationships with others if you make good use of your dreams. But to write a book tai-lored exactly to your personal requirements is far beyond any writers I have ever heard of. David Fontana's *The Secret Language of Dreams* (1994) is prettier than most guides and yet is no closer to reliable and rigid definitions of symbols than the tackiest little pamphlet in paper covers, the dream-book that looks as if it had been lithographed from stale bread. The dreams of little girls in Kansas do not have the same "vocabulary" as, for instance, those of men in The Klondike (see Brad Evenson in the *Ottawa Citizen* 17 June 1998, A 4). The dreams of blacks and whites, of young and old, of Baptists and Buddhists are all different.

However, we do have lists of What The Dream Symbols Mean. Go ahead and play with them, or hire a professional to spend a lot of hours and a lot of your hard-earned money working out the current implica-tions of the fact that your mommy locked your favorite doll in a trunk when you misbehaved at age three. Or discover with a shout of *Eureka!*—you have vacuumed your messy mind—why you keep having that recurring dream in which you are at a church social and you see your older brother pee in the punch when no one else is looking.

I'm going to rush right past the one where you fall downstairs with a vase of yellow flowers or the one where you have to defend yourself against *It*. Remember your dreams through whatever method you pre-fer, and pay a healthy amount of attention to them.

We undoubtedly are still interested in dream interpretation as one way to know ourselves. (Sandra Shulman's *The Interpretation of Dreams and Nightmares* came out in 1973.) Few if any books meet my criteria: Where did you get that? How do you know it is true? Just *who* says Tea means unforeseen circumstances?

This reminds me of a pretentious woman I met recently who stated that "Paris is Virgo." When I asked her what that meant and where she got that information, she announced she could argue with me but was above that. She fell silent, which is about as good, I suppose, as conceding to my unexpressed wish for her to shut up.

Use a published dream-book. They are mostly all alike. Plumbing your depths is going to be hard work. It is not just a question of looking up the answer in some unoriginal, cheap paperback.

CHINESE DREAM INTERPRETATION IN THE THREE KINGDOMS PERIOD (AD 220–264)

Once upon a time a man consulted Chou Hsuan, the dream interpreter, saying: "Last night I dreamed of straw dogs." He asked what this meant. Chou Hsuan said it meant that he would soon eat a nice meal. And that happened.

The man reappeared to say he had dreamed again of straw dogs. "Be careful," Chou Hsuan warned him. "You may fall from a carriage and break your legs." And that happened.

A third time the man came to say he had dreamed of straw dogs. "Be careful," Chou Hsuan said, "or your house will burn down." And that happened.

Finally the man confessed to Chou Hsuan that he had never dreamed of straw dogs at all. "I just made that up to test you," he said.

"That makes no difference," Chou Hsuan responded. "The spirits moved you to say those things and that is the same as if they had appeared to you in dreams."

"When I told you three times I had dreamed of straw dogs," the man continued, "you gave me three different interpretations. Why was that?"

"Straw dogs," Chou Hsuan reminded him, "are sacrificial offerings. First they are part of a ceremonial feast. Then they are discarded, thrown into the road where they are run over by carriages. At last the straw is gathered up and burned. That is why three dreams of straw dogs, whether you had the dreams or not, are to be read as I read them and why what they foretold came to pass as you have reported to me."

HORRORSCOPE

Don't say you don't glance at the horoscopes in the paper. More Americans read horoscopes than editorial pages. I put this in to remind you that dream-books and astrology are alike. They are popular and useless.

Here's a quote from one of Bob Brezney's breezy columns—I claim I read him for his wit—relating to dream interpretation:

> CAPRICORN (Dec. 22-Jan.19): As I woke up this morning, a voice from my dream said, "Tell Capricorn that the juggler should go for the jugular." Let's analyze the symbolism of that enigmatic oracle. A juggler is skilled at an art that looks simple but takes a lot of practice. With a light touch and burning concentration, the juggler improvises buoyant stability in the midst of bubbling flux. Maybe the informant in my dream was suggesting that this is the frame of mind you should be in as you close on your prey.

DIFFERENCES OF OPINION

One time I was writing a book that had to discuss astrology. My publisher paid for horoscopes of myself from half a dozen of the leading US and UK experts. They disagreed to an alarming extent, and I was forbidden to run these horoscopes side by side, even without comment, on the grounds that I had not warned the experts that "I would hold them up to ridicule in print."

You may have to do the same with dream interpretations. Despite the fact that dream books copy shamelessly from each other a lot of the time, and the so-called experts don't even bother with explanations. One may say this or that is in the ascendant, whazzis is in the house of whoozis, etc., and then disagree with other alleged experts on what that signifies. There is a famous story of the learned Rabbi Binza who submitted a dream to 24 different interpreters and received 24 different interpretations. The old story assures us that "all 24 interpretations proved correct," but I beg leave to doubt that claim.

If you are not prepared to go through the arduous business of decoding your dream symbols, why not read a few "gypsy dreambooks" and take the answers you like the best? It's a free country!

REFERENCES ON DREAM INTERPRETATION
IN THE POPULAR PRESS

"Do Your Dreams Have Any Meaning? Views of Hans von Brauchitsch [University of Oklahoma Health Sciences Center], *USA Today* 118 (July 1989), 10.

Graves, Ginny. "Dream On: How to Solve Your Problems while You Sleep," *Mademoiselle* 101 (March 1995), 190–193+.

————————-. "What Your Dreams are Trying to Tell You," *Glamour* 96: 8 (August 1998), 190–191.

Haray, Keith. "Language of the Night...," *Omni* 15 (September 1993), 46 – 47+.

"How to Build a Dream," *Psychology Today* 28 (November/December 1995), 47.

Morris, Jill. "Your Dreams: What You Can Learn from Them!," *Good Housekeeping* 204 (April 1987), 12.

"Omni Book of Dreams," *Omni* 12 (November 1989), 1–8.

Williams, Gurney. "What Do Your Dreams Mean?," *McCall's* 125: 11 (August 1999), 98–101.

REFERENCES OF SCIENTISTS

There are too many of these even to create a representative select list, but here are some recent ones that the layman could read:

Arden, John B. *Consciousness, Dreams & Self* (2000).

Blechner, Mark J. "The Analysis and Creation of Dream Meaning: Intrapersonal, Intra-psychic, and Neurobiological Perspectives," *Contemporary Psychoanalysis* 34:2 (April 1998), 181–194.

Buckeley, Kelly. *An Introduction to the Psychology of Dreaming* (1997).

Caroppo, E., *et al.* "Recurrent Oneiric Themes...during Psychotherapy," *New Trends in Experimental and Clinical Psychiatry* 13:4 (October-December 1997), 275–278.

Conigliaro, Vincenzo. *Dreams as a Tool in Psychodynamic Psychotherapy* (1997).

Epstein, Arthur. *Dreaming and Other Involuntary Mentation* (1996).

Ray, Douglas. *Dreams and the Inner Self* (1999).

Langs, Robert. *Dreams and Emotional Adaptation* (1998).

Marcus, Laura. *Sigmund Freud's The Interpretation of Dreams* (1999).

Moustakas, Clark. *Existential Psychotherapy and the Interpretations of Dreams* (1994).

Samson, Anne. "Science, Metaphor and Meaning in the Interpretation of Dreams," *British Journal of Psychotherapy* 14:3 (Spring 1998), 327–336.

JUNGIAN DREAM INTERPRETATION

I like Jung. I warble,

> In the spring a Jung man's fancy
> Lightly turns to thoughts of love.

I strongly recommend you read Jung and maybe Joseph Campbell or even books like these:

Jung, C. G. *Dreams* (1996).
Thomson-Daniel, G. G. & Gabriel Thomson. *A Jungian Dreambook* (1997).

(Do not get hung up on them, for Jung says that "every form of addiction is bad, no matter whether the narcotic be alcohol, morphine, or idealism.")

A DREAM CORRECTLY INTERPRETED

Philip of Macedon, the father of Alexander the Great, reported a dream in which he sealed up his wife's belly. He took this to mean that she would be barren. Aristander corrected him: Philip's wife must be pregnant, because one does not seal up an empty container. And so it was.

SIR THOMAS BROWNE ON DREAM INTERPRETATION

Sir Thomas Browne (1605–1682) was a physician who was very interested in what he called "vulgar errors." On the subject of symbols seen in dreams he wrote in *A Letter to a Friend* (published posthumously, 1690):

> Some Dreams I confess may admit of easie and feminine Exposition: he who dreamed that he could not see his right Shoulder, might easily fear to lose the sight of his right Eye; he that before a Journey dreamed that his Feet were cut off, had a plain warning not to undertake his intended Journey. But why to dream of Lettuce should presage some ensuing disease, why to eat Figs should signify foolish Talk, why to eat Eggs great Trouble, and to dream of Blindness should be so highly commended, according to the oneirocritical Verses of Astrampsychus and [St.] Nicephorus, I shall leave unto your Divination.

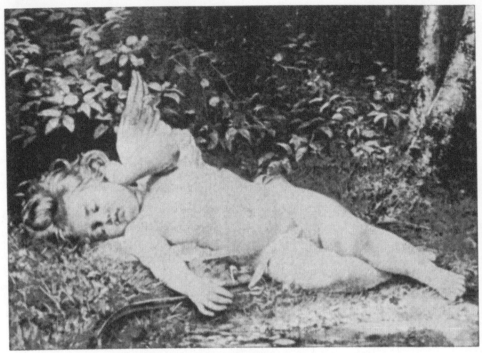

Cupid once upon a bed
Of roses laid his weary head.

Love dreams and puts us in touch with needs and news not known to the waking mind. The gods were said to speak through us in inspiration, to us in revelation, in trance and in ecstatic visions. God or The Devil was said to dictate in inner voices. Conscience was *inwit*. Hypnosis freed other deep forces. Ghosts (or our hidden ideas) spoke in séances of trance mediums and in automatic writing.

25 DREAM INTERPRETERS AT WORK

Baylis, Janice H. *Sex, Symbols and Dreams* (1996).
Bentley, Peter. *The Book of Dream Symbols* (1995).
Boss, Medard. *The Analysis of Dreams* (1958).
Buckland, Raymond. *Gypsy Dream Dictionary* (1999).
DeBarcy, Carlotta. *The Great Dream Book* (1996).
Fink, G. *Dream Symbols A to Z* (1999).
Gold, Solomon. *Erotic Dreams* (1999).
Goldberg, E. *Ultimate Dictionary of Dreams* (1999).
Goodison, Lucy. *The Dreams of Women* (1996).
Grant, Russell. *The Illustrated Dream Dictionary* (1996).
Hamilton-Parker, Craig. *The Hidden Meaning of Dreams* (1999).

Hill, Clara, *et al.* "Dream Interpretation Sessions: Who Volunteers, Who Benefits, and What Volunteer Clients [undergraduate students] View as Most and Least Helpful," *Journal of Counseling Psychology* 44 (January 1997), 53–62.

Interpretación de los sueños. Mexicanos Editores/Panorama Publishing (1997).

Mahoney, Patrick J. "Ben Jonson's 'Best Piece of Poetrie' [his son's ghost seen in a possible dream]," *American Imago* 37 (1979), 69–79.

Moir, T. *Dictionnaire des images, symboles du rêve* (1997).

O'Brien, Jodi & Peter Kollock. *The Production of Reality* (3rd edition, 2001).

Pliskin, Marcia & Shari L. Just, *The Complete Idiot's Guide to Interpreting Your Dreams* (1999).

Prophecies of Paracelsus. Rudolf Steiner Publications (1973).

Recht, Roberta. "The Foundations of an Admirable Science:' Descartes's Dreams of 10 November 1619," *Humanities in Society* 4:2–3 (1981), 203–219.

Reiser, Morton F. "The Art and Science of Dream Interpretation," *Journal of the American Psychoanalytical Association* 45: 3 (1997), 891–905.

Ryans, B. *American New World Dictionary of Dream Language Interpretations* (1999).

Segal, Ora. "[James] Joyce's Interpretations of Dreams," *International Review of Psycho-Analysis* 6 (1979), 483–498.

Spurr, Pam. *Understanding Your Child's Dreams* (1999).

Stewart, B. T. "The Renaissance Interpretation of Dreams and Their Use in Elizabethan Drama," doctoral dissertation, Northwestern University (1942).

Ten Thousand Dreams and their Traditional Symbols. W. Foulsham & Co. (1995).

Todeschi, Kevin J. *The Encyclopedia of Symbolism* (1995).

Most if not all of these books are indeed for "complete idiots," unless a little commonsense can be put into play.

A CAVEAT ON DREAM INTERPRETATION

A French writer on the occult (Paul Lacroix), writing under the pseudonym Jacob, ended his obscure nineteenth-century book on dream interpretation with this straightforward statement:

There is in all things a golden mean which must continually be sought and, when it is found, adhered to. When we consider the art of dream interpretation let us always remember this final axiom: that what may be perilous to admit blindly need not be systematically rejected. Root out errors and prejudices, but on the condition that we do not offend reason by too much credulity in the place of false gods let us not set up an utter void.

Don't be too credulous, always question, and always ask *how* people know what they so dogmatically state to be true, but never be rigid or throw out the baby with the bath water. My grandmother had an expression, rather surprisingly crude for a lady of her formality: "There's something in that, as the Irishman said when he put his hand into the pot."

There's a little truth in most outrageous things. Even if it were totally impossible to link any useful meanings to the images in dreams—which I do not think is the case—it would still be notable that since mankind first started keeping records there has been superstitious belief. It used to be said that the very first writing of the world consisted of two records discovered in ancient Egyptian tombs. One dealt with making women's cosmetics and the other with reading fortunes in people's palms. Both still make money hand over fist.

In Danish folklore, if you tread on a loaf of bread you will wake up in a fairyland. Superstitions had to come from somewhere, prompted by the governing force of dreams, which is wish fulfillment.

Superstitions may be foolish, even pitiful. However, superstitions exist and need to be noted, and the fact that they are widely believed is incontestably significant. All those dream-book writers, copying slavishly from each other, prove that there is a big market for dream interpretation books of all sorts and any quality.

There are many things people believe that I do not believe. I keep telling that to people who ask about the occult books I write, but *I believe that people believe these things*—and I believe *that* is well worth considering. People are my favorite puzzles and, as the old English saying goes, "there's nothing queerer than folk."

WHAT THE DREAM MEANS MAY BE SHOCKING

John Eugene Unterecker in his biography of the poet Hart Crane (1899–1932), *Voyager* (1969), gives us some idea of the troubled mind of the homosexual author of *The Bridge*. Crane committed suicide by jumping off a boat at sea after a short and difficult life. Unterecker gives

ASTROLOGASTER,
OR,
THE FIGVRE-CASTER.

Rather the Arraignment of Artlesse Aftrologers, and Fortune-tellers
that cheat many ignorant people vnder the pretence of foretelling things to
come, of telling things that are paft, finding out things that are loft, &x.
pounding Dreames, calculating Deaths and Natiuities,
once againe brought to the Barre.

By Iohn Melton.

Cicero. *Stultorum plena funt omnia.*

Imprinted at London by *Barnard Alfop,* for *Edward Blackmore,* and are
to be fold in *Paules* Churchyard, at the Signe of the
Blazing-Starre. 1620.

An English book of 1620 arraigns astrologers and fortune-tellers "that cheat" many
ignorant people under the pretense of "foretelling things to come." The public still
spends many millions of dollars in the United States each year—and great sums of
money in Britain and everywhere else, too—on horoscopes, "expounding Dreames,"
and such.

us this description of one of Crane's dreams. Unusually (for Freud showed that we often much disguise the true meanings of our dreams) in this dream there is a shock of recognition about the horrific content. Unterecker states of Crane that:

>...he had the feeling, long after he was awake, that it was something he had actually experienced. He had gone to bed exhausted, and when he [apparently] woke up, he was in his old room on 115th Street [in New York City].
>
>He got up, remembering that he had to hunt for something in the attic, and as he stumbled through the dusty attic—half awake—he kept trying to remember what he was looking for. Whatever it was, it was in a trunk.
>
>He was sure of that. It was very dark in the attic, but when he found the trunk, there was enough light for him to see that it was full of his mother's clothes. He started rummaging through them, looking for whatever it was he was looking for, pulling out dresses, shoes, stockings, underclothing. But the trunk was so full it seemed as if he would never find what he was after. There was so much to look at that when he found the hand, he hardly realized that it was a human hand; but when he found another hand and a piece of an arm, he knew there was a body in the trunk. He kept pulling out piece after piece of it, all mixed in with the clothing. The clothing was covered with blood. It was not until he had almost emptied the trunk that he realized he was unpacking the dismembered body of his mother.

Here the attic symbolizes the mind of the as the basement in Poe's *The Fall of the House of Usher* is a symbol of the deep recesses of the mind. Poe's building has a crack in it, the fatal flaw in the whole Usher family and especially in Roderick, the last of the Ushers. The trunk seems, like the trunk of Blanche Dubois in *A Streetcar Named Desire*, to be the repository of memories. The dismembered body of his mother points pretty surely to a psychopathology or haunting guilt.

TRY YOUR HAND AT INTERPRETING THIS DREAM

In addition to the dream above, in Donald Hall's *Oxford Book of American Literary Anecdotes* (1981) we find this reminiscence by the critic Edmund Wilson (first seen in his survey *The Twenties*, 1975) of e.e. cummings (1894–1962) and John Dos Passos (1896–1970):

They had once taken a trip to Spain together. When we got to a town, Cummings said, I'd want to go out to the square or somewhere to see if I could find something [he meant a girl]. Dos would never go with me—he'd say, "I'll just stay in the hotel here, I think." One day I said to him, "Dos: don't you ever think about women?" No. "Don't you ever dream about sex?" No. What I went through with that man! He'd wake me up in the night groaning and throwing himself around in his sleep. I'd say, "What's the matter, Dos?" He'd say, "Why, I thought there were some beautiful white swans overhead." One day I said, "You know, sometimes sex appears in dreams in very much disguised forms. You may be dreaming about sex without knowing it. Tell me one of your dreams—what did you dream about last night, for example?" He said, "Why, I dweamed I had a bunch of aspawagus and I was twying to give it to you." This had evidently stopped Cummings in his tracks.

THE DANGER OF A PROPHETICAL DREAM MISINTERPRETED

Caesar: Calpurnia here, my wife, stays me at home.
  She dreamt last night she saw my statuë
  Which, like a fountain with an hundred spouts,
  Did run pure blood, and many lusty Romans
  Came smiling, and did bathe their hands in it.
  And these does she apply for warnings and portents
  And evils imminent, and on her knee
  Hath begg'd that I will stay at home today.
Decius: This dream is all amiss interpreted;
  It was a vision fair and fortunate:
  Your statue spouting blood in many pipes,
  In which so many smiling Romans bath'd,
  Signifies that from you great Rome shall suck
  Reviving blood, and that great men shall press
  For tinctures, stains, relics, and cognizance.
  This by Calpurnia's dream is signified.
Caesar: And this way have you well expounded it.

The devious and flattering misreading of the dream by Decius Brutus convinces ambitious Caesar, embarrassed at being persuaded by a woman's dream to hide from danger, to go to his death at the hands of the conspirators. Shakespeare in his *Tragedy of Julius Caesar* shows, as he does in *Macbeth* and in other plays, that the death of the protagonist is brought on by a flaw in his character as much or more than by any opposition from others. We are the victims in tragedy of our own weaknesses, not the strength of others. We must not permit those weaknesses to blind us to the true meaning of warnings when these are clearly given to us, not even, perhaps, to be so foolish as to brush aside woman's intuition.

Symbols in dreams are often as commanding as the Parisian occultist's shop sign in Karl Grune's *Die Strausse* (The Street, German, 1923). The actors in this expressionist film still are the john (Eugene Klöpfer) and the hooker (Audegede Nissen). Because Grune during World War I lived with soldiers whose language he could not speak, he concentrated on "a pictorial language as communicative as the spoken one."

IS IT POSSIBLE?

Rainer Maria Rilke (1875–1926) wrote some challenging thoughts in *Aufzeichnungen des Malte Laurids Brigge* (1910, translated by J. Linton in 1930 as *Notebooks of Malte Laurids Brigge*) that might well give us pause as we look to dream analysis to delve into deep matters of human consciousness.

> Is it possible that nothing important or real has yet been known or said? Is it possible that mankind has had thousands of years to observe, reflect, record, and allowed those millennia to slip by like the recess interval at school in which one eats a sandwich and an apple?
>
> Yes, it is possible.
>
> Is it possible that despite our progress and discoveries, we still remain on the surface of life…?
>
> Is it possible that these people know with perfect accuracy a past that has never existed? Is it possible that all the realities are nothing to them, that their life runs on unconnected with anything, like a watch in an empty room?

WOLFGANG PAULI

This famous twentieth-century physicist attached mystical significance to the numbers 3 and 4 and was always looking for symbolism as a key to meaning, in his dreams as well as in waking life. Carl Jung interpreted some 1000 of Pauli's dreams for him, which Pauli found useful in developing his exclusion principle and other ideas. An interesting book on Jung is M. L. von Franz's *C. G. Jung: His Myth in Our Time* (translated by William H. Kennedy, 1998).

Jung disagreed with Freud on the meaning of all sorts of dream symbols. I believe that Jung was the more subtle, if more puzzling, scientist. For one thing, he saw the complexity of encoding and was completely aware of a fact that most of us—including authors of "dream dictionaries"—forget, and that is that symbols are not simple signs but multifaceted and shifting.

FREUDIAN ANALYSIS

This is a complex subject, worthy of a book and not a mere entry here, but, in a nutshell, Freud thought dreams were a valuable key to the unconscious but greatly distrusted them. He believed they were encoded, if not censored, and that their subliminal content was, down deep, not what at first appeared, latent but not obvious. This led him to demand that patients free associate to give him some clues as to the hidden meaning of the dreams that dealt in a roundabout way with sexual repressions and traumas, erotic urges and wounds which the dreamer could not or would not present clearly and unambiguously.

On top of that, he feared that while reporting the bizarre events of a dream the dreamer might consciously hold things back or distort them to make the dream more coherent and even less revelatory of guiltily held secrets.

Freud did not trust the patient. Freud was trying to wrest from the dreamer, the only person who had the answer, and at the same time a person who might very well not want to face the answer, what the truth really was. He strove to get the dream out of the dreamer in its actual rather than elaborated or truncated form.

I would not go so far as a friend of mine who, encouraged by his friends to "get some help," saw a psychiatrist and returned from the first visit triumphantly announcing that "He didn't get a word out of me for the whole hour!" But I do not, myself, feel the need, so long as there are friends, to hire a friend to listen to me, and in fact I have some things I know about (and others I do not, I suppose) that I have no intention of chatting about with anyone, least of all a "non-directive" type who will not hand me directions for definite improvement. I guess I would be a hard case to tackle.

One thing Freud was aware of pretty much from the start was that in dream symbolism there might be evasive, complex wordplay. That would, naturally, be different for German-speaking patients on the couch than English-speaking ones. Let me try something in English. Traditionally, dreaming of eating raspberries means that you think people are making unkind remarks behind your back. Whoever came up with that I do not know. Ms. González-Wippler repeats it without qualifying it. But let us see if we can discover how that works out.

First of all, there is the Cockney rhyming slang: in England *raspberry* was short for *raspberry tart*, which rhymes with *fart*. In America, too, to *give someone the raspberry* is to insult them by making with your mouth an imitation of the sphincter releasing a fart. (Were you aware what the rude noise was all about? Most people are not.)

So raspberries appear in your dream as the red fruit but really stand for the rude sound: people are mocking you, but not straight out to your face. (You may not be paranoid. They may really be doing it.) The reaction to you is unkind, and swathed, as you see, in a sort of rejection by you. Or raspberries could mean something altogether different.

Another thing often present in disguise in dreams is sex. Freud loved to think about sex. The layman has tended to think that Freud was obsessed with sex. No, Sigmund, that cigar of yours is not "just a cigar;" we are on to you! You couch potentates! You are so devious! They say that when one psychiatrist says "Hello" to another he passes in the street the first one ponders, "I wonder what he meant by that!"

Granted, dreams are in code and psychoanalysis is a kind of crypt-analysis, so the practitioners have to be subtle and sensitive. I have always regarded psychoanalysis as demanding rather more understanding of the culture than of science. I must confess, too, that it worries me that so many Jews, however much assimilated, are so prominent in the field of psychoanalysis that it may be to some extent too Jewish a social science for an overwhelmingly Christian society, if not a kind of reformed Jewish religion to some degree, science as substitute for religion altogether, which is precisely what Freud most approved of. I think the psychiatrist and myself, a literary critic by profession, are in the same business, so we have lots in common, though our faiths differ.

To my way of thinking, the talking cure of psychoanalysis is really a kind of literary criticism designed to improve the writer's style by sound advice based upon close reading of his texts. It seems to me that the great challenge of psychoanalysis is the same as that of the literary critic (be sure you are honoring the text, not reducing the text to pretext) and the teacher of creative writing (don't try to make the student write as you, the teacher, would write if the piece were yours, because it isn't).

There is also a kind of literary criticism that descends into mere symbol hunting. I have often repeated the story that Mary McCarthy told about a paper she was given by a student when Ms. McCarthy (a famous author) was teaching creative writing at Bennington. The student submitted a short story, on time, but added this apology: "I didn't have time to go through it and put the symbols in."

The story is told of a psychiatrist who showed a patient a straight line and asked what it reminded him of. The patient said, "A phallus." The psychiatrist said he could understand that. What was the meaning of the circle? "A vagina." Well, yes. And the meaning of the cross? Sex for that, too.

At this the psychiatrist balked, "There is no way that could suggest sex. You, dear sir, are a sex fiend."

"Me!," remonstrated the patient. "It's *you* who are drawing all the dirty pictures."

ONEIROMANCY

From my first book in the Barricade Books series on the occult, *The Complete Book of Superstition, Prophecy and Luck* (1995), here is most of what I wrote about the system of divination by means of dreams that was offered by St. Nicephorus, Patriarch of Constantinople, in ninth-century Greek. I am not going to take much from that book but I cannot resist giving you this:

> An eagle means that your dream "whether happy or tragic, is a warning from God."
>
> A cock means: "your dream will soon come true;" a fish means bad news for your plans.
>
> Eating new-baked bread means "imminent misfortune;" a present means "imminent success."
>
> Holding a bee means "your hope will be disappointed;" a wasp means "danger, attacks."
>
> Walking slowly means "success won with difficulty;" walking straight, "triumph."
>
> Meeting a loved one means "a very hopeful augury," the same as eating grapes.
>
> Talking with a king means "your plans will not mature;" kissed by a king means "you will enjoy benevolence, favor and support of powerful persons."
>
> Burning coals mean "harm at the hands of your enemies."
>
> Flying means "a journey in a foreign land." If your feet are cut off it means a bad trip awaits you.
>
> Holding a book means "you will rise in the world"....

And so on. Holding a book by this saint or any other dream-book in advance of dreaming, it seems to me, will probably have some effect on the symbols you encounter in your dreams. Be careful.

One last example from my longer list: "If you see yourself dead, your troubles will soon be ended." Which way, pray tell?

TO HAVE DREAMS OF DEVILS AND DEMONS

I don't know why you would want to do this, but if you insist, check my *Complete Book of Devils and Demons* (1996). There you are told you can effect this by putting laurel leaves under your pillow, omitting your nightly prayers, or rubbing your eyelids with the blood of bats. I warn there and I repeat the warning now: "Bats are often rabid." Magic involves danger, to mind and body.

THE CONTEXT OF DREAMS

In studying dreams, perhaps the most important aspect that has so far been sadly neglected is the framework in which the dreamer operates.

As with autobiography, the cultural context needs to be taken into account along with the mind of the individual. See what I have to say elsewhere on Adler, and what I dared to say above about Freud the secular rabbi.

What you dream has a lot to do with what language you speak, how old you are, where you have lived and live now. No single dream-book can fit your particular case exactly. No two people are exactly alike (though we may be less singular than we think we are!).

No wonder some of those Viennese patients of Freud look so odd to the rest of us!

THE GYPSY DREAM-BOOK

I have consulted a great many of these ratty little pamphlets, new and old, and many slick paperbacks and hardcover books. It was fun. Here I want to justify the time spent on my research, maybe even to provide you with a good new toy or a tool, by putting down in black and white some synthesis of all the alleged wisdom. Here goes. Repeat: One Size Fits All is a bad idea. Nonetheless, I shall attempt to be more specific than the granddaddy of all dream-book soothsayers, Artemidorus Daldianus, some of whose sooth, I must say, still is knocking around, unattributed.

Actually his compendium of dream symbols was just an accumulation of stuff that had been building up centuries before he came along, and his material is being repeated, to a surprising extent, in the piles of books on dream interpretation that pour from the presses year after year.

I reiterate my advice to keep a dream journal, to think about dreaming before you go to bed and to write about dreaming when you get up in the morning. Recall what you can. You may well find that you get better at recalling your dreams. With a dream journal you will have something substantial to interpret. Even *Glamour* (February 1983) and *'Teen* (August 1995) have recommended keeping a dream journal, so there *must* be something in it, right? Seriously, it is a good idea. Don't you want to know as much about yourself as you can find out? You don't have to tell other people!

Here is what you need to get started on dream analysis at home. I shall limit myself to a dozen items or less under each letter of the alphabet. As an author, I do not wish to put my so-called gypsy colleagues (many of whom write under pseudonyms and, as far as I can tell, are not gypsy fortune-tellers at all) out of lucrative business. Never blame the peddlers even of trash; blame the market that supports them.

Really, if you look closely, you will see that I give more than a This=That list; you will learn a lot about the general nature of dream symbols as well as some specifics. As usual, now that you have bought my book and crossed my palm with silver, I shall offer you a reading that is at least as informative as it is entertaining. The gypsies reverse the emphasis, usually. Now that I have tipped my hand, may I see yours? Hmmm. Very *interesting*. Now from my own list:

A

Accident. Like a suicide, an accident may be a call for help or just a play for attention. Your dream may be warning you about some place or person or physical state or object you fear. You will probably feel better if you carry over a warning into your waking life. Did you cause the accident or become the victim of it? Where does responsibility lie? As always, Take Care!

Actor, Acrobat, any other performer. You may be exhibitionistic and starved for applause. Problems: you may have forgotten your lines, have the wrong costume (or too revealing a one), have difficulty getting to the theater, fear some or all of the audience, or *really* break a leg. If you are very successful in your dream, be careful of overconfidence. Auditions may betray insecurities. They say in the theater a bad dress rehearsal means a good opening night, but a bad audition means rejection from the get-go.

Alligators. Danger. It's the crocodile that wants to eat you, but the average person doesn't know that. Symbols need not be based on any fact.

Addition. If you are adding up numbers, particularly if it is difficult or you get wrong answers, you may be concerned about business or other connections.

Adultery. Are you feeling guilty? In any case, do not discuss this dream with your Significant Other. The old song went, "You tell me your dream, and I will tell you mine." Not always the best idea.

Animals. Wild animals may suggest danger or lustful desires. Pets may suggest friendship and companionship. I presume you are not sexually attracted.

Angel. Blessing, good news. Does the angel facially resemble anyone you know?

Ape. Some so-called experts suggest this is a symbol of a friend that threatens or will disappoint. Is our acquaintanceship a planet of the apes?

Apple. Temptation. Red apples, good luck. Rotten apples, thwarted deals. Eve.

Arrow. Festivity. Phallus. Who is shot where with the arrow? Who is shooting it?

Auction. Suggestive of business deals. Are you winning, being outbid, happy with your purchase? What is being contested?

B

Baby Carriage. Do you desire (or fear) pregnancy? Maybe you just want to be babied.

Banana. Penis. Tom Crisp's *Dream Dictionary* (1990) says "male penis," which strikes me as sexual ignorance and bad editing.

Beads. Vanity, insecurity. If the string breaks and they are scattered, loss. See Necklace.

Beauty. "Every man [and, presumably, woman] creating the beautiful appearance of the dream world is an artist."

Bicycle. Sex or other sports. Riding up hill=difficulty. Riding downhill= either a free ride of some sort or things going downhill for you.

Bird. Happiness if, for example, a bluebird, but there are also birds of prey, which are ominous, parrots that talk (gossip), and so on.

Black. Death, disappointment, mourning (since we stopped wearing white at funerals).

Blind. Does any sighted person at all dream of being blind? What do the blind see in dreams if formerly sighted or never sighted?

Book. Symbol of wisdom, authority. The titles of the books on the shelves in libraries or people's homes are significant, in life or in dreams. Dreaming of a book you cannot find, cannot open, or cannot understand signals frustration in getting some information you want.

Box. Sex, secret, treasure, surprise, confinement, and more.

Boy. Fathers-to-be dream more of boys than women do.

Bride. Seeing yourself as a bride is pretty obvious, unless you are male. Obviously, as in real life, men and women have different "vocabularies."

Broom. Cleaning up, phallus (witches' broomstick), desire to be rid of something.

Bugle. Call to action. It wasn't playing *Taps*, I hope.

Bull. Machismo, sexual proposal. In the sense of "lies," who is lying and why?

Butterfly. Happiness (if it comes to you), bad luck (if you squash it). The unattainable.

Button. If missing one, you may need to be more careful, or to find an attentive lover. Silver and gold buttons=wealth. One source says: "cloth-covered covered button, take care of your health." Who thinks up this stuff?

C

Cage. Possession, immobility. See Jail.

Canada. Why is your dream set in Canada? Must be something personal. But some countries have popular reputations that do influence dream symbolism. One example: Tahiti=hedonistic escape.

Cat. Female—with claws.

Candle. Phallus, tradition, religion, wish.

Candy. To receive candy is to get affection and admiration, to be tempted. To give candy is to court disappointment, to try to seduce, to appease.

Cane. Phallus, assistance, authority. In UK may suggest a beating.

Car. We use cars for all sorts of things besides transportation, including prestige, sex, tailgate parties, sex, cruising, sex, escape, and sex. Parts of the car can even be sexually suggestive. The color and style matter: a red convertible is a mistress or an attempt to recapture youth; an SUV makes a statement (or carries a load of stuff); a family car is a marriage and its responsibilities. Or do you dream you are on a motorcycle?

Cave. Female (or homosexual bottom). Desire to hide from the world or, conversely, to explore.

Circus. Are you taking the kids to the circus, looking at a freak show (they don't really have those anymore, just with Jerry, Maury, and such on TV), performing on the high wire? The carnival is the world of escape and entertainment; the circus is life. Are you a ringmaster? A clown?

Cock. Artemidoris would read this in terms of the bragging rooster heralding the dawn. You probably would be influenced by slang and think even the rooster or spiggot to be a phallic symbol. "That's a phallic symbol," says the sophisticated man. "Ooo," replies the naïve girl, "but do you know *what it looks like*?" Or are there any naïve girls around anymore?

Computers. Our generation naturally is familiar with machines that previously were unknown, but dreams have always driven technology and technology has always appeared in dreams, sometimes threateningly. Are you the master or slave of the machine in your dreams? Do you worry about computer crashes the way your parents and grandparents worried about airplane crashes, the way your great-grandparents worried about railroad accidents?

Confessing. Unburdening, gain, happiness.

Corpse. Is it of someone you dislike? Are you responsible for this unfortunate state someone else is in? Are you the corpse?

D

Dagger. Danger, phallus.

Defilement. In your dreams you are not usually taken advantage of without you somehow wanting to be. In life, "She asked for it" is absolutely no justification for rape, but in dreams rape may mean the fulfillment of desire, and any defilement may possibly be in some way satisfying. Men often cloak urges to be "had" in elaborate covers.

Devil. Temptation, flattery, danger.

Dirt. Defilement, humiliation, frustration of good housekeepers.

Ditch. Falling in indicates debasement, jumping over is "getting over."

Divorce. Wish fulfillment.

Doll. Insecurity, loneliness, sentimentality. If inflatable, sex.

Door. Opportunity if open, obstacle if closed, and an ancient book says that if the door of your house falls off you must expect a loss.

Dove. Peace, luck, love. Pigeons have a different signification.

Drinking. If it is alcohol, you want to celebrate and you may not be having enough fun, (or too many troubles you won't face,) in your waking life.

Drowning. A call for help or just attention, a desire to have your sins washed away.

Dying. Dreamers seldom wish to die; most frequently those who dream of dying are looking to live less stressed and more appreciated lives. They want to be sympathized with, taken care of.

E

Eagle. Ambition, predatoriness. See Flying. Or it could be a golf term.

Eating. This can be a cover for oral sex or for non-sexual greed. See Meal.

Eden. It is pleasant to rollick in some Edenic landscape, to get away from it all.

Egypt. Many people find the Land of the Pharaohs (known only from the "OK, Pharaoh" movies—even William Faulkner was guilty of one of these) irresistibly romantic. People whose present lives are so unimpressive they want to have had past lives like to think they were Cleopatra (never the garlic-chewing, sweaty guys who put up the pyramids). Dreams can have a lot of Egyptian costumes, scenery, symbols.

Eight ball. Sometimes our dreams use clichés like "being behind the eight ball" literally. There you are behind the big black unfortunate obstruction. When examining the language of dream symbolism never neglect slang, proverbs, catch phrases, and other words you may not see in your desk dictionary.

Einstein. Historic figures that embody useful concepts—this one, of course, is "genius"—often occur in dreams, as do real people with interesting physical appearances that you happen to see in the street, on the soap operas, in the movies, and on risqué cable television or girlie or meat mags.

Elephant. In ordinary life the elephant is a symbol of memory (actually, revenge, "never forgets") but in dreams you are thinking about power, sexual domination, all that jazz.

English. This is not a dream symbol but I want to put it here to make a point and a pun. First, the language(s) people dream in do much to shape the symbols (often dictated by wordplay). Second, dreams put a little english (spin) on reality, so things are not as simply cause-and-effect nor as plain as they might be. Remember it is not dream reading but dream *interpretation.* "Reader response," as they say in literary criticism, goes far to determine the meaning of the text, which is only partially—some critics say not a bit—fixed.

Error. Do you possibly dream of making mistakes, getting things impossibly wrong?

Escape. If you do escape, you expect to get out of present troubles. If you don't escape, you fear you may not—and you may face criticism, gossip, scandal, etc.

Examination. Life is a series of tests and in dreams we are prone to think of these as school examinations for which we are inadequately prepared, etc. Facing an exam and having no clue, being totally unprepared, is a common nightmare.

Execution. So much guilt, you might be better off dead, you think. But you do not wish to die. Executing someone else means simply getting him or her out of the way, nor truly wanting them dead.

F

Falling. Sex, fear, fear of sex, etc.

Father. Authority figure or gracious protector and advisor, do you want

to kill him? Men and women look on fathers in different ways, even in dreams. Does your lover resemble your father?

Feet. Submission. The oldest books say big feet mean bad luck; sex, for fetishists.

Fence. Symbol of both protection and exclusion and of imprisonment or obstacle.

Fire. If you dream of fire, wake up; something may be burning. Your business burning down is said to be good luck. (Are you an arsonist trying to rob the insurance company?) Fire=good luck, charred ruins=expect desolation.

Fishing. However strenuous it may be, it means relaxation, as in "gone fishin'".

Floating. You expect to "get over." You are hopeful of outside support.

Flying. Freedom, escape, sex.

Fox hunting. Unwise sexual pursuit.

Friday. Accusation, dignity.

F*****g. If you dream of it, you are not getting enough of it. That simple. Or maybe, as they used to say about smoking, you are "doing it more and enjoying it less."

Funeral. Good luck, unless it is yours, in which case you may not wish to be dead but just better appreciated. If it is raining at the funeral, that's good. Maybe you are trying to overhear what the mourners are saying about you, but remember you are writing their dialogue, so this tells you not what these people think but what you think they think of you.

Fur. Money. But mink is said to mean "falsehood," fox "treachery," and skunk (according to Zolar) means: "Some man will fall in love with you." OK, I guess, if you are female—or gay.

G

Gag. You feel it is hard to express yourself. Someone is controlling you.

Gang. If you dream of belonging to a gang, you need new friends.

Gems. See Jewelry.

Genitalia. Come on, now, what did you think I would say? Watch out for slang-word disguises and double entrendres, puns, other evasions. It could be as subtle as a jelly roll.

Gift. Giving, you may be trying to reconcile with someone. Receiving, you may feel unappreciated.

Gnome. Unless this is seen in a British garden, this is a good sign, as are dwarfs, elves (sometimes disguised as elm trees), and leprechauns. Trolls are not so good an omen; they can mean mischief.

Grass. A nice lawn stretching before you promises good things. If you have any trouble walking on it, expect obstacles to your desires, but they can be overcome. Uncut lawn? Work not done.

Grave. An end to something but not necessarily a death. Do you hope you will see an enemy in the grave? Finding yourself in a grave is, oddly, a good omen.

Green. Jealousy, envy, new beginnings, money, outdoor life, ecology, inexperience.

Gun. Phallus, violence, fear.

Gutter. Get your mind out of the gutter. In a dream, you may be trying to become less immoral. You may feel you are at a low point in life.

Gypsy. Fortune telling, but your fortune may be misleading. If you get to pay for the reading, however, it is to be regarded as more reliable. Gypsies may have had interior motives in including that touch, just as I suspect psychiatrists have in insisting that you pay enough so that it is difficult and pay for visits you miss.

H

Haircut or Hairdressing. Vanity, desire to improve your appearance. Too close a cropping or a bad hair day, debasement.

Hatchet. Violence, lies. Burying the hatchet means making peace. But if you find yourself making pieces, what are you so angry or desperate about?

Hell. Trouble, change. Zolar says being in hell is "good times coming." Why? He adds that running away from hell means "joy" but returning from hell is "disappointment." Some confusion here, it seems. See *Zolar's Encyclopedia and Dictionary of Dreams* (1963), perhaps somewhat more eccentric than most of the many such books.

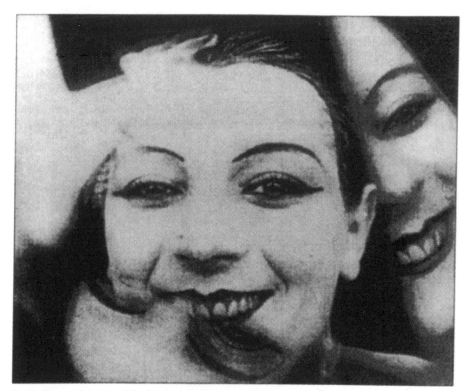

Le Ballet mechanique (Mechanical Ballet) was a ground breaking film of 1924. In it, cubist painter Fernand Léger (perhaps working with an American cinematographer, Dudley Murphy) created a kaleidoscope of 300 shots in a mere 15 minutes of silent, black and white film. This movie is *not* about dreams, but the way it jumbles, distorts, and relates images in some degree resembles dreaming. The language of dreams even when it seems to be straightforward is a language foreign to our daily life. It needs translation.

Help. To dream of receiving help is a sign you need it.

Hero. To dream you are a hero shows you want to be one. Wake up and do something wonderful.

Hilarity. You need to relax and take life less seriously. "A little laughter now and then/Is relished by the best of men." Lighten up when you wake up.

Hoax. To perpetrate a hoax shows you are vengeful. To be the victim of a hoax may suggest you are of a suspicious nature or are afraid of someone.

Holiday. You may be in need of relaxation. If you fear the holiday, you are probably feeling guilty about something.

Home run. To hit one is to score a definite success. Of course you may just be dreaming of something you cannot really accomplish.

Honey. Sweetness, experienced or desired.

Horse. Macho male, sex. If you are riding a horse it may be a desire for sex or for power. It is possible that for you sex and power are inextricably intertwined.

House. Shelter, family, retreat. For some reason I cannot fathom, dreaming that your house is on fire is a good omen, but smoke is a signal of danger.

Hyacinth. Narcissicism. Like the daffodil, symbol of self-love.

I

Ibis. Strange birds whose names you hardly knew you knew may crop up in dreams. Each bird has its own meaning, sometimes several meanings, from cheerful robin to scary vulture. This once-deified bird suggests what you might associate with Egypt.

Incense. You smell danger. Have you noticed how acute your sense of smell may become in dreams?

Indignation. In dreams we sometimes get angry over the most inexplicable things. The secret is to discover what the prompting to anger really is.

Infitada. Dreaming that you are caught up on some foreign brawl just underlines the not infrequent tendency of dreamers to borrow from the current news. You may be simply starved for excitement or you may be expressing a political or other opinion.

Initial. On occasion, in dreams initial letters of some symbols' names suggest the initial of a person's name, but you are keeping things tightly wrapped up, aren't you? Why is that?

Insects. Small things that bug you.

Investigation. If you are the subject of investigation, particularly if you do not know why, you may be harboring paranoid delusions. If you are investigating something you are, naturally, curious about the truth of the matter. Why?

Island. Isolation, protection, ostracism, escapism, lack of enough friends.

Ivy. Constancy.

J

Jail. Punishment, confinement, frustration, fear of or enjoyment of homoerotic fantasies.

Jam. Something good or, in the case of traffic, bad, a frustration of your wishes.

Jewels. Danger, vanity to be punished, covetousness to watch out for, insecurity.

Jigsaw. Do you have all the pieces of the puzzle? What is the overall picture?

Jockstrap. Sex, desire to excel at sports or to be regarded as macho.

Jump. To have to take a jump means to be confronted with a necessary but fearful decision or action. We jump into situations, jump ship, jump to conclusions, even jump over difficulties.

Junk. Your life is too crowded. Call the Salvation Army to pick up.

K

Key. Solution to a problem, power. Lost keys=impotence.

King. See Lion.

Kiss. Sex. Every human relationship is some kind of sexual relationship. Who are you kissing? Politely or sexily?

K-Mart. Most dreams have to have definite locales and these may be familiar places suggested practically at random or they may be deeply significant. It is always important to distinguish the crucial detail of a dream from the insignificant one. To what extent, for instance, is this particular store a key to meaning, if at all?

Knife. Phallus, violence, danger.

Knot. Problem. Personal entanglement.

Klu Klux Klan. Are these guys after you? What have you done? Are you one of them, engaged in a forbidden activity, your identity protected by a hood?

L

Lake. Sex. Are you in a boat, canoe, swimming, drowning?

Leaving. Escape dreams are common, but be sure you know what you are running away from, and why, and what you are running into. Maybe you do not want to go to the trouble of leaving and would be content just to dream about it. Not every dream is a call to action.

Letter. Oddly. Letters received in dreams are rarely read! Not getting a letter means disappointment.

Lettuce. Danger.

Lingerie. Femininity.

Lion. King, top, oppressor, danger.

Lock. Protection, obstruction, frustration, confusion.

Lottery. If you dream of winning the lottery you harbor foolish hopes of reward without effort. Wake up.

Luck. If you dream of bad luck, you ought to be careful but take more responsibility for what happens to you. Good luck? You wish!

Lust. Sex, rape.

M

Mask. Who was that masked man in your dream? Do you dream of shucking responsibility by wearing a mask (or assuming another identity)? Do you dream of unmasking someone, finding the truth?

Meal. Eating with someone means reconciliation. Overeating may mean you are on a diet.

Melons. Female breasts.

Milk. Abundance, comfort, semen. Spilled milk is lost chances or past failures.

Money. Dreams of getting or losing money are very common. Either one may be wish fulfillment. This may be the place to say that in dreams we do not only wish that things will be better for us; sometimes, for one reason or another, we predict and even urge bad luck, loss, defeat, putdowns, etc.

Mortgage. Any burden, but especially a financial one you cannot handle. Another dream about money or the lack of it. But also about control: "Marry me," said the villain we hissed in the old melodramas, "or I shall foreclose on the mortgage."

Mother. Mother means love and protection to most of us. I presume you do not dream of a sexual connection. Mother is often replaced in dreams by a symbol.

Mountains. Desire to achieve, huge obstacle to be overcome, hideaway, breasts.

Movies. Do you run movies in your dreams? Do movies you have seen while awake influence your dreaming? Do you want to be a movie star?

Mud. Misfortune. On you, it signifies calumny, ill luck.

Murder. Do you really want to kill someone or do you just find them an annoyance? Why would anyone want to murder you? If you die in the dream you just want to forget everything that is bothering you.

Mystery. Dreams themselves are puzzles. If you are on some investigative trail in your dreams it may mean there is some answer you are seeking in life. If you are challenged to put together the pieces of a jigsaw puzzle, what is the "big picture?"

N

Nakedness. Vulnerability, insecurity, sex.

Naked woman. Good luck.

Necklace. Peril.

Negro. An old French book suggests that seeing a Negro in your dream portends "illness." As usual, it does not say why that should be so. I include this one to remind you that times change. Seeing an African-American in your dream would not be at all unusual in the U.S., nor a black in many other countries.

Numbers. Some people try to dream of lucky numbers. You are truly lucky if you are not one of those who plays lotteries where the odds are ridiculous. The influence of the cabala—Jewish letters of the alphabet were also used as numbers, which connected words with numbers (hence 666=The Mark of the Beast)—introduced numerology into the interpretation of dreams. Some dream-books give numbers for symbols. Forget that. Just play the same number an infinite number of times and it will come up. Or take your dollar and give it to someone needy. They could be angels, right?

Nutcracker. Fear of castration. Desire to solve a puzzling problem.

O

Obelisk. Phallus.

Obituary. Are you reading or writing someone else's? You want to get rid of them. Are you reading your own? Are you glad to be freed of some problem or duty?

Office. What relation does the office of your dreams bear to the one in which you work? Don't take office problems and office politics to bed with you.

Oil. Flattery, slipperiness, reconciliation. Rub down with scented oils? Sex, you lucky dog, you hedonist!

Old. To see yourself as old may not be a bad thing; think of the alternative. White hair (especially if you do not have white hair) is said to be an encouraging sign.

Oleander. Poison.

Ombudsman. You wish you had a fair, objective person to turn to for a decision.

Omission. Insecurity, guilt, disappointment in oneself or others.

Omnipotence. Dreams of glory, watch out if you start to believe in the compliments heaped upon you too much. As a famous sportsman, Vince Lombardi, said, you are in trouble when you start to believe the hype spoken of you.

Onerousness. In dreams we frequently are carrying great burdens. We may be feeling sorry for ourselves in our present circumstances or fear demands will be made upon us. Does anyone assist you with your load? Do you get to put it down?

Opening. Sex, opportunity (especially windows and doors).

Oranges. Illness, but from an old book published in a time when oranges were a treat and given to the sick. Today orange juice and oranges are in a different category. The symbol can have individual meanings. I always associate tangerines with Christmas. They brightened up the icy winters of my youth. A friend tells me an orange was always found in the toe of her big Christmas stocking. Orange color suggests fecundity, conceit, assertiveness, Princeton.

P

Palm branch. You will be accused—unless it is Palm Sunday. Remember that a palm branch might have a meaning for a Roman Catholic it does not have for a Jew or a follower of Islam or an atheist living in Palm Springs.

Parade. In your honor? Lucky you. Just marching in step with the rest? You are desirous of community, maybe conformity. Just watching from the sidelines? Is that what you think you are doing in life?

Peaches. Sex, rewards.

Performer. Do you want to be exhibitionistic? Or are you a blushing violet fearful of getting up there and forgetting your lines, falling off the high wire, etc.?

Purple. Illness.

Pushing. Struggling, resisting, victimizing.

Q

Quarrel. A common dream involves repeating some argument you had but in the dream getting the better of the opponent, slinging some really telling lines, etc.

Queer. Are you acting homosexual in your dreams, afraid of being accused of sexual deviation, or does *queer* here just mean unusual, strange, exotic, weird?

Question. Are you asking (searching for truth) or being questioned? Are you afraid you do not have the answer. See Examination.

Quirk. Do you find yourself exhibiting in your dream some unusual desire or behavior you might not countenance, or dare, in waking life?

Quince. Any exotic fruit bespeaks a desire for sensuality, but this is a bitter one.

R

Rack. Torture, questioning, bed.

Racket. In the sense of noise, anxiety, several other senses, due to the fact that this, in common with other English words, may have more than one meaning, from tennis to mob crime. Dreams can play one meaning against another, so be cautious in arriving at conclusions.

Rags. Are you afraid of being poor, dressed in rags? Are you in ragged clothes when all around you are well dressed?

Red. Danger, or happiness if you happen to be Chinese. Colors have different significances in different cultures: to the Chinese, yellow is the royal purple.

Rent. Inability to pay the rent suggests fear of not meeting obligations, fear of losing security, stability.

Return. Forgiveness, apology, guilt, security.

Rinse. Cleansing, shucking guilt or burdens.

Roaming. Are you anxious at being lost or enjoying freedom of movement?

Round. Vagina. Oval may mean the same.

Ruin. You may fear financial collapse or be grateful for removal of pressure.

S

Scarlet. Blood, danger, sin.

Sex. Sex. For all their love of encoding, sometimes dreams are very direct and give us what we feel we are lacking. There must be some people who have more fun in bed asleep than they do awake.

Shackles. Impediments to your desires, exculpating circumstances.

Slut. A career you wish you had embarked upon?

Snake. Penis, deceptions, lies, betrayals.

Soaring. See Flying.

Space rangers. Some people engage in science-fiction adventures in dreams.

Stadium. Are you the athletic hero, the cynosure of all eyes—or do you want to be?

Stairs. Going up, going down, sliding down the banister—some interpreters say it's all sex. Maybe it simply means you want to rise in the world. Or step down from an uncomfortable position.

Star. Another dream of glory? A symbol of guidance, approval, etc.?

Strangers. Naturally strangers as well as friends and relatives (cute distinction in that old phrase!) turn up in your dreams. Where do you think you got faces for them? Coming upon a dead stranger means a loss of your property. Do the strangers in your dreams ever turn up in reality?

Svengali. Do you dream you are in the grip of some hypnotic person? Does this excuse inappropriate behavior or serve as a substitute for talent or willpower?

T

Tarantula. Some people are terrified of bats, spiders, snakes, and so on, and your unconscious knows all about what scares you the most. It is liable to do its work, whatever that may be, with these small terrors. Try dreaming that you can charm these creatures, immobilize them, and make them go away. Try to take care of yourself in your dreams; it might spill over into your waking life.

Terrier. The mind, like a terrier, can get a hold of something and worry it, refusing to let go. Dreams can similarly fix on a problem and make all sorts of use of it, refusing to change the subject. You are struggling to see your way through some difficulty.

Terrors. In our peaceful lives, we seek the excitement of rides at the amusement parks, horror movies, scary stories, monsters in comic books and on television. In dreams we do not have the sense of being safely strapped in, nor the confidence that the horrors are just flickers on the screen, or contained behind the television's glass. Dreams seem really to be happening. We can awake in a fright. But we usually are not mauled or murdered in our dreams. It's anxiety disorder, not physical attack. With a little reflection, we can examine the nightmares and determine what realities they represent. Do you have a particularly frightening dream, a recurrent nightmare? It is trying to tell you something. Next time the monster comes at you, try to summon the "cool" to ask.

Thirst. This may possibly be symbolic but most likely you need to wake up and drink a glass of cold water. Wine before bed can make you thirsty in dreams. It is also bad for apnea (interrupted breathing during sleep).

Thirteen. At the back of your mind are a host of superstitions you may truly believe that you do not believe. But 13, and broken mirrors, and black cats crossing your path, and more, may clutter your dream world. Be brave and analytical.

Tied up. A sense of helplessness, or the gratifying feeling that you are not responsible for action.

Time. This is handled in odd ways in dreams. But even in our waking hours, time expands and contracts. There is a story—how reliable I cannot discover—that Einstein explained relativity by saying that when a pretty girl is sitting in your lap a long time seems like a short time and when you accidentally touch a hot stove a short time seems like a long time. Recently, physicists have been redefining time and, suggesting that it is merely a human invention attempting to explain motion and change.

Torment. Are you tortured in a dream? Are you refusing to reveal some secret? What is it? Do you have no information but cannot convince the torturer that you are not holding back something? The kind of torture is also significant. If there is a sexual element, that bears consideration.

Tornado. Hurricanes, tornadoes, all kinds of violent storms may stand for turbulent mental states, like the whirlwind in *The Book of Job* or the storm in *King Lear*.

Train. You have heard of a "train of thought." Have you ever thought what a train may mean in a dream? Is it a means of escape or a commute, a symbol of freedom or running on determined tracks? Do you worry about being late for your train, going off the rails, that you have no ticket, that something ominous or happy awaits you at your destination, etc.? These days you can substitute a bus or an airplane in your dreams for the trains that figured so largely in the Victorian imagination. Technology creates new symbols, all the time.

Tree. Family, shelter. Tree with leaves or flowers=good. Barren tree=bad. The type of tree is significant: a blasted oak is not a Christmas tree. May you flourish like the green bay tree.

Turkish bath. Your bedroom may be too warm. Temperatures, noises, smells, all sorts of exterior influences are woven into the tapestries of dreams. Some people burn incense or scented candles to affect their dreams but unwatched fires are ill advised.

Twin. Do you dream of having a twin—maybe an evil sister? This may indicate a certain Jekyll & Hyde aspect in you. If you actually have a twin, do you both ever have similar dreams? Do you believe there may be some kind of psychic bond between you, like the Corsican Brothers of the old melodrama?

U

Umbrella. Protection, dignity.

Uncorking. Release, revelation.

Underwater. In the unconscious.

Undressing. Revealing, dropping pretenses, coming clean. Dreams in which we are unclothed are common.

Uniform. Control, authority.

Uphill. Difficulty.

Uproar. Violent emotions often erupt in dreams.

Urn. Watch for punning (earn, yearn, even Urnings) allusion (your pal Ernie?)

V

Vacation. Maybe you need one more than you thought.

Vagabond. Bespeaking a desire to escape routine or responsibility.

Vampire. Monsters from the media and legend often show up in our dreams but may be stand-ins for actual fears or persons we dislike. We disguise things, I repeat.

Venice. If we have been there, some memory of the place, but it can also stand for our fears of death or ideas of decadence.

Vigil. Dutifulness, anxious waiting.

Viper. Snake in the grass, hidden danger. Watch your asp.

W

Watch. To be watching for something is to be anxious, and so is checking your watch for the time.

Water. Maybe you are just thirsty. Always have a glass of water before going to bed. Also, it helps to get you up on the morning. Water is life, forgiveness, rededication, and much more. Being baptized is to be born again, freed from sin and guilt.

Wedding cake. Minor disappointment.

Window. Opportunity. A broken window is a dashed hope. Sex.

Wine. Struggle ahead.

Wolf. Danger, predator. But in some cultures the wolf is the wise counselor, the totemic protector.

Worm. Penis, debasement. See Snake. Seldom today the old symbol of death.

X, Y, Z

X-ray. Seeing into things.

Yacht. Escape, "champagne dreams," wealth.

Zoo. You are a visitor, you are curious. You are in the cage, you feel trapped.

MORE ABOUT INTERPRETING

In Virginia Woolf"'s great novel, *To the Lighthouse*, Mr. Ramsay thinks of thought as an alphabet. Which letter are you on?

Once again I remind you that we each have our personal psychologies, so looking up a thing in anyone else's dream book is not any guarantee that the underlying truth will be revealed. Still, whatever connection you can make with the coded products of your own unconscious will certainly be of some help to your conscious life. Therefore, do not be afraid to analyze your dreams.

Try to recall them, try to work out what they may be telling you, as well as you can. In this, as in everything you do, combine caution with courage. May I suggest in this very practical business that you take the attitude of Machiavelli who wrote "one judges by result."

As you or your therapist works, it should never be forgotten how tentative dream analysis still must be. "It has been left to me," Freud wrote not so very long ago, "to draw the first crude map" of what his colleague Fleiss called "the scene of action of dreams," another world "different from that of waking ideational life." We are still just on the first stages of what Freud thought of as a journey.

MORE GYPSY DREAMING

You have been patient if you got this far (unless you immediately turned to the end). I have a habit of doing that with detective stories, because it saves me the trouble of reading most of them. You deserve a break today! So here, my dears, are very brief and often-alleged meanings attached to dream symbols you may encounter.

Go ahead. Play with them. It cannot hurt unless you take this too seriously. "There are few things more exciting to me," wrote Henry James in *The Art of Fiction*, "than a psychological reason."

It is indeed interesting to try to dig out the psychological reason for this or that symbol in your dream. Of course whenever you look inward, look out! You may find something you won't like.

Most people have too many negative dreams. Sexual symbolism is especially frequent but not especially difficult to spot. You immediately caught on, I suppose, to that big long thing and that big round thing that were the symbols of the World's Fair in the thirties, not to mention shooting milk out of those squirt guns the kiddies run around with. But, I keep repeating, your dream may call for something more than a patent cliché or a tired entry in a derivative dictionary of symbols. Well, if you must have them, here are some of the most familiar "what does it mean?" puzzles. To list all that are possible is impossible.

Abandonment. Are you being abandoned (anxiety) or abandoning someone else (hope of relief of a burden, guilt)? Freud says our major latent content (as opposed to surface, so-called manifest content) of dreams revolves around either sex or abandonment—or both.

Abscess. A festering problem.

Abuse. Are you abusing someone (you dislike or fear them) or are they abusing you (you fear or dislike them)?

Acceptance. Usually wish fulfillment, especially if sex is involved.

Accident. You are afraid of something; avoid it.

Accusation. Are you accusing someone you dare not confront in real life (this is then compensatory) or is someone accusing you (why do you feel guilty)?

Acorn. Some big new thing is going to come from a small beginning, usually very positive for you.

Actor. To dream you are performing is exhibitionistic but not bad news. How are you going over? Do performers from TV or the movies turn up in your dreams? Do you, too, want to be a celebrity? Feel small now?

Adder. There's a snake in the grass. Can you identify your enemy? Danger.

Adultery. Wish fulfillment or fear of destabilization of your relationship with a Significant Other Being. If it's the SOB who's being adulterous, obviously you do not trust them. Never charge them with infidelity. Nothing makes another person angrier than that and if they are actually guilty they get even angrier.

Advice. Who is giving you advice in your dream and do you feel you want to take it? If you find yourself advising others, it may be you with the problem.

Almonds. A good sign. Blossoms? A very good sign!

Altar. Often suggests marriage. Of course if you are being sacrificed on a pagan altar, you are afraid of enemies. Who are these people? Do you wake up on time?

Ambulance. Help is on the way.

Ambush. You are aware of danger and for some reason are headed right for it.

Amethyst. Good fortune, perhaps an unexpected gift. If you lose an amethyst, bad luck.

Ancestor. Tradition, duty, feelings of inadequacy.

Anchor. Hope. This is a traditional symbol—but did you know the tradition?

Angel. Messenger with good news or new protection, some angels can bring warnings of danger, which you should heed.

Animals. Each has a special symbolism. Friendly lions and fat pigs are good. Dogs usually are good. Stay away from ravenous predators in dreams, bulls, bears (also on Wall Street). Apes are bad luck, gorillas threatening, monkeys amusing.

Antiques. Are you buying or selling your past? Does all that fancy furniture mean you have wealth (be careful you hold onto it) or want it (out of pride, not for any good you could do with it)?

Apology. Are you making one in your dream? If so, go and make it when you wake up. If you are receiving an apology, it hurts you to have lost a friend or partner.

Apple. It bespeaks temptation, prize, prosperity. See a bad apple? Bad sign. Finding your apple has a worm in it is bad luck. Finding it has half a worm in it is twice as bad.

Appointment. Obligation, being appointed to a better job (ambition, desire).

Apricots. Eating them is a good sign. No one ever says why!

Arabs. Prejudice adds treachery to this symbol of wealth and exotic travel.

Ascent. Rising in the word, passions heating up, getting a lift in life.

Ashes. Destruction and disappointment.

Asylum. Fear of being confined to the loony bin when you are not insane could drive you crazy. Resist taking blame when you are not guilty. Watch out for people who want to get you out of the way by any means possible.

Bacon. Good luck to eat, unless you are Jewish.

Baking. For a woman, this may mean an unexpected "bun in the oven," pregnancy.

Baldness. Bad news in a dream, where the Hair Club for Men and wigs for women may not be available.

Balloon. A lot of hot air has inflated your career, business, etc., and some prick is sure to burst your balloon.

Bandage. Temporary amelioration, wound.

Bare feet. I think it means freedom. Some "experts" say it means failure or many difficulties to overcome.

Barn. Represents storing up necessities, so if it is full, OK; if it is empty, watch out.

Basement. Your subconscious mind. Buried threats, unacknowledged fears, discarded things.

Basket. Many meanings from generosity to male genitals.

Beans. Always bad news, dream-books report.

Bed. Home, comfort, sex. If the bed is clean and inviting, jump in. If the sheets are stained or in disarray, you may be having domestic or sex problems, or both.

Beets. These are often said to bring "good tidings." For God's sake, why? Dream-books never deign to explain. Of course if you have read that beets are good news and then dream about them it is significant. Are dream-books leading you?

Bells. Are they ringing joyfully? Most dream-books say they are tolling for death. Why?

Belt. Said to warn against an enemy soon to appear.

Bird in a cage. Supposedly good fortune. Bird flown and cage empty=death. On the wings of a bird=exhilaration. Birds from Alfred Hitchcock? Ouch!

Blue. The books say prosperity. But the blues are not that, and the mind often plays with language. You may also associate a color with a person.

Bottle. Drink, sexual success.

Bowling. Prosperity or maybe just a reference to low-class sport success.

Bracelet. See Ring.

Breakfast. Watch out for a trap. Or maybe you got hungry overnight.

Breath. Shortness of breath=anxiety. Sweet breath is good, bad breath is bad.

Bride. Dream books say this means money rather than marriage coming to a woman. I doubt this one.

Broom. Opposition will be swept away. Maybe you are cleaning up your act.

Building. In good repair, your life is going well. In ruins, your life has been wrecked or you fear it will be. Bad signs are rickety stairs, broken windows, fallen arches or dangerous ceilings. Something nasty in the basement may signify some evil or threatening thought in your subconscious. The attic is your own head.

Buried alive. Terror at being trapped in a personal or business situation, stymied. Do you escape? Some of us are Houdinis in our dreams.

Butterfly. Happiness. Blue birds and other happy fliers are said to mean joy.

Cabbage. A rocky marriage or relationship, money.

Canary. Success, unless the canary dies.

Cancer. To have cancer in a dream and be cured means you expect to escape from a big threat.

Candle. Burning bright=good sign. Snuffed out=unpleasant termination of something, perhaps of a life. Anything else shaped like a candle. Enlightenment.

Canoe. Paddling your own canoe of course means being independent. Moving along with another in the canoe means marriage or a relationship. If the canoe capsizes, expect the marriage or relationship to end.

Capture. If you are held captive you fear restrictions or exploitation. If you hold another captive one dream-book says "you will associate with people of low moral caliber." I don't see why.

Car. If you are a passenger, you are in some situation just going along for the ride. If you are behind the wheel, you are in charge. If you are stuck on the road—no gas, flat tire, etc.—expect an impediment to your career progress or realize that you are doubtful about success. One must say somewhere here –and this is as good a place as any—that the deepest *you*, not some wise and *outside* sources, are presenting good or bad, optimistic or pessimistic messages. Dream-books never tell you that, and that is a very great failing in all of them.

Carpet. The expression "to be called on the carpet" means to be in trouble and to have people "roll out the red carpet" for you means to be honored. But will you get honored or do you just yearn to be honored?

Carrots. Happiness. Male members.

Caterpillars. Symbols of untrustworthy persons. In seventeenth-century England some politicians were called "Caterpillars of the Commonwealth."

Cave. Danger, hidden threats, sex.

Celery. Good when green and crisp. Limp celery could be a sexual symbol.

Check. To receive one is to expect money. Surprise! To pay out checks may mean either loss or facing up to duties.

Cheese. Disappointment. The British say "hard cheese" for tough luck.

Cherries. Happiness. "Life is just a bowl of cherries" (but all some people get are the pits).

Chocolate. See Sweet food. Sometimes associated with compliments or good providers. In the Royal Navy "to get a bar of chocolate" means to be praised by a superior.

Cigar. Phallus, happiness or wealth.

Circus. Bad luck.

City Hall. Conflict you can't win.

Clay. Bad news for your sex life. Fear of death or deterioration?

Clothes. Are you happy and well dressed or in rags and unhappy? Are you anxious about how other people regard you? Are you in a uniform of any sort, with obligations? Are you showing off and desire to be impressive? Is someone trying to get clothes off you? Figure that one out. Have you mislaid your clothes and are running around naked (unprotected)?

Clouds, dark. Bad prospects.

Coffee. Trouble in sexual relationships. Coffee grounds, somehow, are supposed to be good luck. On what grounds I cannot guess.

Comet. Bad news "out of the blue."

Corpse. Not your death but certainly bad news about someone else. In a coffin, debt.

Couch. Pipe dreams, relaxation, psychiatry, comfort.

Cream. Wealth, sex.

Cross. Trouble, suffering.

Crown. Not power but loss.

Cut. Termination, treachery, loss. Insult, wound, termination.

Daybreak. Happy beginning. Is something dawning on you at last?

Driving. Control, sex drive, ambition. See Car. If someone else is driving you may feel taken care of, oppressed, kidnapped, useless, etc.

Egypt. Mystery, death. A different meaning in, say, Israel?

Engine. Energy, motivation.

Explosion. Ejaculation, orgasm. Fear of injury or death in war.

Fleeing. Avoidant behavior, the experts say. Avoiding what, exactly? Successfully? Try to make your dreams portray you as happily running toward something rather than frightened, running away from something.

Flooring. Basic support. Bare boards, tile, carpet, or what?

Funeral. Look at the weather; a wet day is good luck. See Funeral above.

Fun Fair. You may think your sexual relationship is shaky. You may wish for tawdry distractions.

Furnace. Testing, passions.

Garbage. If in your dream your wife is nagging you to take out the garbage that could have lots of domestic messages, including something to do with the old Southern expression regarding getting your ashes hauled. Never miss the chance of trying to connect a symbol with a common expression, joke, pun, etc.

Garlic. Prosperity. No, I don't know why. Once again, no one ever explains.

Ghost. Does the ghost want you to do something or to do something for you? This is about duty and can be a warning of danger.

Heat. Warm feelings, passions. Maybe your duvet is too heavy, the room overheated.

Indian. From India, spirituality. From America, naturalness, tribal warfare.

Junkyard. Memories, wasted opportunities, unworkable things.

Kinky. One man's kink is another man's ordinary aberration. If you are happy or horrified with kinky practices in your dreams you may wish or fear to be very unusual. Or maybe you just get over kinkiness by dreaming.

Kitchen. Home, food, even drudgery or a passion to redecorate.

Loneliness. Get a life.

Lunar eclipse. I put this one in just to make the point that no matter how big a dream list some book gives you, you are quite capable of coming up with some vivid dream experience the book does not mention at all. I once dreamed of feeding ice cream to a camel. No gypsy came to my aid in making sense of that one. I even dreamed of trying to dream that again and was unable to do so.

Mother. Just one entry under M can set you the task of thinking this word means to you, especially if you are male and did not quite get out of the Oedipal stage when you reached age 6.

Odors. Pleasant odors are a good sign. Unpleasant ones—well, you can figure it out.

Older. If you are older in your dreams you fear that the future holds failure for you.

Ovation. You are hungry for praise.

Oven. Womb, pregnancy or "something cooking" in some other aspect, change of character.

Photographing. Upcoming disappointment in a close friend. Fear of loss.

Playing cards. Gambling, fate, opportunity, risks. Hearts mean "emotions," love; Diamonds "wealth;" Clubs "fear, hunger, sex, violence;" Spades "body, sensuality."

Pyramid. Death, greater awareness. See Egypt.

Pumpkin. Lots of bad news, says Zolar; others may disagree. Growing, Zolar says, means "dishonor," picking "death of a relative." Buying a pumpkin pie "treachery and revenge," eating it "serious disease." Why, oh why? Never any explanation!

Purple. Honor, wealth, distinction, happiness, and (some say) loss.

Rabbit. Promiscuous sex, pregnancy, vulnerability.

Ram. Horny. Always think of dream language in terms of slang, too.

Ring. Marriage. Boxing ring=conflict. Are you winning or being beaten up?

Rollercoaster. Sometimes life seems like this safe but scary ride. Try to concentrate on the fact that the thrill is not dangerous.

Sailing. Clear sailing means clear sailing. A stormy voyage points to danger or doubt.

Detail of a painting by Murillio in The Prado.

Slap. If you slap someone in a dream, of course you are angry with them. Are you slapped?

Snake. Penis. See Adder.

Stealing. If you steal in your dream, what is it you take? Do you feel guilty, happy to get away with it, fearful of being apprehended and shamed?

Sweet food. Happiness, while sour tastes mean disappointment.

Target. Vagina, or goal. The name of a store?

Thunderstorm. Just one of the many bugaboos left over from childhood.

Travel. You may be desirous of escaping boredom or an uncomfortable situation or you may want adventure. Travel by air suggests sex needs.

Trench. Insecurity, trap, defense, stuck in a rut.

Underwear. I suppose that some people who are so reserved that even in their dreams they will not permit themselves to appear totally naked may find themselves in their underwear. Are they insecure, humiliated? Or could a fetish be involved? Lingerie can appear in sexy dreams with some frequency.

Vat. One source says an empty vat means "wealth." Why? British dreamers may want to think about VAT (Value Added Tax). All symbols are society specific.

Victory. Winning a battle in a dream signifies the hope or the likelihood of winning an important contest in your waking life.

Volcano. Eruption of concealed emotions, passions.

Vomiting. Bringing up unpleasant things.

Wager. You bet and win. Better to take this as wish fulfillment than as a guarantee. If you dream of losing, you believe you will.

Warm bath. Warning of miscarriage. For males, you may have wet the bed.

Web. A convenient example to raise the question, necessary with each and every symbol, "In what sense?" The worldwide web? A spider web, symbol of trapping, not of communication or interrelating at all?

Win the lottery. Wish fulfillment. Winning anything may signal you think yourself deserving but perhaps ill-served.

Wool. Warmth, motherhood, protection, fuzzy thinking.

Wrong. Do you feel accused? Contrite? Misunderstood? Victimized? Do you desire to set things straight, pay off a debt, right an injustice? Good Luck! We hope to live under a rule of law, but law and justice are not the same thing. Cheer yourself with the thought that most of humanity does *not* get what it deserves, where would you be in a perfectly just world?

Many dreamlike images distinguish Danish director Benjamin Christensen's famous *Häxen* (Witchcraft, Sweden, 1921).

Zipper. This can even have a sexual connotation. More things than you would credit actually do. But, *pace* Freud and his followers, there is more than sex there. In the 100,000 dreams that one expert calculates the average person will experience there is a staggering number of possible symbols.

With the observation that dreams often are ambiguous or even work by contraries, and that important ones may not be recalled while trivial ones may, I leave you with that gypsy dream-book list of augury impedimenta, perhaps not the most dignified but indubitably a very familiar aspect of writing about dreams. My list here has necessarily been arbitrary and selective but the "definitions" in this little lexicon are, I assure the reader, not my inventions but much repeated ones in literature. These days you can even get such a "dictionary" online, for this is the basic money-spinner (as the British say) in connection with dream reading—unless you count the psychoanalytic and psychological counseling industries.

Listen. That's enough of this. Yes, there are many common dream symbols, many of them pretty obvious. But what you really need is your own personal dictionary of dream symbols. Make it, starting now. You can do it. I hope to have inspired you to start.

IN CONCLUSION

There is a chapter on prophetic dreams in the first book in this series, *The Complete Book of Superstition, Prophecy, and Luck* (1995). What I have given you here is the "gypsy dream-book" of the type that floods the market. However, here you get it with a context, with a twist. Now you can look up your dreams with full knowledge of how to recall and examine them and in the full light of a warning that dreams work in mysterious ways to deliver their message—though deliver they do. You are well advised, not simply superstitious, to follow the very ancient tradition of paying attention to each and every one of them you can recall. Women recall more dreams than men do but both sexes dream about the same, although the lexicon of symbols may be different in each case. If the stereotypes have any validity, I urge men to try to be more sensitive, more feeling, and women to be more literal and logical. But I assume that if the Creator wanted men and women to be exactly alike He would not have created two sexes. I have done my best to craft this book for both.

Well, that is the conclusion of *The Complete Book of Dreams and*

What They Mean, still another book in the series, and still another book among the million that will be published worldwide this year. This book was researched and written and published in ways that very soon in this new millennium will become obsolete. The future is well beyond anything of which we now dream!

Now that you have finished the latest book in the series, you may wish to read the whole. I predict you will enjoy the experience. You may also wish to know that next comes *The Complete Book of Sex Magic*.

THE END

Index

adrenergic chemicals, 189
Africa, dreams,
among primitive people, 90
in divination, 106
significance of, 156
in women's literature, 170
African-American folklore, 171
Agee, James, 198
agrimony (in folklore), 163
Alfred Aethling (death dream), 35
Allah, sender of true dreams, 155
American dream, 162
and nightmares, 148
American proverbs, 174
Amerindian dreams, 16-18
Amphyction of Athens (1497 B.C.), 289
An Occurrence at Owl Creek Bridge, 260-269
Anderson, George K., 112
anthropology, 90
Apocalypse Maybe, 1999: (novel), 92
Archer, William, 129-130
Aristotle
on predictive dreams, 159
theories of dreams, 68-69, 72
art depicting dreams, 154, 158-159, 168-169, 184
Artemidoris (2nd century B.C.), 290

Artemidorous Daldianus, 307
Arthur (King of Britain), 274-285
Asclepius, god of healing, 66-67
Association for the Study of Dreams, 66
astral projection in sleep, 164-165
astrology and dream interpretation, 293
astronaut, dreams in space, 46
Australian aborigines, 51, 96
automatic writing, 172-174
Bacon, Sir Francis, 97
Barca, Pedro Calderón de la, 166
Béguin, Albert, 179-181
Beowulf, dream of Hrothgar, 157-158
Bergman, Ingmar
Persona, 188
The Virgin Spring, 208
Wild Strawberries, 188
Berryman, John, 142
Bible
dream material in, 113-115
use in dream interpretation, 97, 107-108, 289
Daniel interprets dreams, 110-112
Deuteronomy - observing dreams prohibited, 96, 101
Genesis - Pharoah's dreams, 98-100, 144
Job, 109-110

Joel, 149
Proverbs – "where there is no
  vision", 161
Vulgate (Latin), 155, 189
Bierce, Ambrose, 260-269
blood circulation, 69
Blake, William, 147
Boccaccio, Giovanni
  Il Corbaccio (dream vision), 137-138
  The Decameron on dreams, 165
body language 77-78
Bosch, dream imagery, 158
Bradbury, Ray, 192
brain
  brain waves, 88-89
  reticular stem, 66
Browne, Sir Thomas (1605-1682), 149,
  295
Buñuel, Luis (movie director), 202
Bunyan, John 145
calf-skin, yellow, 273
Campbell, Joseph, 77
Cardano, Girolamo, 20
Caribbean religious cults, 106-107
Carroll, Lewis, 39, 205
Chaldean dream interpretation, 289
Charcot, Jean-Martin, 76-77
Chaucer's use of dream visions, 136
China
  dream interpretation, 292
  dreams in literature, 141
cholinergic chemicals, 189
Chou Hsuan, 292
Christ
  see Jesus Christ
Christianity
  in dream poetry, 142
  Emperor Constantine's dream, 13-
  14
Christmas Eve folklore, 154-155
Cicero (Marcus Tullius)
  on dreams, 156
  Dream of Scipio, 135
cinema and dreams, 187-227
clairvoyant dreams, 80-81
Coleridge, Samuel Taylor
  composing poetry in a dream, 83

Kubla Khan, written in a dream,
  131-132
collective culture, 56
collective unconscious, 74, 77
  Jung's theory of, 172
Confucious on dreams, 15, 19
conscience in dreams, 121
conscious mind, 74
Crane Hart (poet), 298-299
Creation as a dream, 96
creativity and dreams, 184
*Crime and Mentalities in Early Modern
  England*, 122
da Vinci, Leonardo, on daydreams, 31
Dante (*Divine Comedy*), 130
daydreaming, 35
de Sade, Marquis, 55
death
  in dreams, 313
  Makar's Dream, 243-259
  among primitive peoples, 179
Decameron (Boccaccio), 165
deep sleep, 116
  and dream sleep, 82
déja vu, 83-84
Delphi, oracle of Apollo, 108
demons in dreams, 29, 119, 121, 306
Der Tad in Venedig (Death in Venice,
  1913), 229-230
Descartes on dreams, 19, 84
Devil (The)
  appearing in dreams, 70, 72, 176,
  312, 306
  false dreams from, 41
devils, dreams of, 306
Diderot, Denis, 145-146
divination, 114-115, 306
Dickens, Charles, 82, 150
djinn (genies), 155
Don Juan in Hell, 168
Dos Passos, John, 300-301
"dream community", 14
dream diary, 57
Dream Encyclopedia (1995), 90
dream interpretation
  see interpretation of dreams
dream journal, 288, 307-308

dream lines (Australian aborigines), 96
Dream Lover: Transforming Relationships, 291
Dream of Gerontius, The, 139-140
Dream of John Ball, A, 140
Dream Master, The, 178
Dream of Owen O'Mulready, 269-271
Dream of Pilate's Wife, The, 133
Dream of Rhonabwy, The, 272-285
Dream of Scipio, The, 156
Dream of the Rood, The, 141-142, 145
dream prophecy, 16
Dream Songs, 142
dream states, 68
dream vision, 135-137
dream witnesses, 122
dreaming and thinking, 35-36
dreaming of the future, 78-79
Dreaming (journal), 66
Dreamplay, The, 140
dreams
    ancient authors on, 16
    astronauts in space, 46
    categories of, 40-41
    caused by God or Satan, 72
    caused by weather or planets, 72
    Christian history, 13-14
    in cinema, 187-227
    color in, 46-47
    context, 307
    control of, 57-58
    divinatory, 97-98
    effect on unborn children, 88
    exterior influence, 38
    getting what you want from, 48-49
    learning how to control, 90
    long and short, 83
    lucid, 20
    meaning, 13
    methods to inspire, 269
    in police work, 23
    in pregnancy, 117-118
    presence of flowers and plants, 75
    reasons for, 14
    recall different for men or women, 339
    scientific discoveries in, 61
    short stories about (100), 230-232
    television documentaries, 191
    time in, 38
    work from, 20
    writing down, 39-40
Dreams (novel), 169
dreams come true, 43
dreams under hypnosis, 88
dreams while dying, 263-269
dreams, in movies
    see movies, dreams in
Dreams: God's Forgotten Language (1968), 124-125
dumb cake (folklore), 155
dying in a dream, 157
Egypt
    interpretation of dreams in, 289-290
    significance in dreams, 313
electroencephalogram, 88-89
Eliade, Mircea, 96
Elizabethan theory of dreams, 73
Emotions as source for dreams, 34
encoding dreams, 303
ending a dream, 83
erections (in deep sleep), 83
Ethelred the Unready, 35
extra sensory perception (ESP), 81
fairies in dreams, 118
fairytales about dreams, 177
Fall of the House of Usher, 300
Fellini, Frederico, 193
Finnegan's Wake, 142
Folklore concerning dreams, 156-158, 161-162, 163-165, 167, 171-177, 179
    Amerindian, 17-18
    African American, 171
    agrimony to induce sleep, 163
    Danish, 298
    Irish, 269-271
    magical routes to inner space, 155
    marriage partners, 155, 161, 171
    sleeper's soul, 156-157, 222-223
    Welsh, 272-285
    Korean, 156
Fontana, David, 291

Forgotten Language, The (1951), 114

Foxley, William, 41

Frazier, Sir James, 156

Freud, Sigmund
  analysis of dreams, 87, 123, 142, 303-305
  dreams as reports from the unconscious, 30
  Interpretation of Dreams, The, 35-36, 65, 288
  map of dream interpretation, 329
  mistaken, 62, 287
  psychoanalysis as sacrament, 39-40
  as secular rabbi, 305, 307

Fromm, Erich, 114

Fuseli, Johann Heinrich (Henry) 1741-1825, 159

Galen, Greek physician, 69

Gaskill, Malcolm, 122

Gaudier-Brzeska, Henri, 181

gems influencing dreams, 67

God
  communication through dreams, 100-102, 110, 112
  appearing in dreams, 26, 152
  in *Makar's Dream*, 253-259
  murder in the name of, 124

Golden Bough, The, 156

González-Wippler, Migene
  Dreams and What They Mean to You, 290-291
  symbolism of eating raspberries, 304

Goya, Francisco, 158

Guest, Lady Charlotte, 272

gypsy dream-books, 307-308

gypsy dreaming, 329-339

Haiti, dream interpretation, 108

Hare, Augustus, 164-165

Hauffe, Fredericke, 59

Hebrew literature, 104-105

Henry I, King of England, 28

Henty, G.A., 44

History of Witchcraft, 124

Hobbes, Thomas, 29, 149

Homburg, Prinz Friedrich von, 167

horoscopes and dreams, 293

Huxley, Aldous (nightmare), 168

Hypnos, Greek god of sleep, 96

hypnosis
  and extended sleep, 184-185
  dreams under, 88
  in movies (*see* movies, hypnosis in)
  movies about, 219-221
  neurology and psychology of, 76-77

Hypnotic Investigation of Dreams, 89

incense
  for good dreams, 122
  transcendental states, 126

incubus, 119, 158

insomnium, 40

inspiration (gods speaking through people), 173

Interpretation of Dreams and Nightmares, 292

interpretation of dreams, 103-114, 287-339
  by Amphyction of Athens (1497 B.C.), 289
  astrology, 293
  Bible, 107-108, 189, 289
  books, alphabetical list, 296-297
  Chaldean, 289
  China, Three Kingdoms Period, 292
  cliches, 329-339
  divination, 306
  Egyptian, 289-290
  encoding, 303
  Haiti, 108
  Hebrew literature, 104-105
  Jung, Carl, 295, 303
  Montaigne, Michel de, 291
  origins, 289-290
  in the popular press, 294
  psychoanalysis, 305
  raspberries in, 304
  references of scientists, 294
  sexual repression and trauma, 303-304
  Sir Thomas Browne on, 295
  Talmud, 289
  vocabulary, 291

Islam, soul leaving body, 155
James I, King of Scotland, 143-144
Jesus Christ
    appearing in dreams, 116-117, 145
    birth foretold in dream, 115
Johnson, Dr. Samuel, 148, 159
Jonson, Ben, 43-44
Jordan, Neil, 193
Joyce, James, 142
Julius Caesar (wife's dream), 301
Jung, Carl
    unlike Freud, 77
    believes dreams, 87
    collective unconscious, 172
    interpretation of dreams, 295, 303
Kabbalah, 103-104
Kafka, Franz, 20
    Metamorphisis, 43
    A Country Doctor, 53
Kant, Emmanuel, 30
Keats, John, 154
King, Martin Luther, Jr.
    "I have a dream", 55, 148, 162
Koran, revelation in dream, 102-103
Korolenko, Vladimir Galaktionovich
    (1852-1921), 233
Krishnamurti, 181
Kuan Yin, 24
Kubla Khan, 131-132
La Vida es Sueño, 166
Lalibela, King of Ethiopia, 25
Langland, William, 170
Leave Your Mind Alone, 40
legends concerning dreams, 177
LeGuin, Ursula, 209
Lewis, James R., 90
Liddell, Alice, 205
Lincoln, Abraham
    dream of coffin in White House, 44
Lindberg baby kidnapping, 23
Literature of the Anglo-Saxons (1949),
    112
literature, dreams in, 156, 159, 165-
    170, 178-181, 184
long sleep, 41
Looking Backward 2000-1887, 184-185
lottery
    dreams to predict winners, 170

winning in dreams, 320
luck in dreams, 23
Lyakhov, Valdimir, 46
Mabinogion (Welsh legends), 141, 272-
    285
Macaulay, Lord Thomas Babington,
    162-163
Macbeth, 121
Madách, Imre, 168
Magi, dreams, 113-114
magic
    condemned in Old Testament, 101-
        102
    to induce dreams, 117
Magic Flute, The, 132
Makar's Dream (short story), 233-259
Mandela, Nelson, 55
Manichean heresy, 95
Mann, Thomas, 229-230
McGregor, Dion, 184
Mesmer, Franz Anton, 89, 220
*Midwife's Maid's Lamentation in
    Newgate, The* (1693), 121-122
Mohammed, dream revelations, 102
Montaigne, Michel de, 149, 291
Moon goddess, 105
moonlight, dreams under, 52
Morpheus, Greek god, 96
morphine, word origin, 96
Morris, William, 137, 140
movies
    dreams in (alphabetical list), 187-
        219
    hypnosis in (alphabetical list), 219-
        221
    famous dreams of, 225-226
    silent, dreams in, 194-197
    watching, in your dreams, 190
Mozart, *The Magic Flute*, 132
Murray, Dr. Margaret, 27
mystery plays, 133-134
mythology, 77, 177
Nebuchadnezzar, 110-112
Nechung Oracle (Tibet), 97
necromancy
    see spiritualism
Newman, Cardinal John Henry, 139-140

Nicene Creed, 126
nightmares
    in art, 158
    books about, 31-33
    and conscience, 121
    Crysolite to prevent, 67
    in folklore (night mare), 56-57
    interpretation of, 292
    Kafka, stories from, 20
    memories when waking, 19
    menstruation, 53
    painted by Fuseli, 159
    preventing, 167
    Stevenson, Robert Louis, 20
    Strindberg's *Dreamplay*, 140
Nostradamus, 92
novelists and dreams, 159-160
Nutcracker Suite, 154
Occult, The (1971), 90
occult references, 181
Occult Review magazine, 90
occult sciences, 73-74
Old English religious verse, 112-113
oneiromancy, 306
Oneiros, Greek god of dreams, 96
oracles
    Apollo, 108
    oraculum, 40
    Tibetan, 97
    trances and dreams, 108-109
Orphic cult, 105-106
Ouija board, 172-173
out of body, 156
Paracelsus, 53
Pauli, Wolfgang, 303
Peto, Les, 291
Phantasms of the Living, 80-81
Phillip of Macedon, 295
philosophers on dreams, 29-31
phrenology, 89
Pickthall, Mohammed Marmaduke, 102
Piers the Plowman, 136-137, 170
Pilgrim's Progress, 145
pineal gland, 90
Plato on dreams, 19, 29
poets and dreams, 49
pornography, dreams in, 224

Præneste, Roman oracle of Fortuna, 108
prayer before going to bed, 95
precognition, 81
premonitions of death, 167
priests in hell, 176
primitive peoples
    dreams among, 17, 90
    religion, 96
    understanding of death, 179
prophecy
    in dreams, 26, 37-38, 90, 92
    literary, 170
    Shakespeare's *Julius Caesar*, 301
prophetic vision, 100-101, 102
Protestant ministry, 124-126
proverbs on dreams and sleep, 161, 174
psychic powers, 22-23
psychic research, 23-24
psychoanalysis
    decoding dreams, 30
    interpretation of dreams, 305
    as sacrament, 39-40
psychology, 34, 64, 77
rabbis, 101
rapid eye movement (REM), 30, 62, 83
recalling dreams, 115
Red Chamber, The Dream of the, 141
religion
    and dreams, 95-127
    primitive, 96
    and science, 126
religious cults, Caribbean, 106-107
Richard III's haunted dreams, 121
Rilke, Rainer Maria, 302-303
Robinson, D.H., 90, 92
Roger of Wendover, 25
romanticism, 179-181
saints, dreams of birth, 117-118
San Francisco Dream House, 33-34
Sanford, Rev. John A., 124-125
Sanskrit dream plays, 167
Schnitzler, Albert (1862-1931), 189
science
    discoveries in dreams, 61
        benzene ring, 84-85
        sewing machine, 85-86

wireless communication, 86-87
on dream interpretation, 294
problems solved while dreaming, 84-87, 130
and religion, 126
study of dreams, 65
science-fiction
dreams in, 178-179
lack of dreams, 155
séances, 123
self-improvement books, 58
Sendak, Maurice, 154
serial dreams, 84
sex in dreams, 54, 119, 146
daydreams, 35
disguised in dreams, 304-305
in fairytales, 153
repression and traumas, 303-304
as sinful, 73
using dreams to transform, 291
shamanism, 16
shango cult
amombahs, 107-108
interpretation of dreams, 106-108
Shaw, George Bernard, 168
short stories, dreams in
alphabetical list, 230-232
Henty, G.A., 44
Shulman, Sandra, 292
Silverberg, Robert, 155
sleep
deprivation, 30
disorder, 34
and health, 66
proverbs concerning, 174
responses to real world, 75-76
Sleep Disorder Centers, 33
Sleeping Beauty, 152-153
sleeping cures, 24
Smith, Adam, 34
Social Dreaming, 36
somnium, 40
Sorge, Reinhard Johannes, 223
souls, 38, 156-157
South America, 90
spiritualism, 123
St. Agnes Eve, folklore, 155, 161

St. Bernard of Clairvaux, 118
St. Dominic, 118
St. Jerome
interpretation of dreams, 155
Vulgate Bible, 189
St. Nicephorus, Patriarch of Constantinople, 306
St. Patrick's Purgatory, 147
St. Thomas Aquinas, 73, 133-134
St. Thomas Eve, folklore, 161
St. Thomas of Canterbury, 118
St. Uncumber, insomnia, 51-52
St.Anselm, 26-27
Stein, Gertrude, 172
Stevenson, Robert Louis, 20
Strindberg, August, 140
succubus, 119, 158
Summers, Montague, 124
superstitions, 298
Swedenborg, Emmanuel, 45-46
symbolism in dreams
alphabetical listing, 309-328
Artemidorous Daldianus, 307
compiled by Artemidoris, 290
evasive wordplay, 304
personal associations, 290-291
in Poe's *Fall of the House of Usher*, 300
Taiping Rebellion, 116-117
Talmud, 104-105, 289
television documentaries about dreams, 191
Terrors of the Night, 73
Tertullian (Quintus Septimus Flores), 72, 106
Tesla, Nicola, 86
therapy revealed in dreams, 79-80
Thurber, James, 40
time in dreams, 326
Toqueville, Alexis de, 180
trance, 97
transcendental states, 126
Trinidad, 106-108
true and false dreams, 133-134
Uncommercial Traveller, The, 82
Unterecker, John Eugene, 298-299
urim and thurim, 101

Van Gogh, 158
van Winkle, Rip, 146
vapors, cause of dreams, 72
Varo, Remedios, 168
videos on dreaming, 227
Villanueva, Alma, 169
visio, 40
visio corporale, 41
visio intellecuale, 41
visio spirituale, 41
vision
    distinguished from dream, 96-97
    in dreams, 135-137
    seeking, 16
Vision of Vasavadatta, 167
visum (apparition), 40
vocabulary of dreams, 291

wakefulness as sign of holiness, 115-116
Wegener, Paul, 193
Weintraub, Pamela, 15
wet dreams, 73, 106
William Rufus, King of England, 25-28
Wilson, Colin, 90
Wilson, Edmund, 300-301
Wise men (see Magi)
witchcraft, 26-27, 123-124
women's literature, 169-170
word origins (*dreme*), 18-19
Woolf, Virginia, 329
writing in dreams, 129-130
yarrow, for divination, 161
Yoruba dream divination, 106
Zelazny, Roger, 178
Zohar, 104-105